TRANS FORMERS
REVENGE OF THE FALLEN

IDW
PUBLISHING

-----Written by Simon Furman--------

--------Art by Jon Davis-Hunt Issues #1, 2, and 4--------

-------Art by Alex Milne Issue #3--------

---------Colors by Kris Carter and Josh Perez--------

-------------Letters by Chris Mowry--------

-------Adapted from the Screenplay by Roberto Orci,
    Alex Kurtzman, and Ehren Kruger--------

----Original Series Edits by Denton J. Tipton--------

--------Collection Edits by Justin Eisinger--------

--- Special thanks to Hasbro's Aaron Archer, Michael Kelly, Amie Lozanzki,
--- Val Roca, Ed Lane, Michael Provost, Erin Hillman, Samantha Lomow,
--- and Michael Verecchia for their invaluable assistance.------

---

------To discuss this issue of Transformers, join the IDW Insiders,
------or to check out exclusive Web offers, check out our site:

---www.idwpublishing.com------

ISBN: 978-1-60010-455-8
12 11 10 09   1 2 3 4

Licensed by:

OFFICIAL
LICENSED PRODUCT

IDW Publishing
Operations:
Ted Adams, Chief Executive Officer
Greg Goldstein, Chief Operating Officer
Matthew Ruzicka, CPA, Chief Financial Officer
Alan Payne, VP of Sales
Lorelei Bunjes, Dir. of Digital Services
AnnaMaria White, Marketing & PR Manager
Marci Hubbard, Executive Assistant
Alonzo Simon, Shipping Manager

Editorial:
Chris Ryall, Publisher/Editor-in-Chief
Scott Dunbier, Editor, Special Projects
Andy Schmidt, Senior Editor
Justin Eisinger, Editor
Kris Oprisko, Editor/Foreign Lic.
Denton J. Tipton, Editor
Tom Waltz, Editor
Mariah Huehner, Associate Editor

Design:
Robbie Robbins, EVP/Sr. Graphic Artist
Ben Templesmith, Artist/Designer
Neil Uyetake, Art Director
Chris Mowry, Graphic Artist
Amauri Osorio, Graphic Artist
Gilberto Lazcano, Production Assistant

"*HOME.* OURS WAS A PLANET CALLED *CYBERTRON* UNTIL THE WAR BROUGHT DESTRUCTION AND MADE EXILES OF US.

"ALL OUR HOPES LAY IN THE *ALLSPARK,* THE REPOSITORY OF OUR RACE'S TIMELOST SECRETS. BUT IT WAS DESTROYED, AND NOW ONLY *FRAGMENTS* REMAIN.

"WE SHELTER ON THIS PLANET IN SECRET, JOINED BY OTHER *AUTOBOT* ALLIES, BUT OUR ONGOING QUEST TO DEFEND THE HUMANS FROM THE *DECEPTICONS* BRINGS A *REVELATION:* OUR WORLDS HAVE MET BEFORE!"

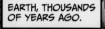

EARTH, THOUSANDS OF YEARS AGO.

...*LIFE?* WHAT PASSES FOR IT ANYWAY.

NO MATTER, SOON...

IS THIS...

KHOOM

...IT WILL BE GONE.

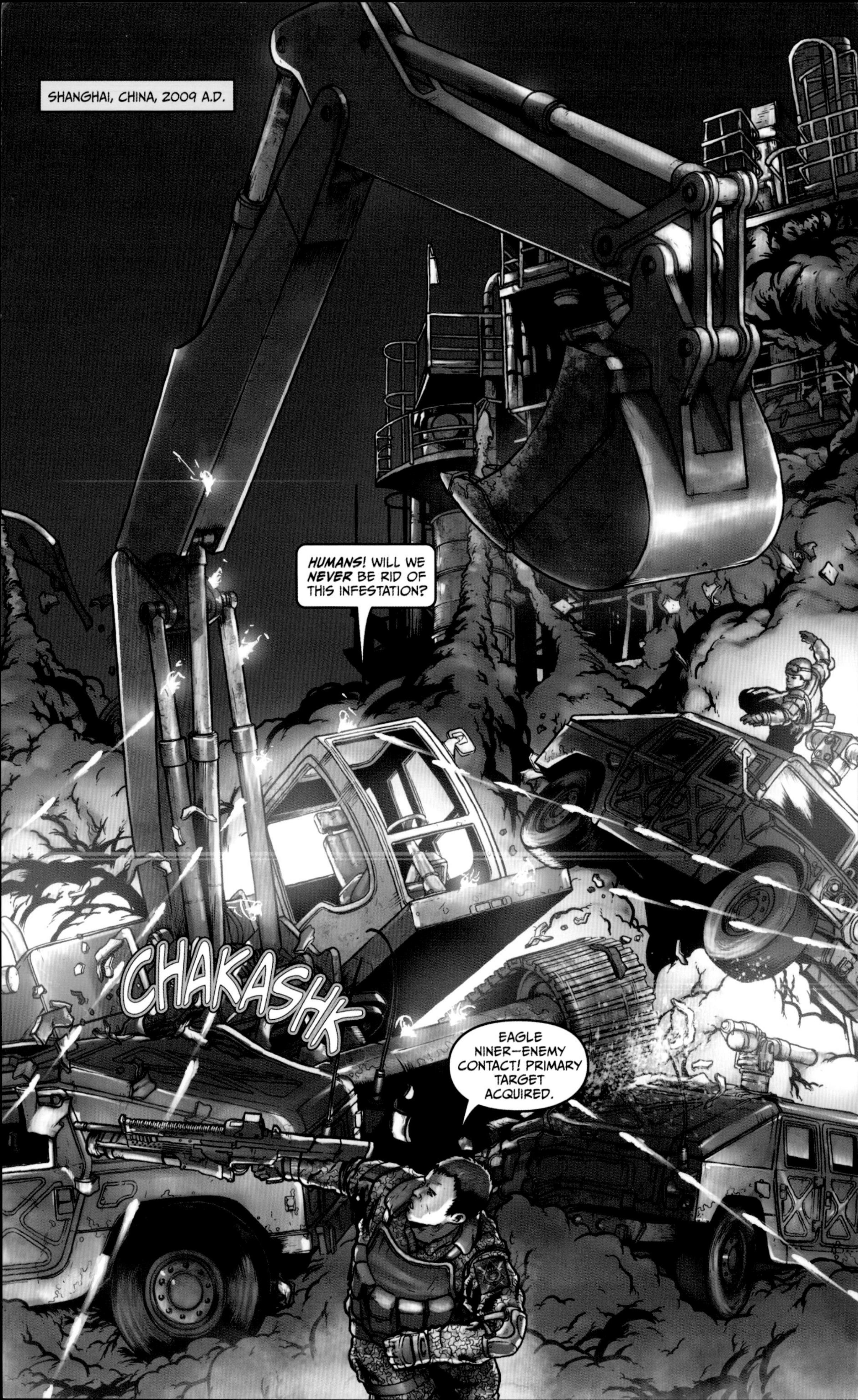
SHANGHAI, CHINA, 2009 A.D.
HUMANS! WILL WE NEVER BE RID OF THIS INFESTATION?
CHAKASHK
EAGLE NINER—ENEMY CONTACT! PRIMARY TARGET ACQUIRED.

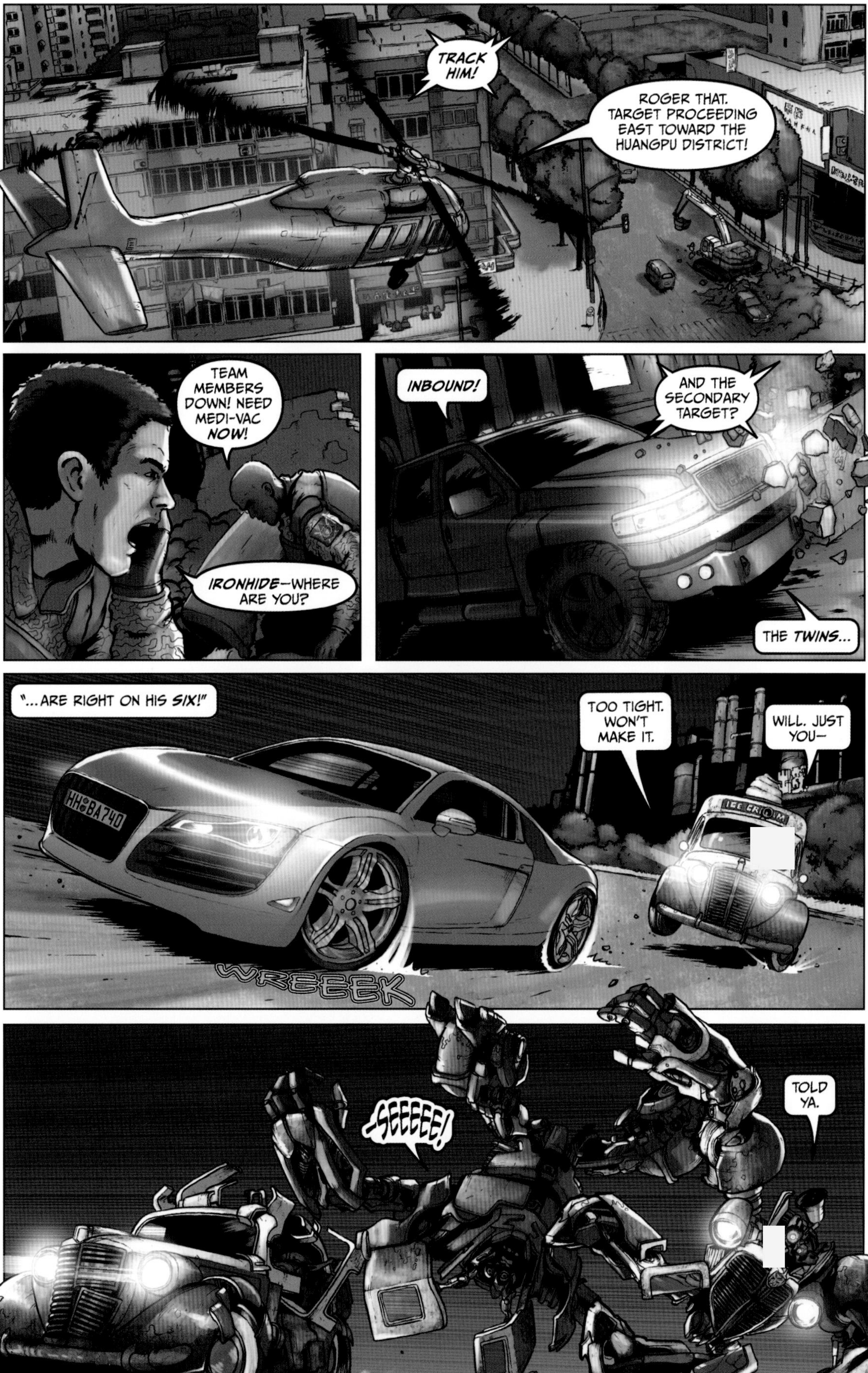
TRACK HIM!
ROGER THAT. TARGET PROCEEDING EAST TOWARD THE HUANGPU DISTRICT!
TEAM MEMBERS DOWN! NEED MEDI-VAC NOW!
IRONHIDE—WHERE ARE YOU?
INBOUND!
AND THE SECONDARY TARGET?
THE TWINS...
"...ARE RIGHT ON HIS SIX!"
TOO TIGHT. WON'T MAKE IT.
WILL. JUST YOU—
WREEEK
-SEEEEE!
TOLD YA.

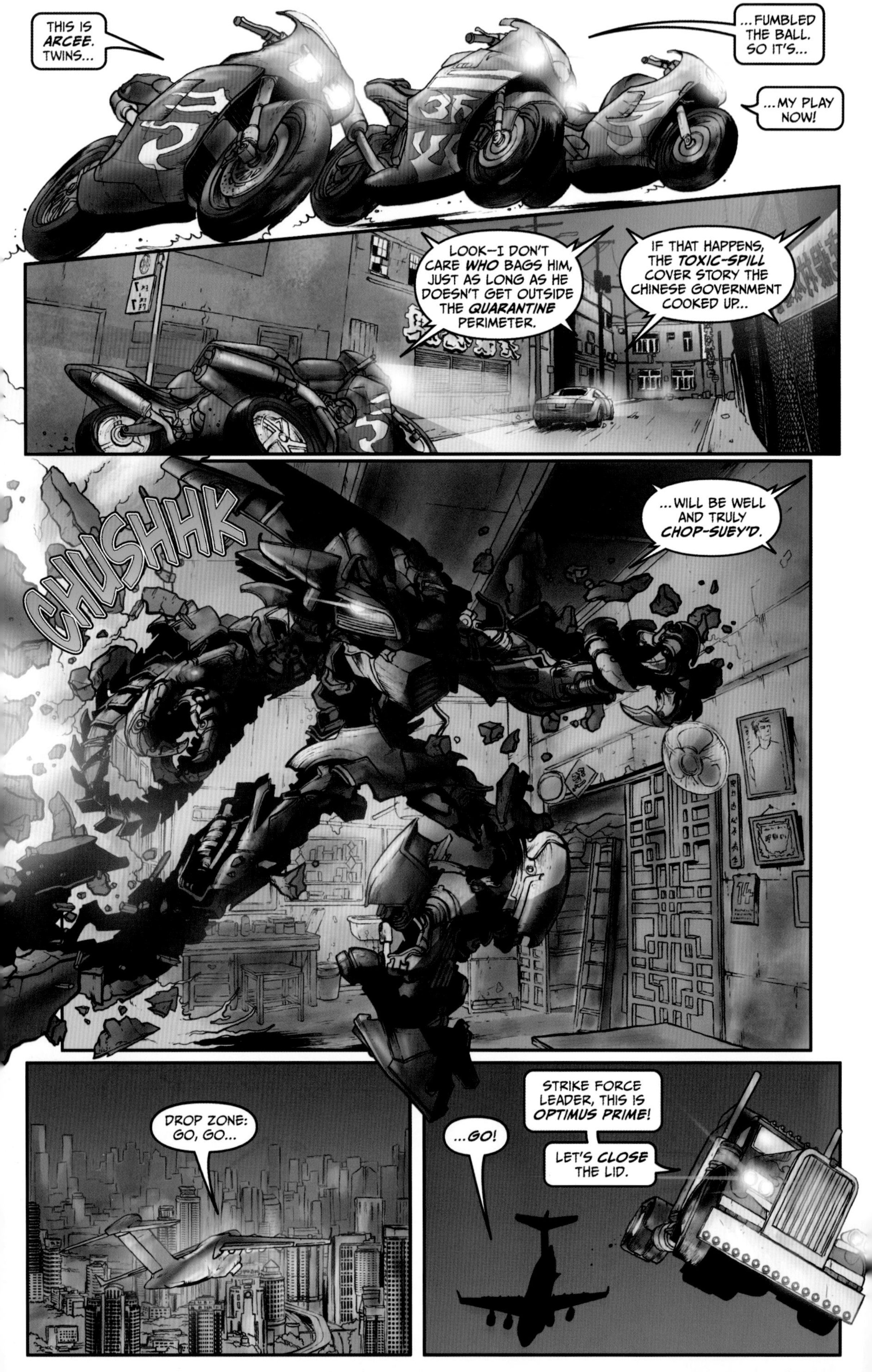
THIS IS ARCEE. TWINS...
...FUMBLED THE BALL. SO IT'S...
...MY PLAY NOW!
LOOK—I DON'T CARE WHO BAGS HIM, JUST AS LONG AS HE DOESN'T GET OUTSIDE THE QUARANTINE PERIMETER.
IF THAT HAPPENS, THE TOXIC-SPILL COVER STORY THE CHINESE GOVERNMENT COOKED UP...
CHUSHHK
...WILL BE WELL AND TRULY CHOP-SUEY'D.
DROP ZONE: GO, GO...
...GO!
STRIKE FORCE LEADER, THIS IS OPTIMUS PRIME!
LET'S CLOSE THE LID.

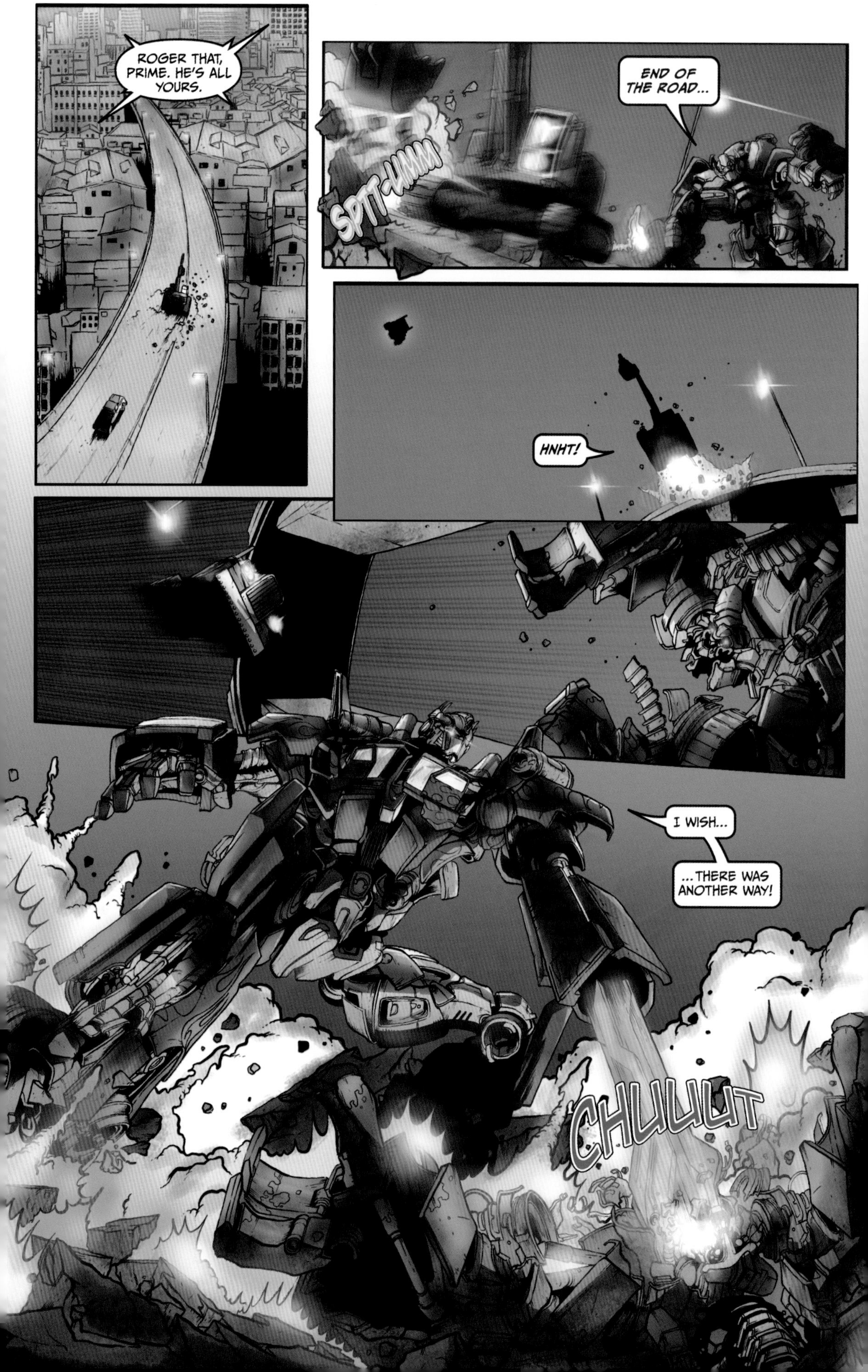
ROGER THAT, PRIME. HE'S ALL YOURS.
END OF THE ROAD...
SPTT-UMM
HNHT!
I WISH...
...THERE WAS ANOTHER WAY!
CHUUUT

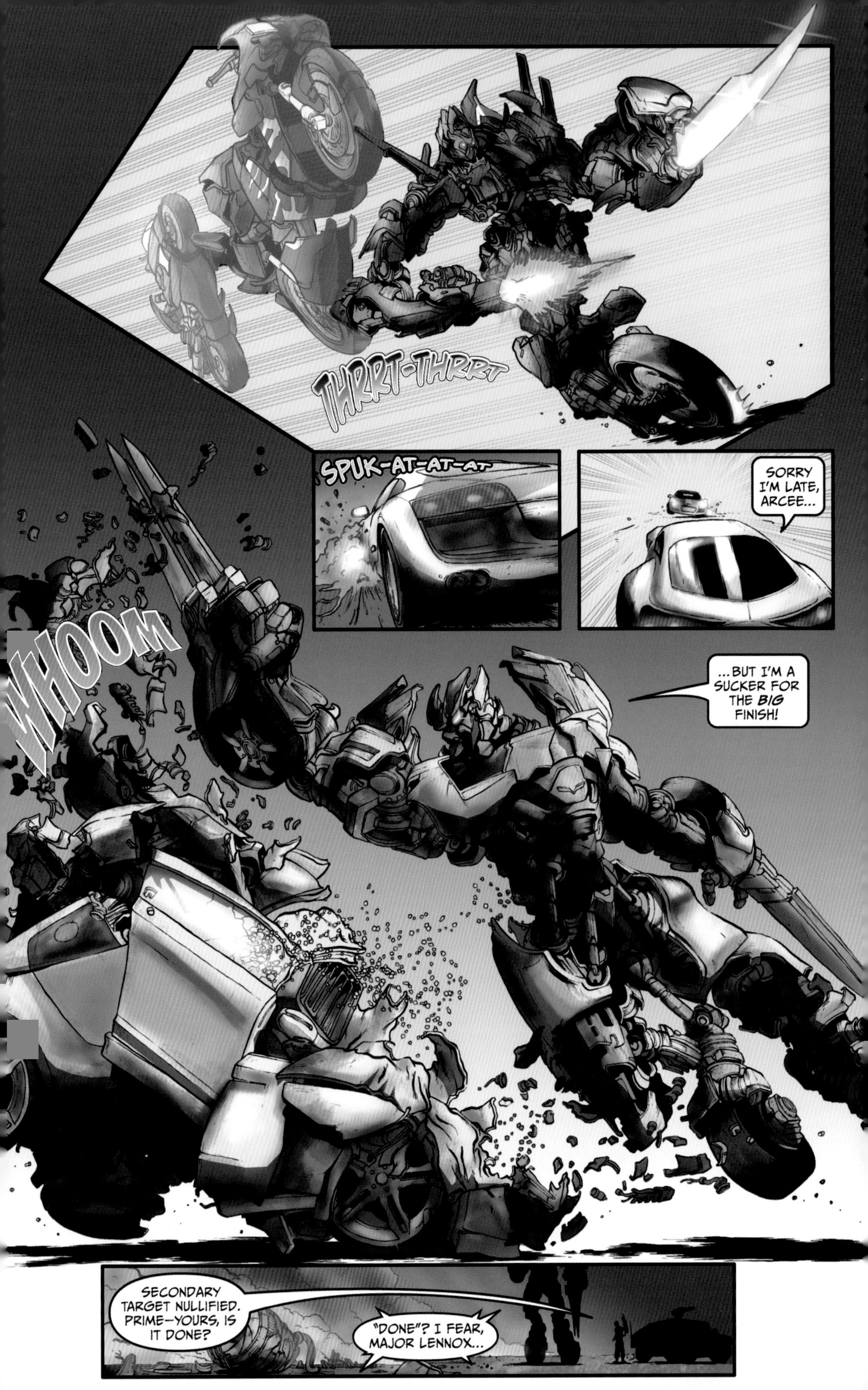
THRRT-THRRT
SPUK-AT-AT-AT
SORRY I'M LATE, ARCEE...
WHOOM
...BUT I'M A SUCKER FOR THE *BIG* FINISH!
SECONDARY TARGET NULLIFIED. PRIME—YOURS, IS IT DONE?
"DONE"? I FEAR, MAJOR LENNOX...

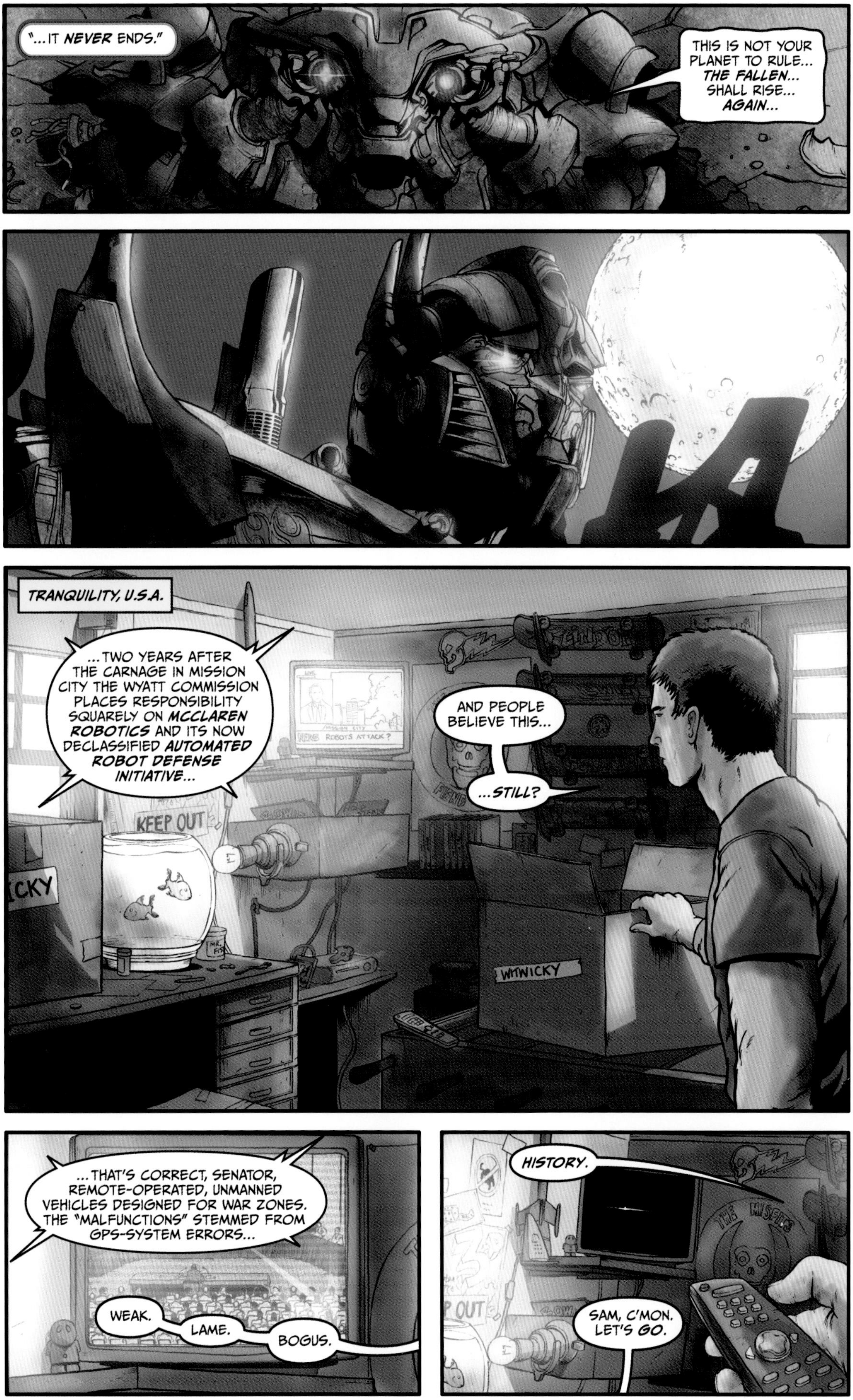
"...IT NEVER ENDS."
THIS IS NOT YOUR PLANET TO RULE... THE FALLEN... SHALL RISE... AGAIN...
TRANQUILITY, U.S.A.
...TWO YEARS AFTER THE CARNAGE IN MISSION CITY THE WYATT COMMISSION PLACES RESPONSIBILITY SQUARELY ON MCCLAREN ROBOTICS AND ITS NOW DECLASSIFIED AUTOMATED ROBOT DEFENSE INITIATIVE...
AND PEOPLE BELIEVE THIS...
...STILL?
KEEP OUT
WITWICKY
...THAT'S CORRECT, SENATOR, REMOTE-OPERATED, UNMANNED VEHICLES DESIGNED FOR WAR ZONES. THE "MALFUNCTIONS" STEMMED FROM GPS-SYSTEM ERRORS...
WEAK.
LAME.
BOGUS.
HISTORY.
SAM, C'MON. LET'S GO.

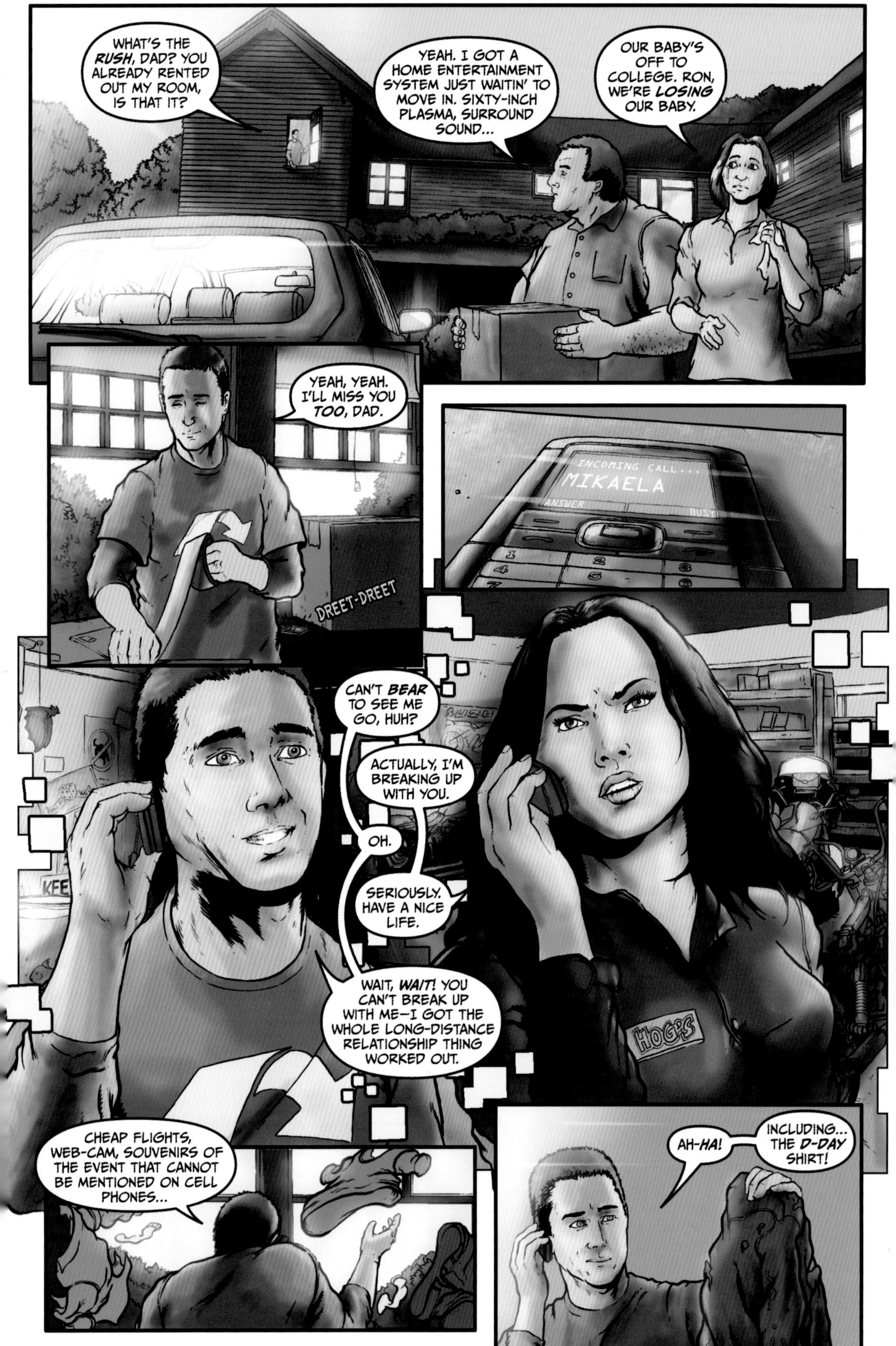
WHAT'S THE RUSH, DAD? YOU ALREADY RENTED OUT MY ROOM, IS THAT IT?
YEAH. I GOT A HOME ENTERTAINMENT SYSTEM JUST WAITIN' TO MOVE IN. SIXTY-INCH PLASMA, SURROUND SOUND...
OUR BABY'S OFF TO COLLEGE. RON, WE'RE LOSING OUR BABY.
YEAH, YEAH. I'LL MISS YOU TOO, DAD.
DREET-DREET
INCOMING CALL...
MIKAELA
ANSWER
BUSY
CAN'T BEAR TO SEE ME GO, HUH?
ACTUALLY, I'M BREAKING UP WITH YOU.
OH.
SERIOUSLY. HAVE A NICE LIFE.
WAIT, WAIT! YOU CAN'T BREAK UP WITH ME—I GOT THE WHOLE LONG-DISTANCE RELATIONSHIP THING WORKED OUT.
HOG'S
CHEAP FLIGHTS, WEB-CAM, SOUVENIRS OF THE EVENT THAT CANNOT BE MENTIONED ON CELL PHONES...
AH-HA!
INCLUDING... THE D-DAY SHIRT!

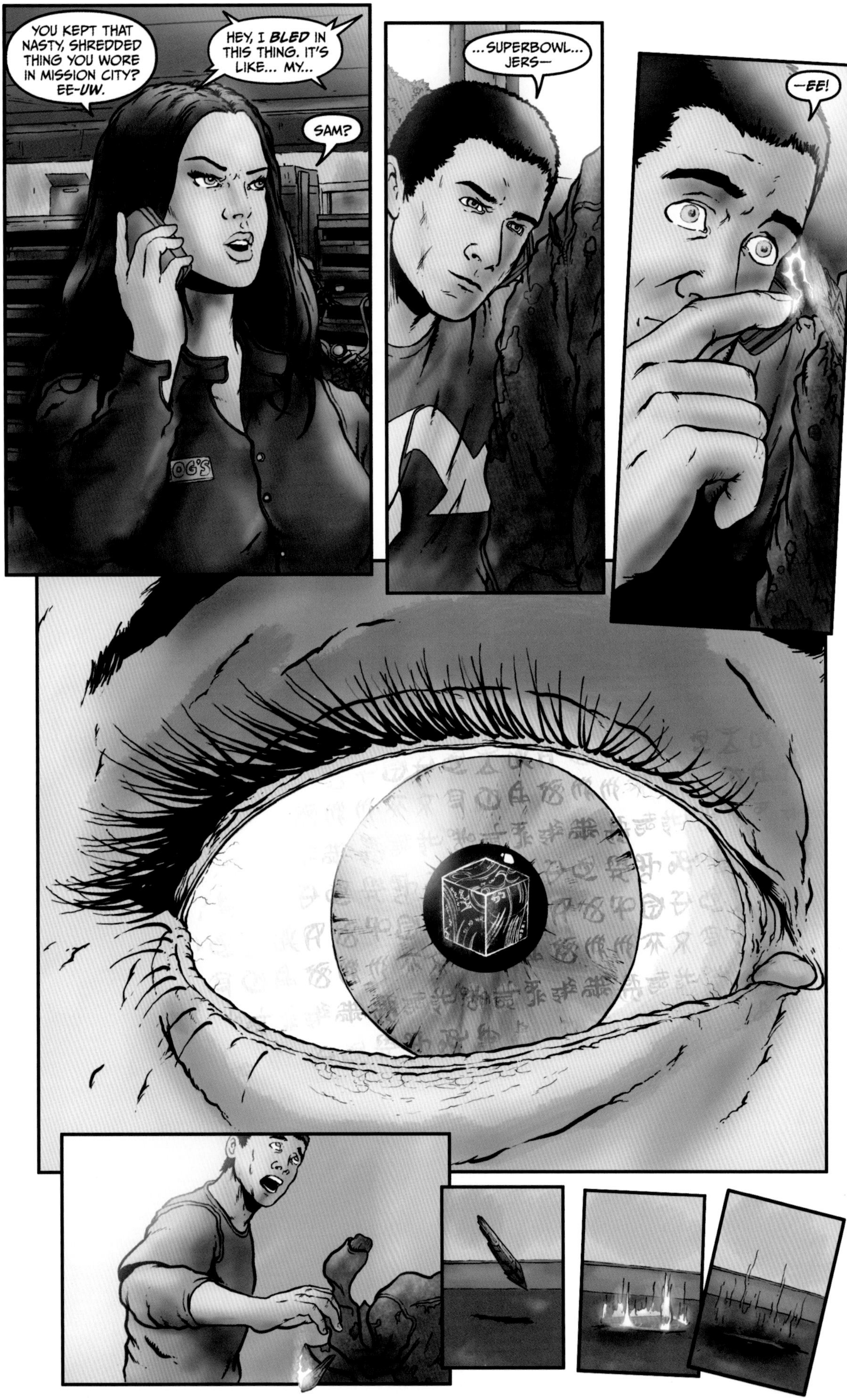
YOU KEPT THAT NASTY, SHREDDED THING YOU WORE IN MISSION CITY? EE-*UW*.
HEY, I *BLED* IN THIS THING. IT'S LIKE... MY...
SAM?
...SUPERBOWL... JERS—
—*EE!*
OG'S

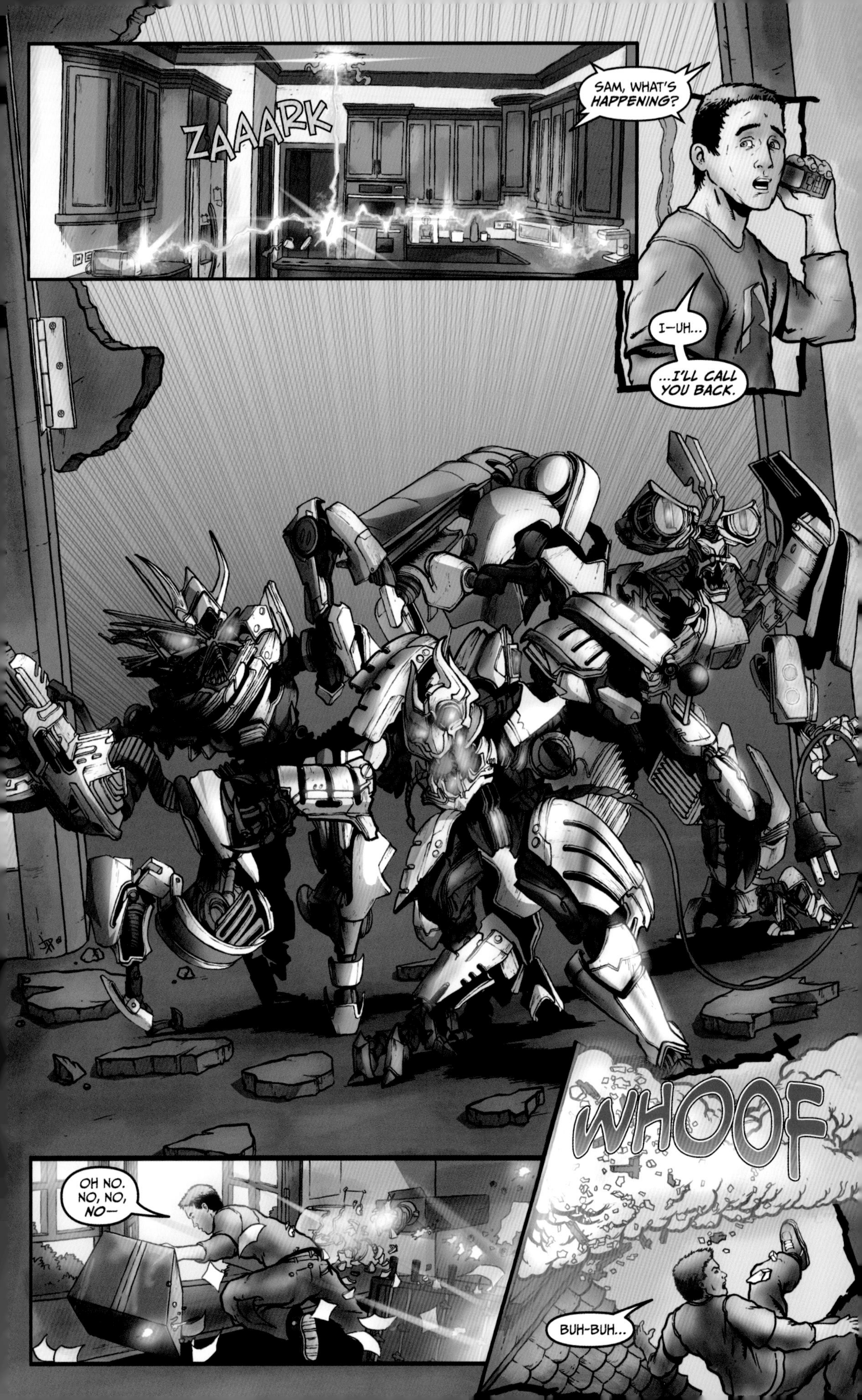
ZAAARK
SAM, WHAT'S HAPPENING?
I—UH...
...I'LL CALL YOU BACK.
WHOOF
OH NO. NO, NO, NO—
BUH-BUH...

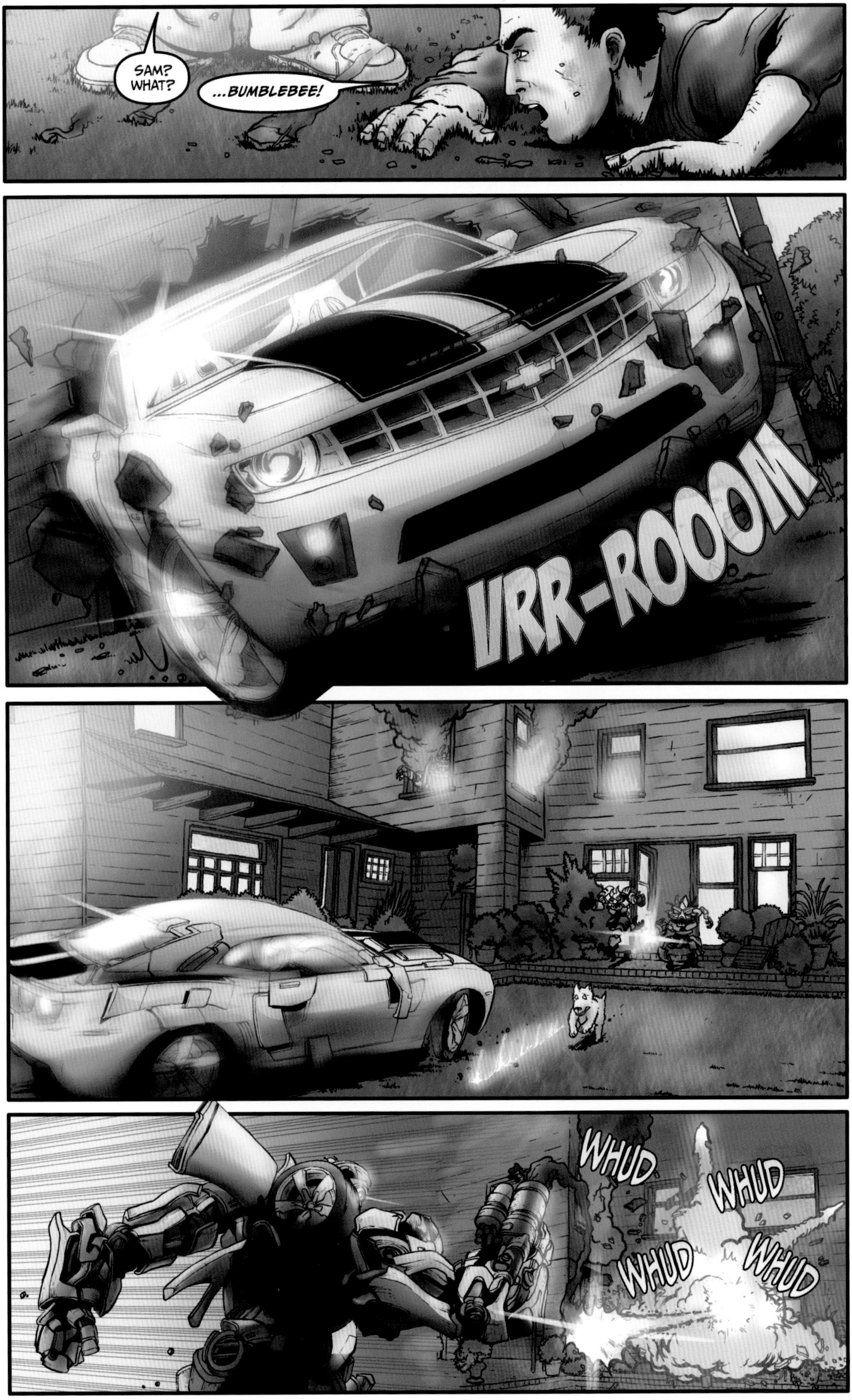
SAM? WHAT?
...BUMBLEBEE!
VRR-ROOOM
WHUD
WHUD
WHUD
WHUD

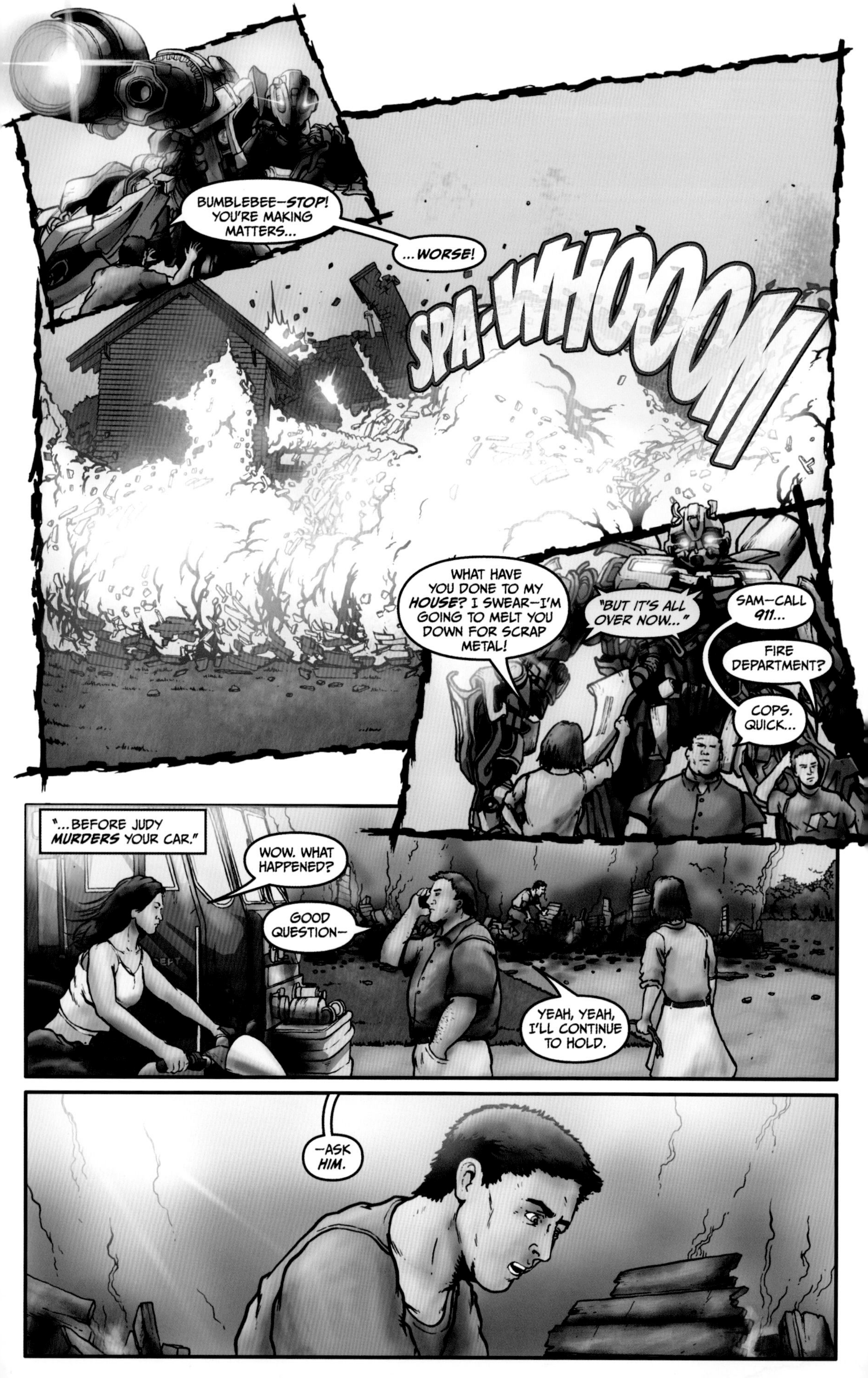
BUMBLEBEE—STOP! YOU'RE MAKING MATTERS...
...WORSE!
SPA-WHOOOM
WHAT HAVE YOU DONE TO MY HOUSE? I SWEAR—I'M GOING TO MELT YOU DOWN FOR SCRAP METAL!
"BUT IT'S ALL OVER NOW..."
SAM—CALL 911...
FIRE DEPARTMENT?
COPS. QUICK...
"...BEFORE JUDY MURDERS YOUR CAR."
WOW. WHAT HAPPENED?
GOOD QUESTION—
YEAH, YEAH, I'LL CONTINUE TO HOLD.
—ASK HIM.

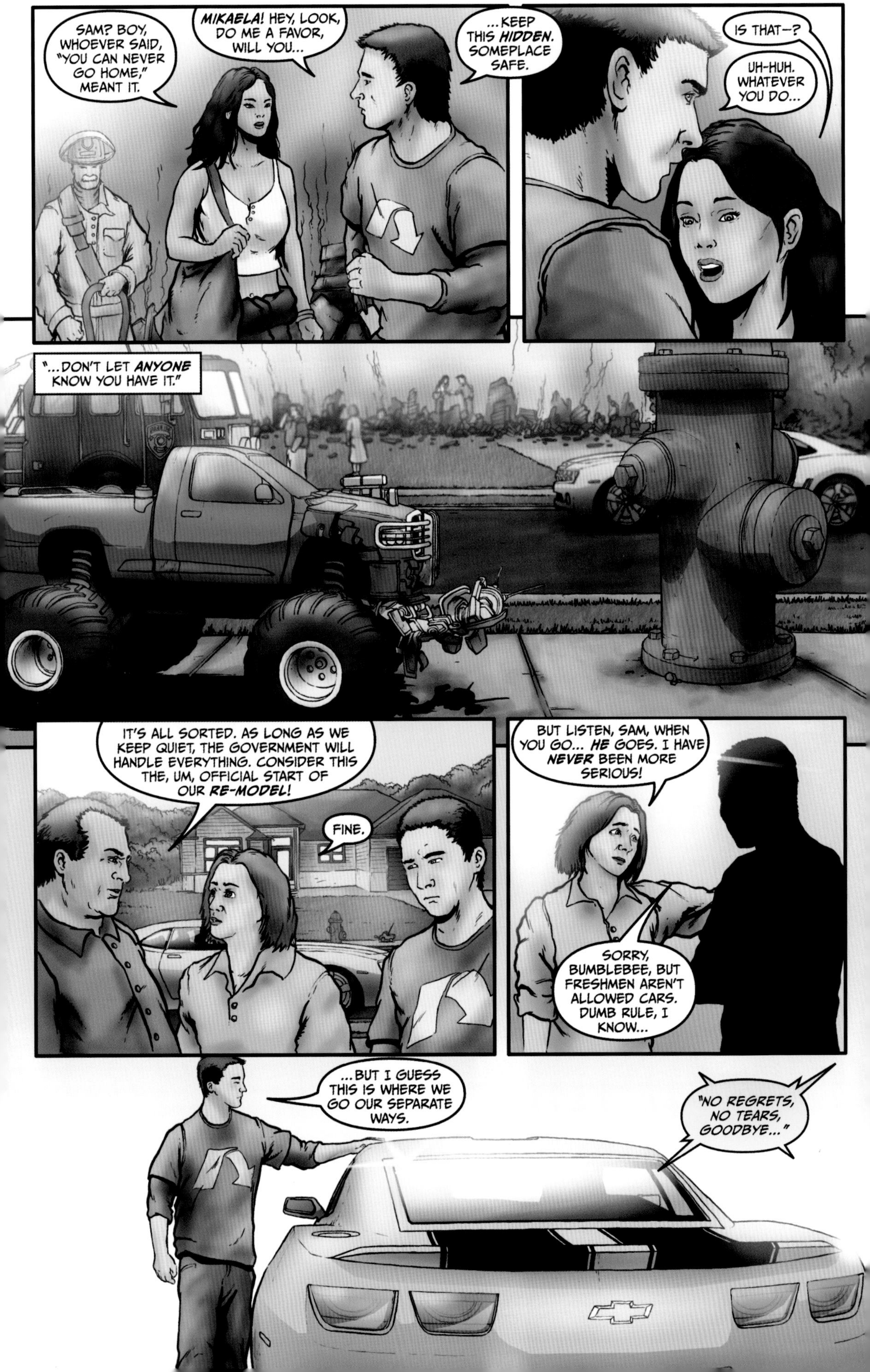
SAM? BOY, WHOEVER SAID, "YOU CAN NEVER GO HOME," MEANT IT.
MIKAELA! HEY, LOOK, DO ME A FAVOR, WILL YOU...
...KEEP THIS HIDDEN. SOMEPLACE SAFE.
IS THAT—?
UH-HUH. WHATEVER YOU DO...
"...DON'T LET ANYONE KNOW YOU HAVE IT."
IT'S ALL SORTED. AS LONG AS WE KEEP QUIET, THE GOVERNMENT WILL HANDLE EVERYTHING. CONSIDER THIS THE, UM, OFFICIAL START OF OUR RE-MODEL!
FINE.
BUT LISTEN, SAM, WHEN YOU GO... HE GOES. I HAVE NEVER BEEN MORE SERIOUS!
SORRY, BUMBLEBEE, BUT FRESHMEN AREN'T ALLOWED CARS. DUMB RULE, I KNOW...
...BUT I GUESS THIS IS WHERE WE GO OUR SEPARATE WAYS.
"NO REGRETS, NO TEARS, GOODBYE..."

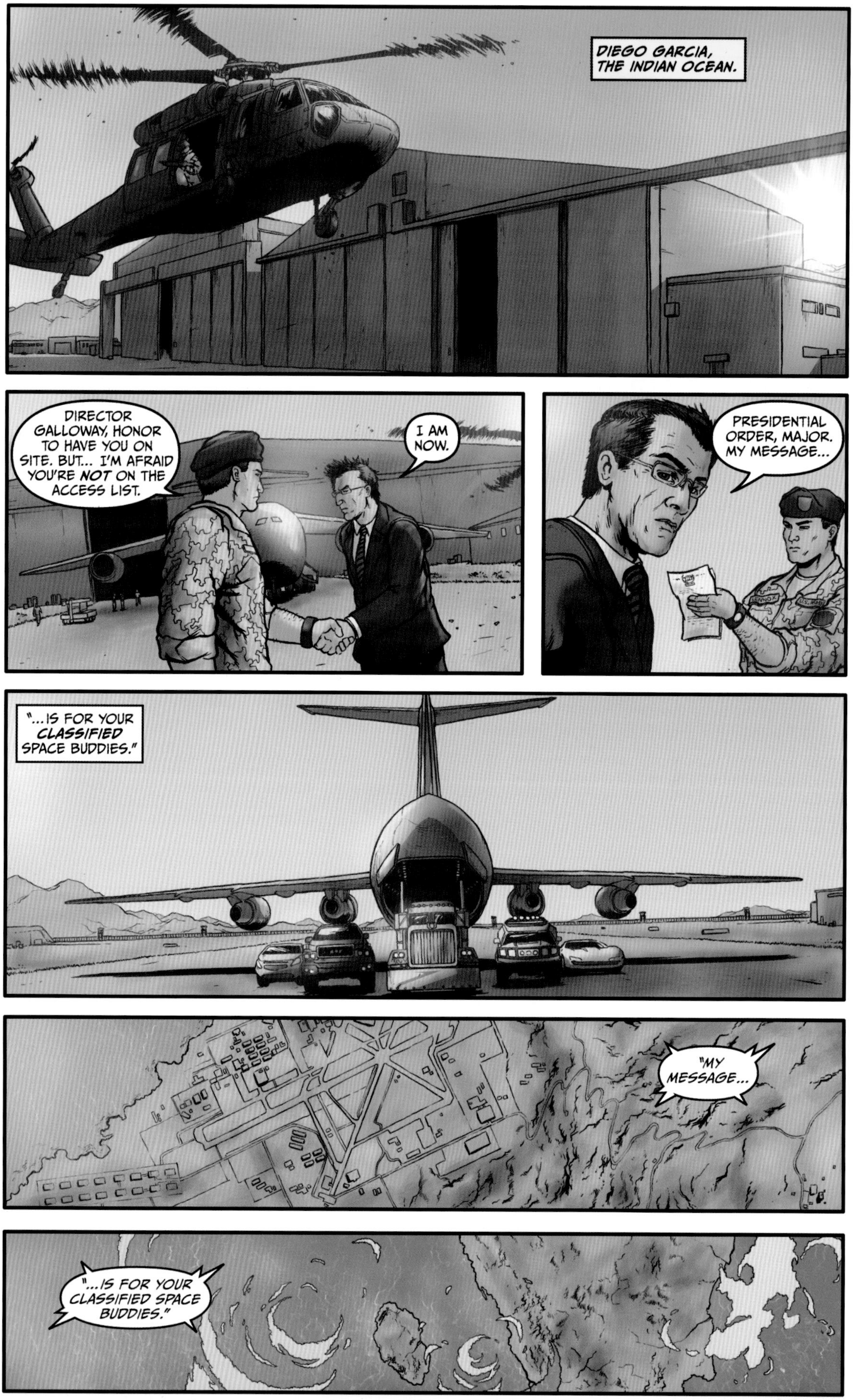
DIEGO GARCIA, THE INDIAN OCEAN.
DIRECTOR GALLOWAY, HONOR TO HAVE YOU ON SITE. BUT... I'M AFRAID YOU'RE NOT ON THE ACCESS LIST.
I AM NOW.
PRESIDENTIAL ORDER, MAJOR. MY MESSAGE...
"...IS FOR YOUR CLASSIFIED SPACE BUDDIES."
"MY MESSAGE...
"...IS FOR YOUR CLASSIFIED SPACE BUDDIES."

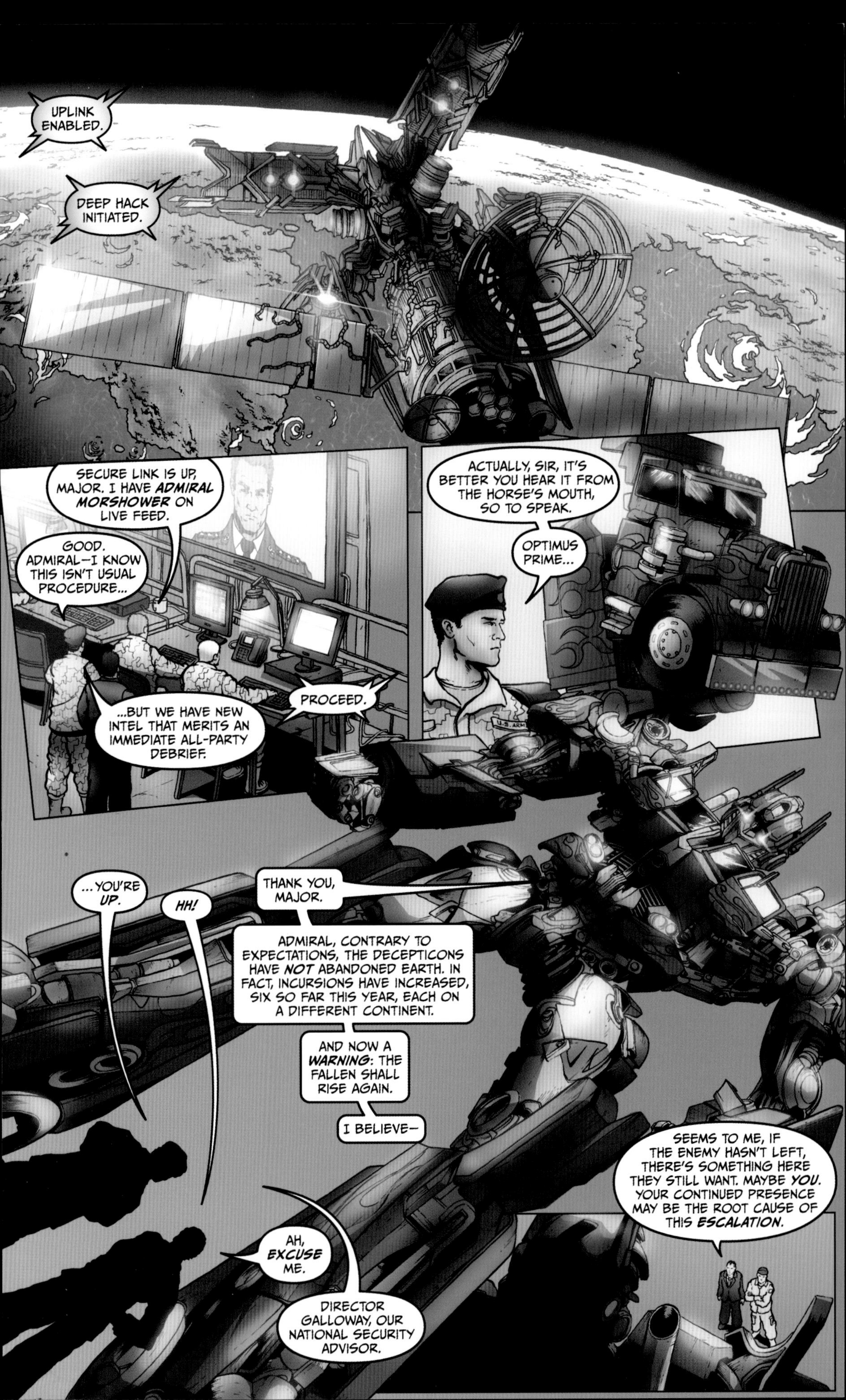
UPLINK ENABLED.
DEEP HACK INITIATED.
SECURE LINK IS UP, MAJOR. I HAVE ADMIRAL MORSHOWER ON LIVE FEED.
GOOD. ADMIRAL—I KNOW THIS ISN'T USUAL PROCEDURE...
...BUT WE HAVE NEW INTEL THAT MERITS AN IMMEDIATE ALL-PARTY DEBRIEF.
PROCEED.
ACTUALLY, SIR, IT'S BETTER YOU HEAR IT FROM THE HORSE'S MOUTH, SO TO SPEAK.
OPTIMUS PRIME...
...YOU'RE UP.
HH!
THANK YOU, MAJOR.
ADMIRAL, CONTRARY TO EXPECTATIONS, THE DECEPTICONS HAVE NOT ABANDONED EARTH. IN FACT, INCURSIONS HAVE INCREASED, SIX SO FAR THIS YEAR, EACH ON A DIFFERENT CONTINENT.
AND NOW A WARNING: THE FALLEN SHALL RISE AGAIN.
I BELIEVE—
AH, EXCUSE ME.
DIRECTOR GALLOWAY, OUR NATIONAL SECURITY ADVISOR.
SEEMS TO ME, IF THE ENEMY HASN'T LEFT, THERE'S SOMETHING HERE THEY STILL WANT. MAYBE YOU. YOUR CONTINUED PRESENCE MAY BE THE ROOT CAUSE OF THIS ESCALATION.

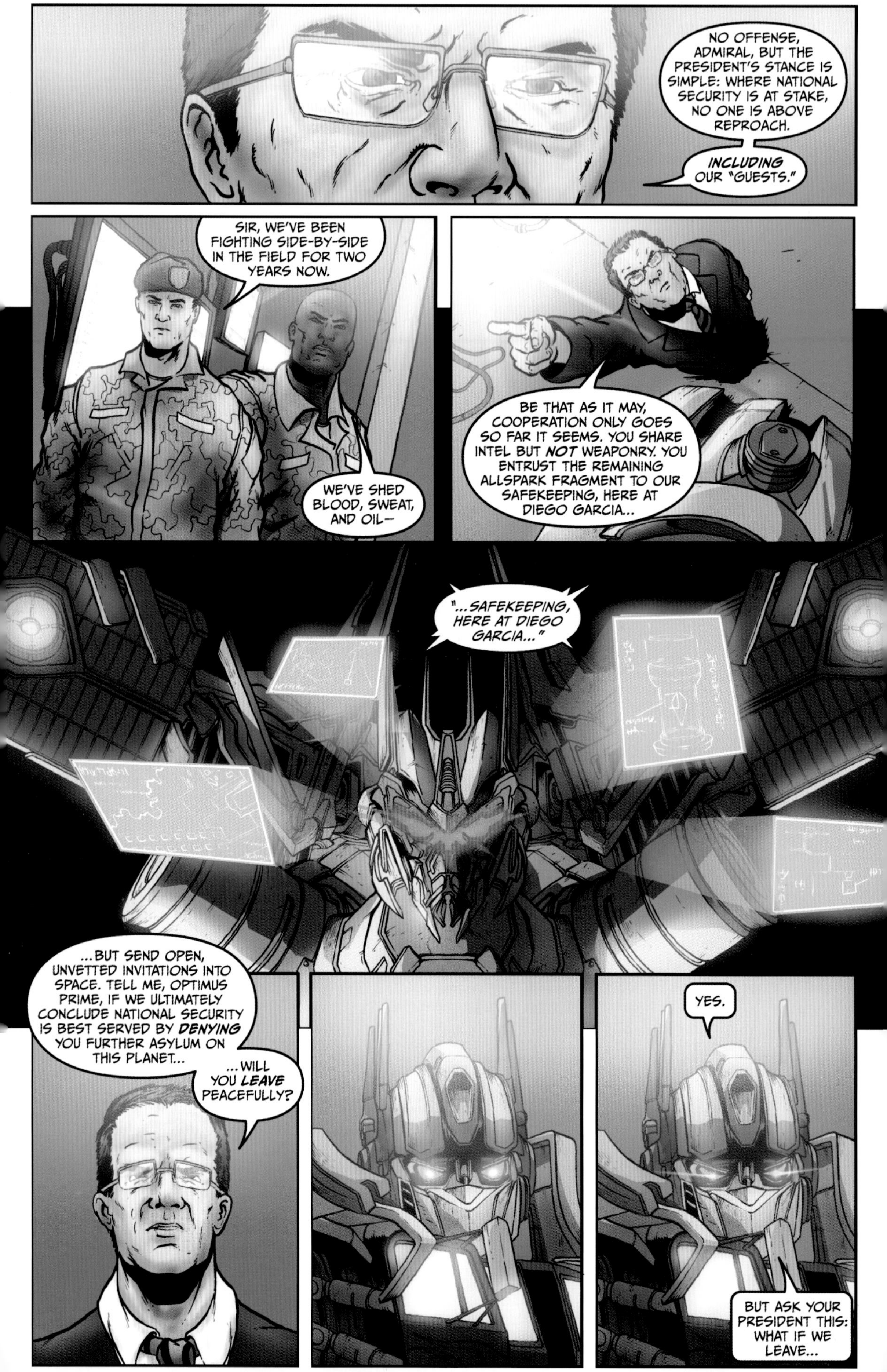
NO OFFENSE, ADMIRAL, BUT THE PRESIDENT'S STANCE IS SIMPLE: WHERE NATIONAL SECURITY IS AT STAKE, NO ONE IS ABOVE REPROACH.
INCLUDING OUR "GUESTS."
SIR, WE'VE BEEN FIGHTING SIDE-BY-SIDE IN THE FIELD FOR TWO YEARS NOW.
WE'VE SHED BLOOD, SWEAT, AND OIL—
BE THAT AS IT MAY, COOPERATION ONLY GOES SO FAR IT SEEMS. YOU SHARE INTEL BUT *NOT* WEAPONRY. YOU ENTRUST THE REMAINING ALLSPARK FRAGMENT TO OUR SAFEKEEPING, HERE AT DIEGO GARCIA...
"...SAFEKEEPING, HERE AT DIEGO GARCIA..."
...BUT SEND OPEN, UNVETTED INVITATIONS INTO SPACE. TELL ME, OPTIMUS PRIME, IF WE ULTIMATELY CONCLUDE NATIONAL SECURITY IS BEST SERVED BY *DENYING* YOU FURTHER ASYLUM ON THIS PLANET...
...WILL YOU *LEAVE* PEACEFULLY?
YES.
BUT ASK YOUR PRESIDENT THIS: WHAT IF WE LEAVE...

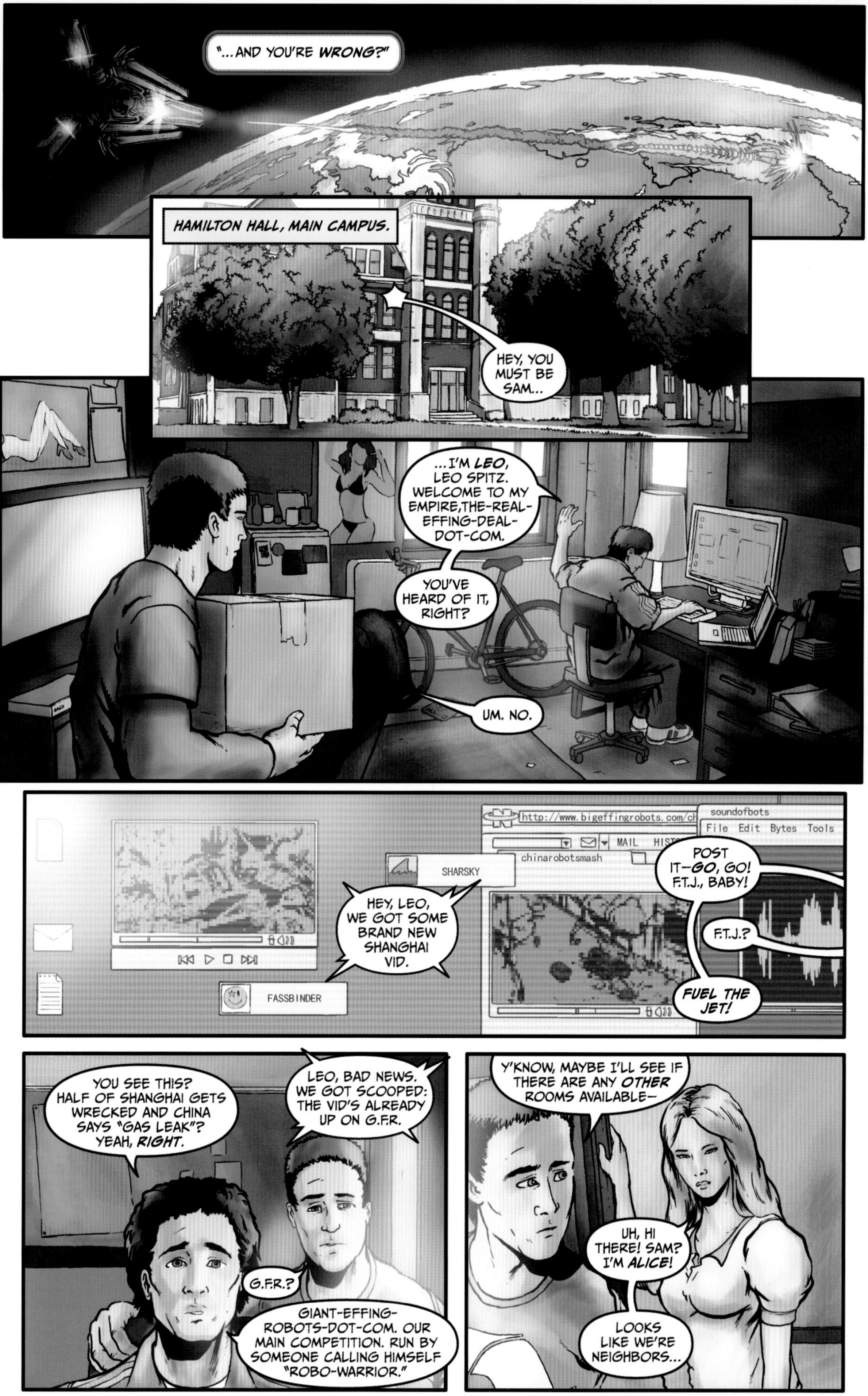
"...AND YOU'RE WRONG?"
HAMILTON HALL, MAIN CAMPUS.
HEY, YOU MUST BE SAM...
...I'M LEO, LEO SPITZ. WELCOME TO MY EMPIRE, THE-REAL-EFFING-DEAL-DOT-COM.
YOU'VE HEARD OF IT, RIGHT?
UM. NO.
http://www.bigeffingrobots.com/ch
soundofbots
File Edit Bytes Tools
MAIL
chinarobotsmash
SHARSKY
FASSBINDER
HEY, LEO, WE GOT SOME BRAND NEW SHANGHAI VID.
POST IT—GO, GO! F.T.J., BABY!
F.T.J.?
FUEL THE JET!
YOU SEE THIS? HALF OF SHANGHAI GETS WRECKED AND CHINA SAYS "GAS LEAK"? YEAH, RIGHT.
LEO, BAD NEWS. WE GOT SCOOPED: THE VID'S ALREADY UP ON G.F.R.
G.F.R.?
GIANT-EFFING-ROBOTS-DOT-COM. OUR MAIN COMPETITION. RUN BY SOMEONE CALLING HIMSELF "ROBO-WARRIOR."
Y'KNOW, MAYBE I'LL SEE IF THERE ARE ANY OTHER ROOMS AVAILABLE—
UH, HI THERE! SAM? I'M ALICE!
LOOKS LIKE WE'RE NEIGHBORS...

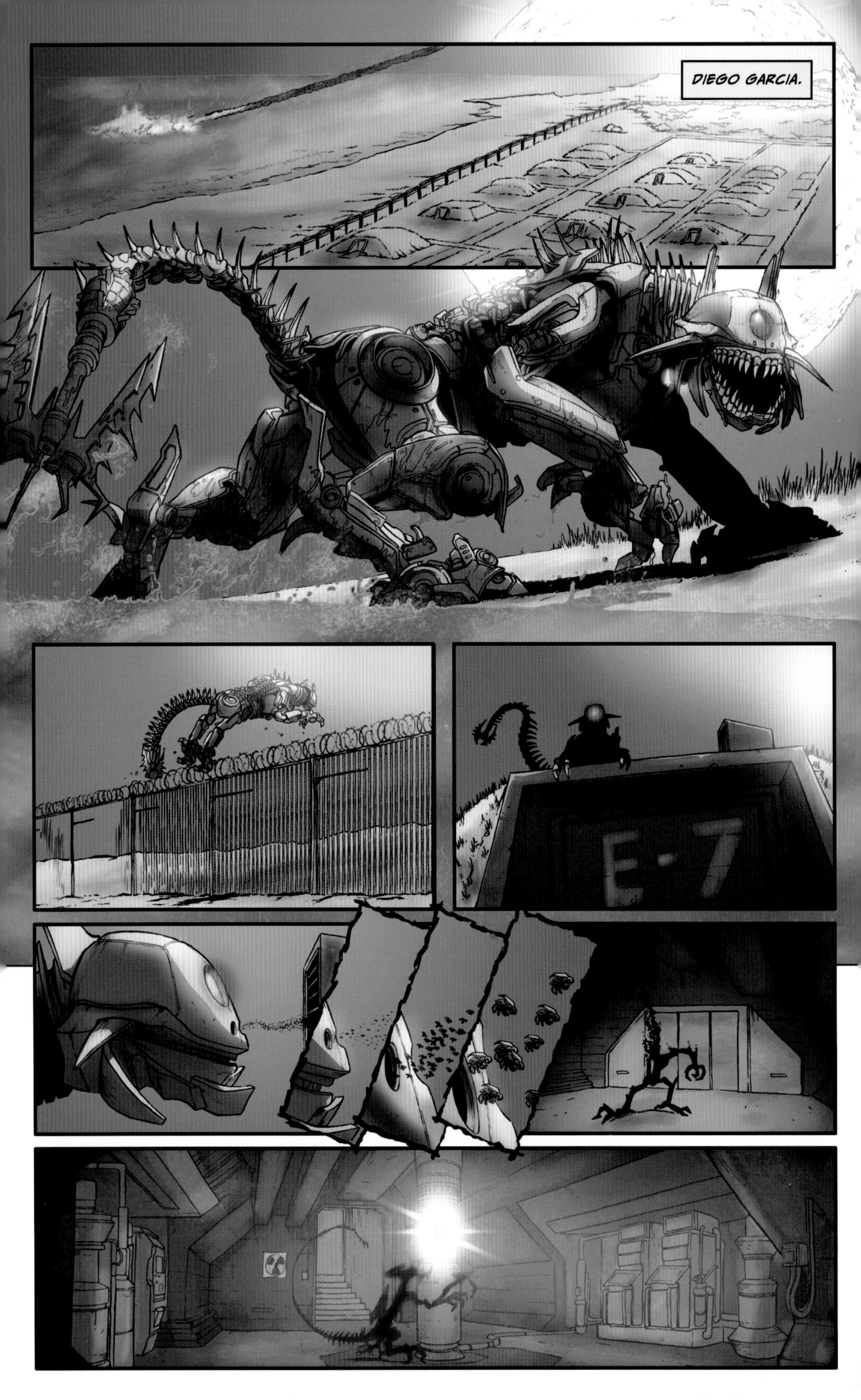
DIEGO GARCIA.
E-7

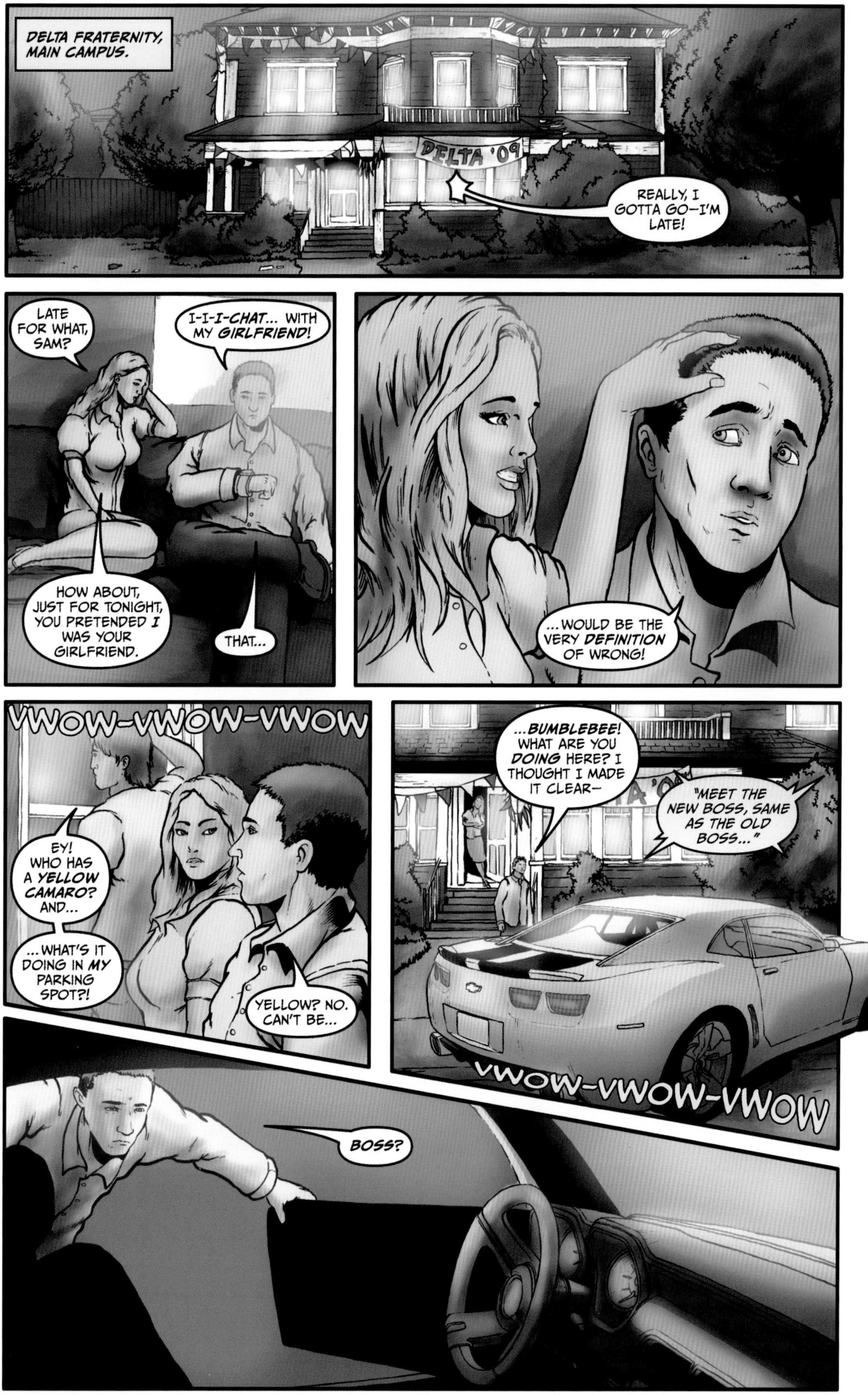
DELTA FRATERNITY, MAIN CAMPUS.
DELTA '09
REALLY, I GOTTA GO—I'M LATE!
LATE FOR WHAT, SAM?
I-I-I-CHAT... WITH MY GIRLFRIEND!
HOW ABOUT, JUST FOR TONIGHT, YOU PRETENDED I WAS YOUR GIRLFRIEND.
THAT...
...WOULD BE THE VERY DEFINITION OF WRONG!
VWOW-VWOW-VWOW
EY! WHO HAS A YELLOW CAMARO? AND...
...WHAT'S IT DOING IN MY PARKING SPOT?!
YELLOW? NO. CAN'T BE...
...BUMBLEBEE! WHAT ARE YOU DOING HERE? I THOUGHT I MADE IT CLEAR—
"MEET THE NEW BOSS, SAME AS THE OLD BOSS..."
VWOW-VWOW-VWOW
BOSS?

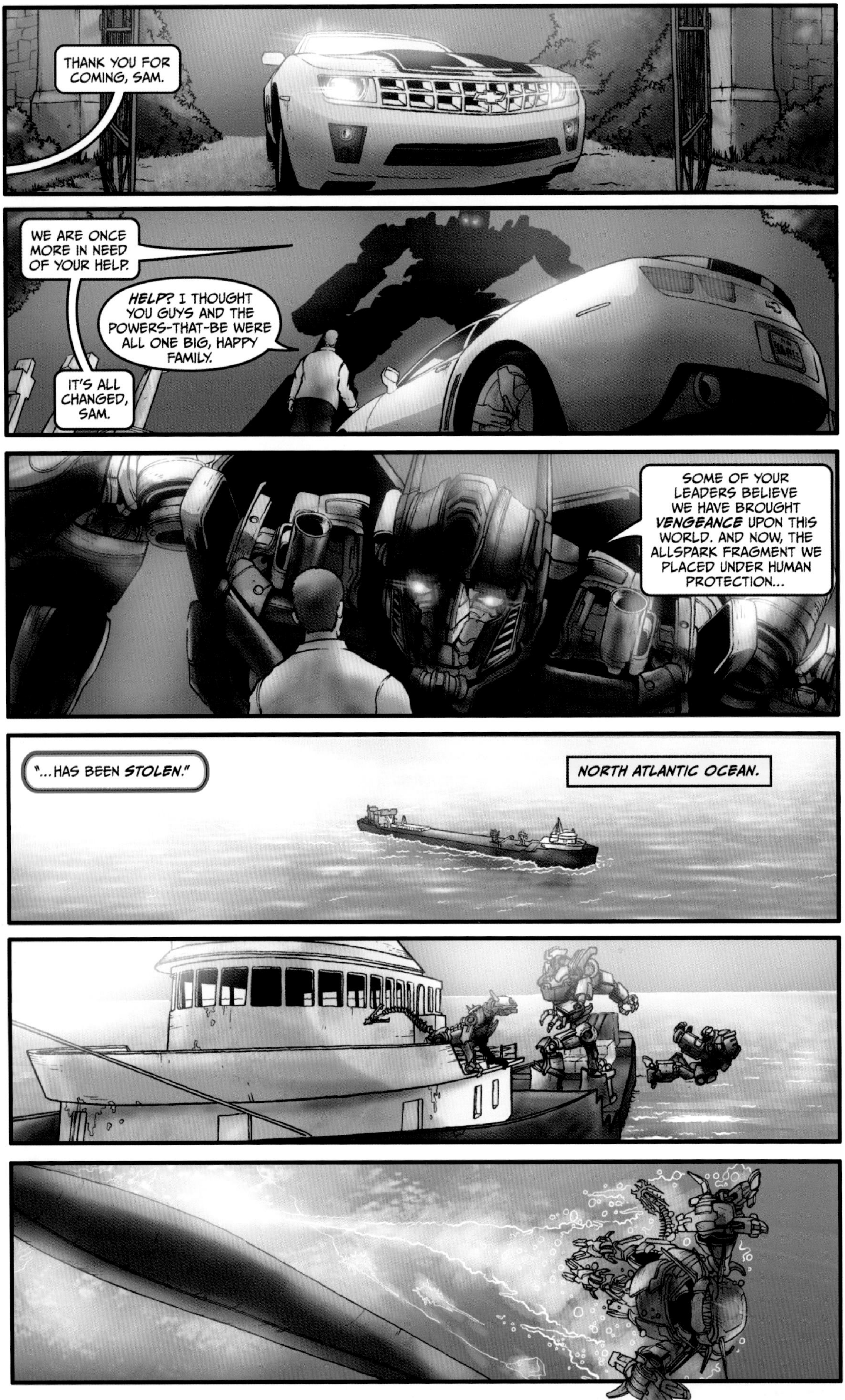
THANK YOU FOR COMING, SAM.
WE ARE ONCE MORE IN NEED OF YOUR HELP.
HELP? I THOUGHT YOU GUYS AND THE POWERS-THAT-BE WERE ALL ONE BIG, HAPPY FAMILY.
IT'S ALL CHANGED, SAM.
SOME OF YOUR LEADERS BELIEVE WE HAVE BROUGHT VENGEANCE UPON THIS WORLD. AND NOW, THE ALLSPARK FRAGMENT WE PLACED UNDER HUMAN PROTECTION...
"...HAS BEEN STOLEN."
NORTH ATLANTIC OCEAN.

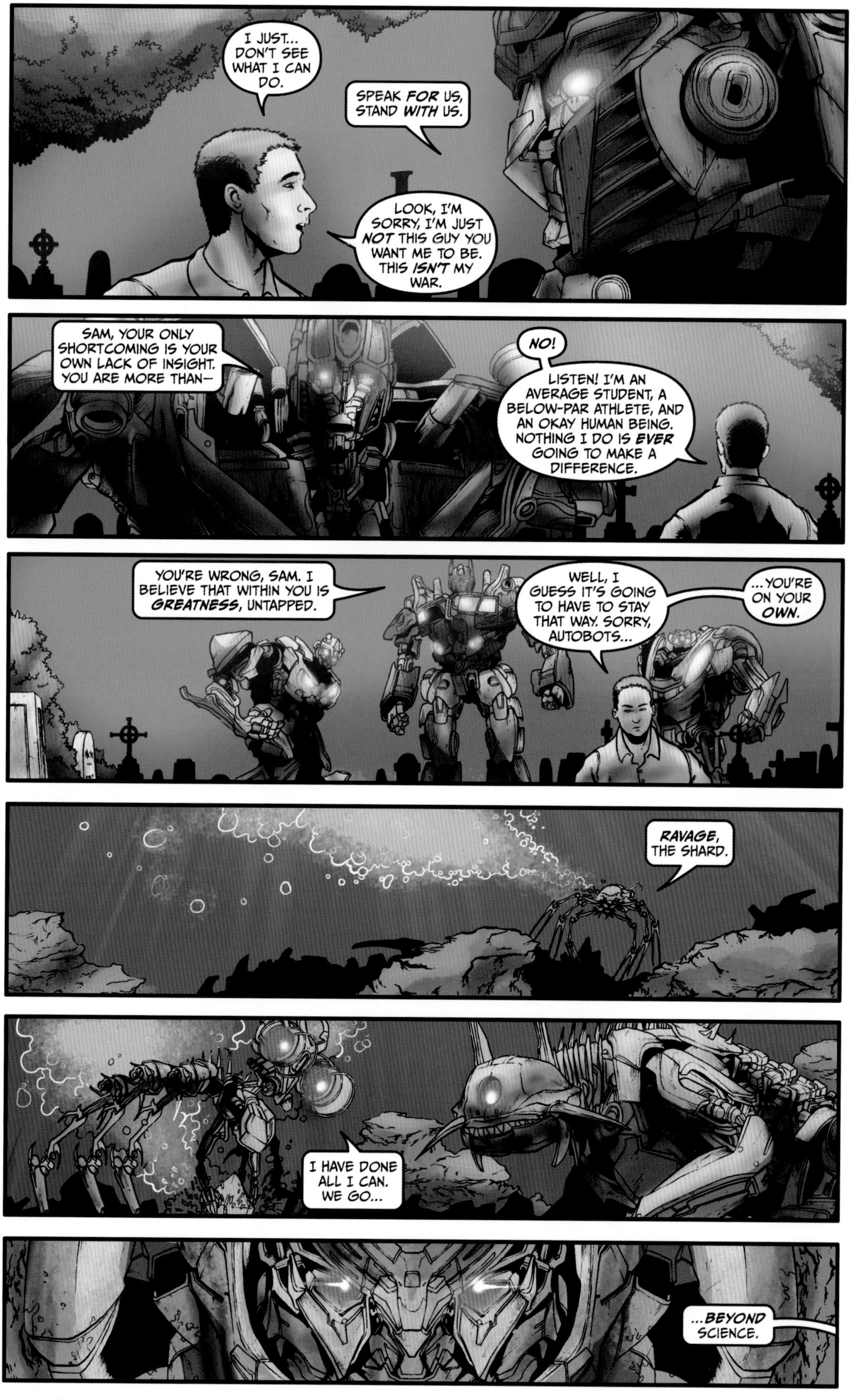
I JUST... DON'T SEE WHAT I CAN DO.
SPEAK FOR US, STAND WITH US.
LOOK, I'M SORRY, I'M JUST NOT THIS GUY YOU WANT ME TO BE. THIS ISN'T MY WAR.
SAM, YOUR ONLY SHORTCOMING IS YOUR OWN LACK OF INSIGHT. YOU ARE MORE THAN—
NO!
LISTEN! I'M AN AVERAGE STUDENT, A BELOW-PAR ATHLETE, AND AN OKAY HUMAN BEING. NOTHING I DO IS EVER GOING TO MAKE A DIFFERENCE.
YOU'RE WRONG, SAM. I BELIEVE THAT WITHIN YOU IS GREATNESS, UNTAPPED.
WELL, I GUESS IT'S GOING TO HAVE TO STAY THAT WAY. SORRY, AUTOBOTS...
...YOU'RE ON YOUR OWN.
RAVAGE, THE SHARD.
I HAVE DONE ALL I CAN. WE GO...
...BEYOND SCIENCE.

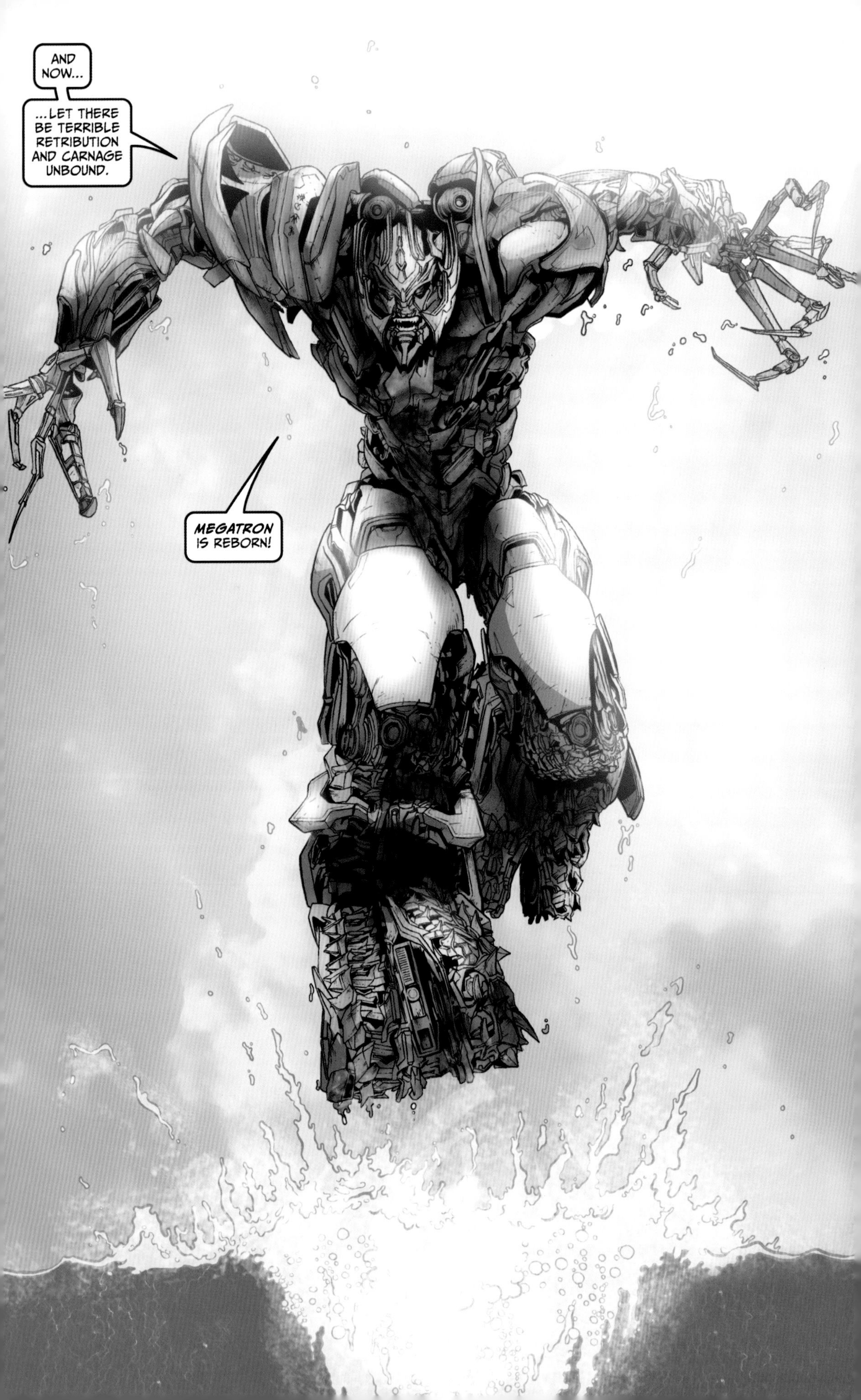
AND NOW...
...LET THERE BE TERRIBLE RETRIBUTION AND CARNAGE UNBOUND.
MEGATRON IS REBORN!

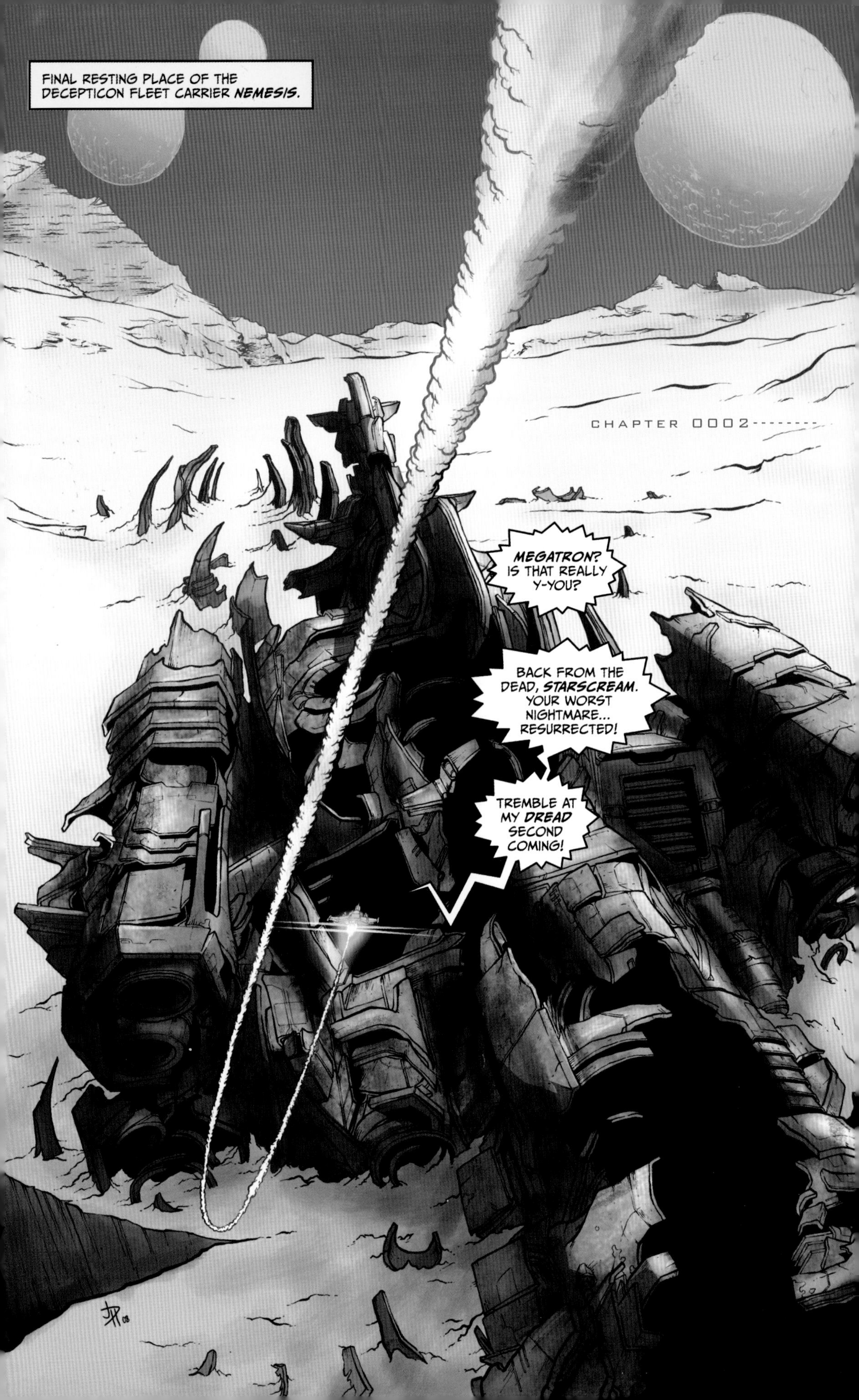
FINAL RESTING PLACE OF THE DECEPTICON FLEET CARRIER *NEMESIS.*
CHAPTER 0002
MEGATRON? IS THAT REALLY Y-YOU?
BACK FROM THE DEAD, *STARSCREAM*. YOUR WORST NIGHTMARE... RESURRECTED!
TREMBLE AT MY *DREAD* SECOND COMING!

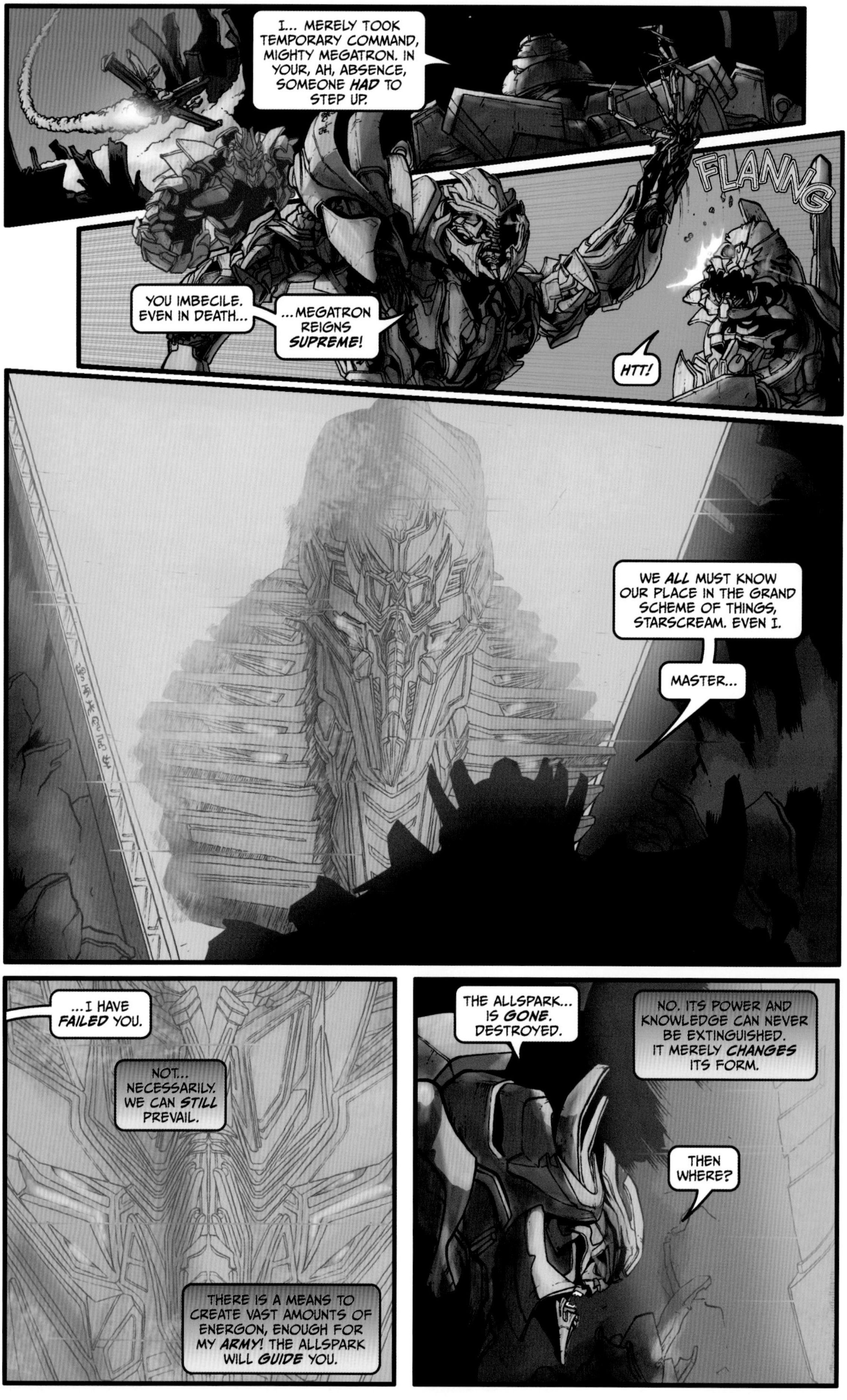
I... MERELY TOOK TEMPORARY COMMAND, MIGHTY MEGATRON. IN YOUR, AH, ABSENCE, SOMEONE HAD TO STEP UP.
FLANNG
YOU IMBECILE. EVEN IN DEATH...
...MEGATRON REIGNS SUPREME!
HTT!
WE ALL MUST KNOW OUR PLACE IN THE GRAND SCHEME OF THINGS, STARSCREAM. EVEN I.
MASTER...
...I HAVE FAILED YOU.
NOT... NECESSARILY. WE CAN STILL PREVAIL.
THERE IS A MEANS TO CREATE VAST AMOUNTS OF ENERGON, ENOUGH FOR MY ARMY! THE ALLSPARK WILL GUIDE YOU.
THE ALLSPARK... IS GONE. DESTROYED.
NO. ITS POWER AND KNOWLEDGE CAN NEVER BE EXTINGUISHED. IT MERELY CHANGES ITS FORM.
THEN WHERE?

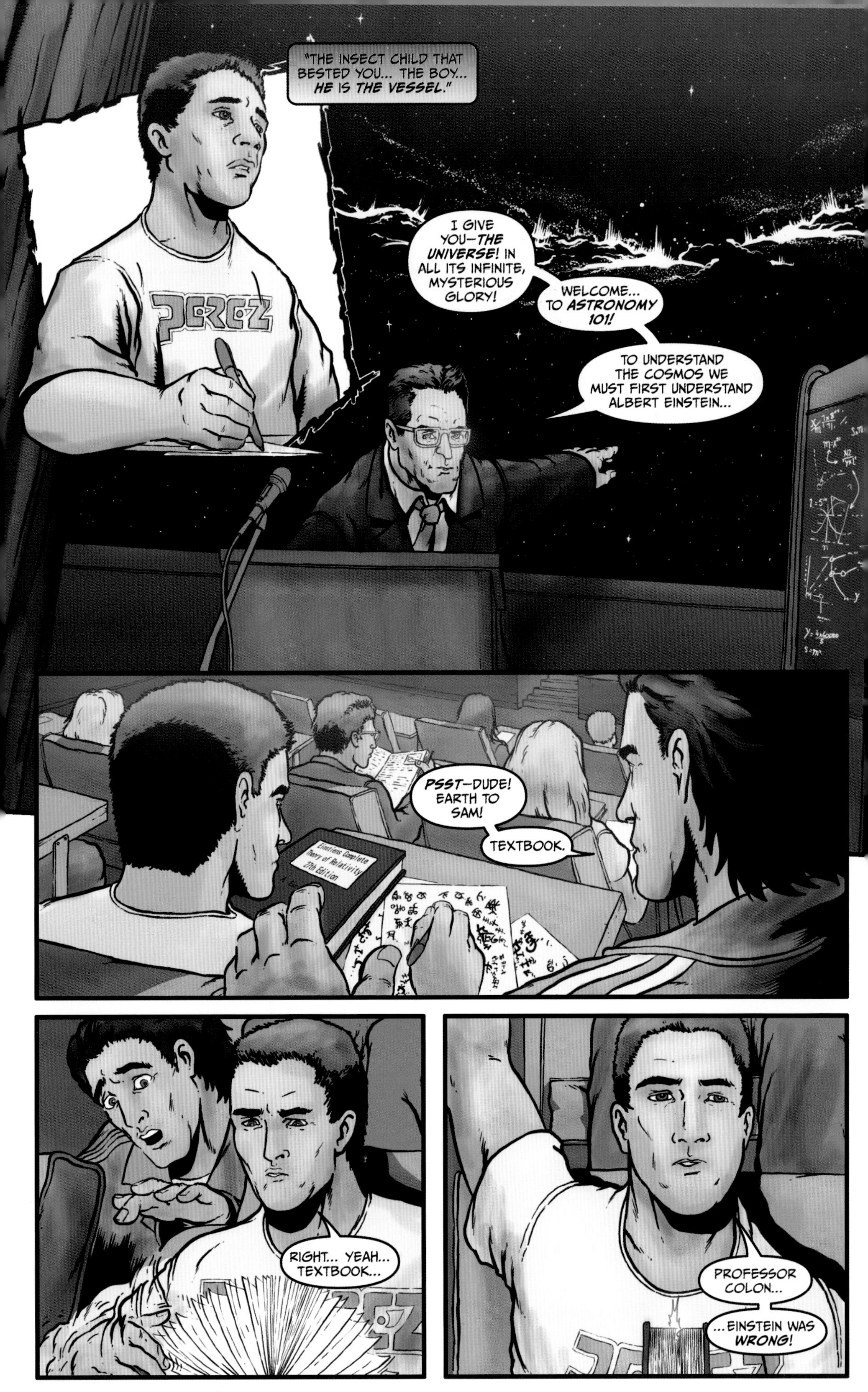
"THE INSECT CHILD THAT BESTED YOU... THE BOY... HE IS THE VESSEL."
I GIVE YOU—THE UNIVERSE! IN ALL ITS INFINITE, MYSTERIOUS GLORY!
WELCOME... TO ASTRONOMY 101!
TO UNDERSTAND THE COSMOS WE MUST FIRST UNDERSTAND ALBERT EINSTEIN...
PSST—DUDE! EARTH TO SAM!
TEXTBOOK.
Einstiens Complete Theory of Relativity 27th Edition
RIGHT... YEAH... TEXTBOOK...
PROFESSOR COLON...
...EINSTEIN WAS WRONG!

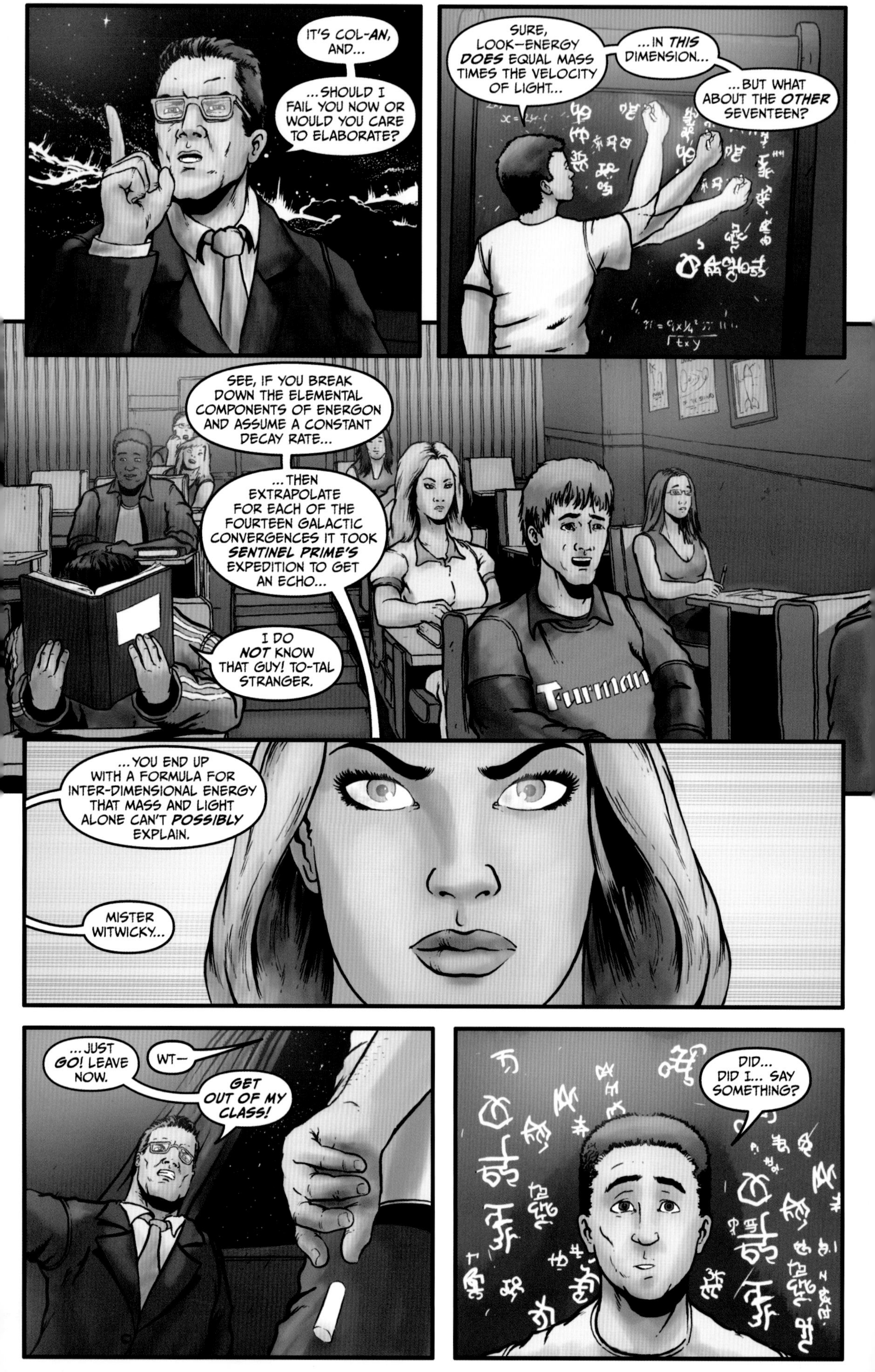
IT'S COL-AN, AND...
...SHOULD I FAIL YOU NOW OR WOULD YOU CARE TO ELABORATE?
SURE, LOOK—ENERGY DOES EQUAL MASS TIMES THE VELOCITY OF LIGHT...
...IN THIS DIMENSION...
...BUT WHAT ABOUT THE OTHER SEVENTEEN?
SEE, IF YOU BREAK DOWN THE ELEMENTAL COMPONENTS OF ENERGON AND ASSUME A CONSTANT DECAY RATE...
...THEN EXTRAPOLATE FOR EACH OF THE FOURTEEN GALACTIC CONVERGENCES IT TOOK SENTINEL PRIME'S EXPEDITION TO GET AN ECHO...
I DO NOT KNOW THAT GUY! TO-TAL STRANGER.
...YOU END UP WITH A FORMULA FOR INTER-DIMENSIONAL ENERGY THAT MASS AND LIGHT ALONE CAN'T POSSIBLY EXPLAIN.
MISTER WITWICKY...
...JUST GO! LEAVE NOW.
WT—
GET OUT OF MY CLASS!
DID... DID I... SAY SOMETHING?

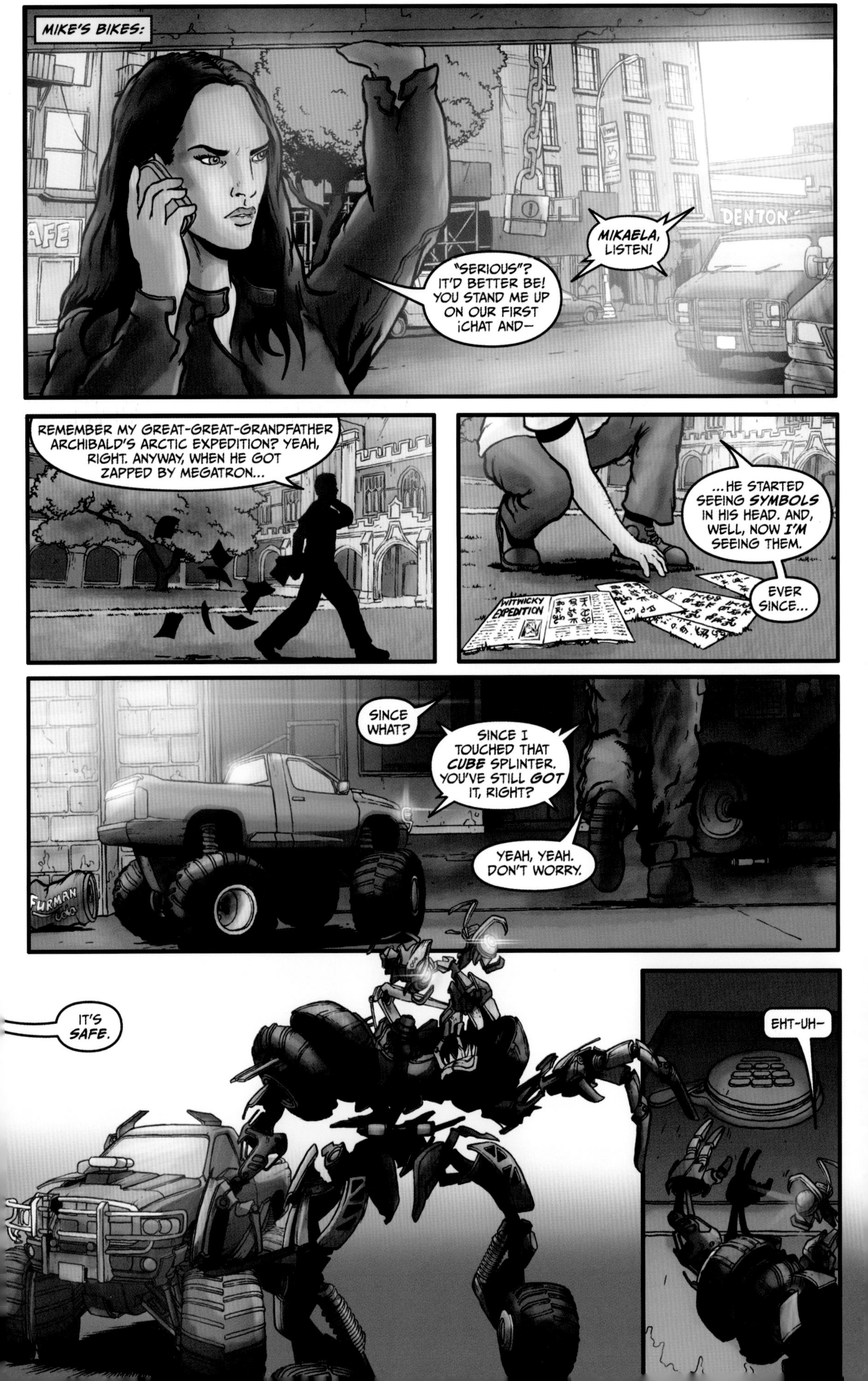

MIKE'S BIKES:
AFE
DENTON
"SERIOUS"? IT'D BETTER BE! YOU STAND ME UP ON OUR FIRST iCHAT AND—
MIKAELA, LISTEN!
REMEMBER MY GREAT-GREAT-GRANDFATHER ARCHIBALD'S ARCTIC EXPEDITION? YEAH, RIGHT. ANYWAY, WHEN HE GOT ZAPPED BY MEGATRON...
...HE STARTED SEEING SYMBOLS IN HIS HEAD. AND, WELL, NOW I'M SEEING THEM.
EVER SINCE...
WITWICKY EXPEDITION
SINCE WHAT?
SINCE I TOUCHED THAT CUBE SPLINTER. YOU'VE STILL GOT IT, RIGHT?
YEAH, YEAH. DON'T WORRY.
FURMAN
IT'S SAFE.
EHT-UH-

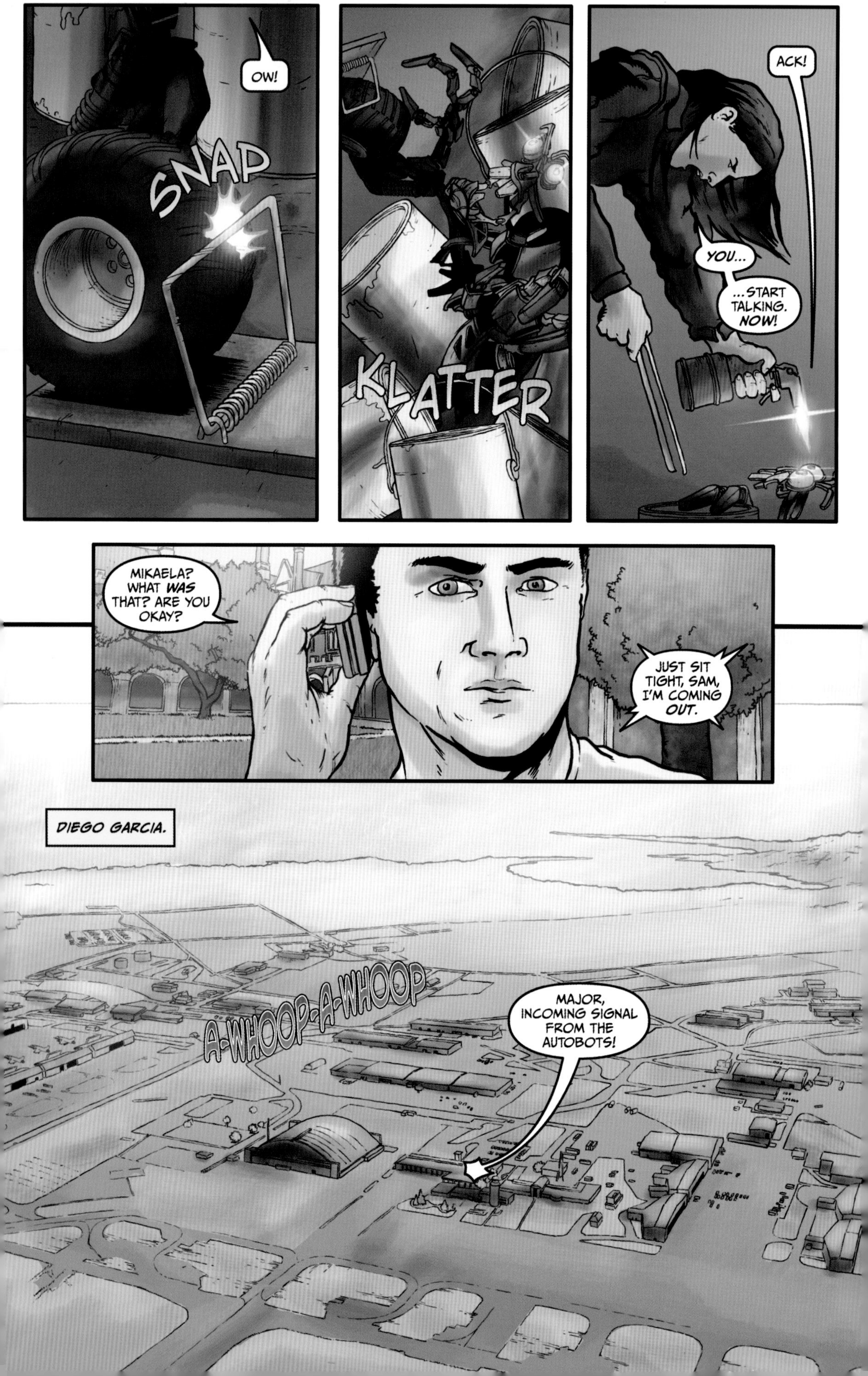
OW!
SNAP
KLATTER
ACK!
YOU...
...START TALKING. NOW!
MIKAELA? WHAT WAS THAT? ARE YOU OKAY?
JUST SIT TIGHT, SAM, I'M COMING OUT.
DIEGO GARCIA.
A-WHOOP-A-WHOOP
MAJOR, INCOMING SIGNAL FROM THE AUTOBOTS!

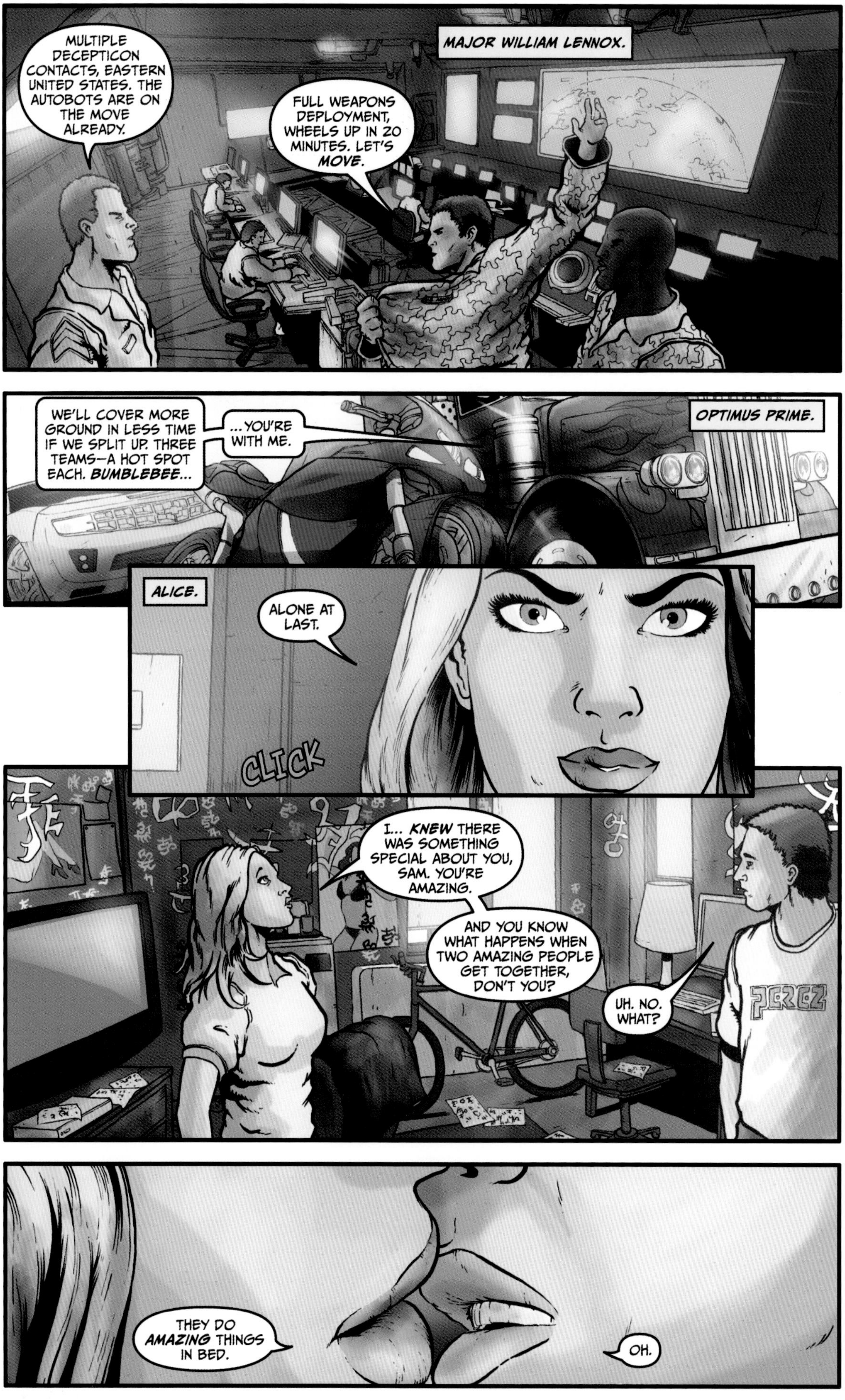
MAJOR WILLIAM LENNOX.
MULTIPLE DECEPTICON CONTACTS, EASTERN UNITED STATES. THE AUTOBOTS ARE ON THE MOVE ALREADY.
FULL WEAPONS DEPLOYMENT, WHEELS UP IN 20 MINUTES. LET'S MOVE.
OPTIMUS PRIME.
WE'LL COVER MORE GROUND IN LESS TIME IF WE SPLIT UP. THREE TEAMS—A HOT SPOT EACH. BUMBLEBEE...
...YOU'RE WITH ME.
ALICE.
ALONE AT LAST.
CLICK
I... KNEW THERE WAS SOMETHING SPECIAL ABOUT YOU, SAM. YOU'RE AMAZING.
AND YOU KNOW WHAT HAPPENS WHEN TWO AMAZING PEOPLE GET TOGETHER, DON'T YOU?
UH. NO. WHAT?
THEY DO AMAZING THINGS IN BED.
OH.

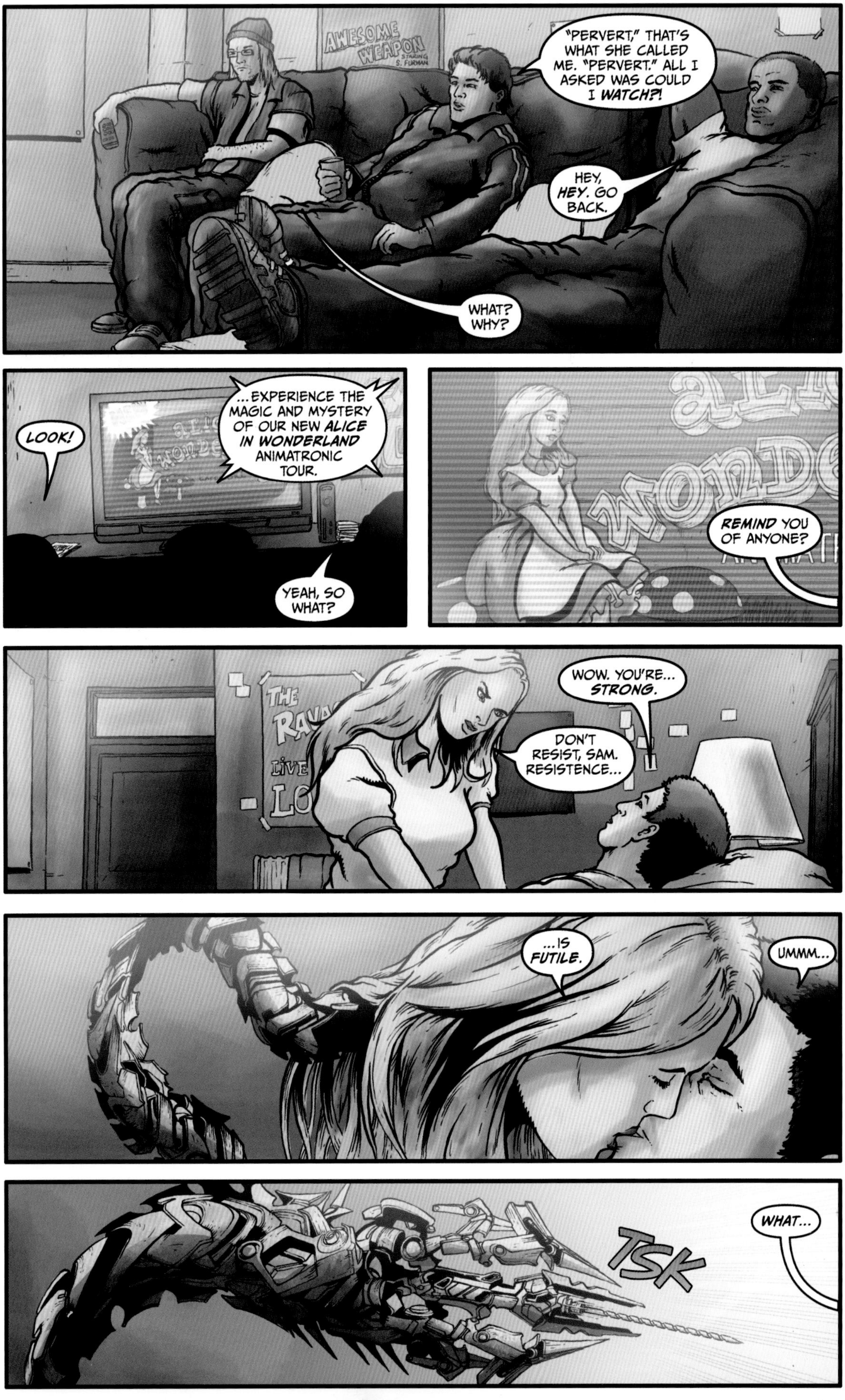
AWESOME WEAPON STARING S. FURMAN
"PERVERT," THAT'S WHAT SHE CALLED ME. "PERVERT." ALL I ASKED WAS COULD I WATCH?!
HEY, HEY. GO BACK.
WHAT? WHY?
...EXPERIENCE THE MAGIC AND MYSTERY OF OUR NEW ALICE IN WONDERLAND ANIMATRONIC TOUR.
LOOK!
YEAH, SO WHAT?
REMIND YOU OF ANYONE?
WOW. YOU'RE... STRONG.
DON'T RESIST, SAM. RESISTENCE...
...IS FUTILE.
UMMM...
WHAT...
TSK

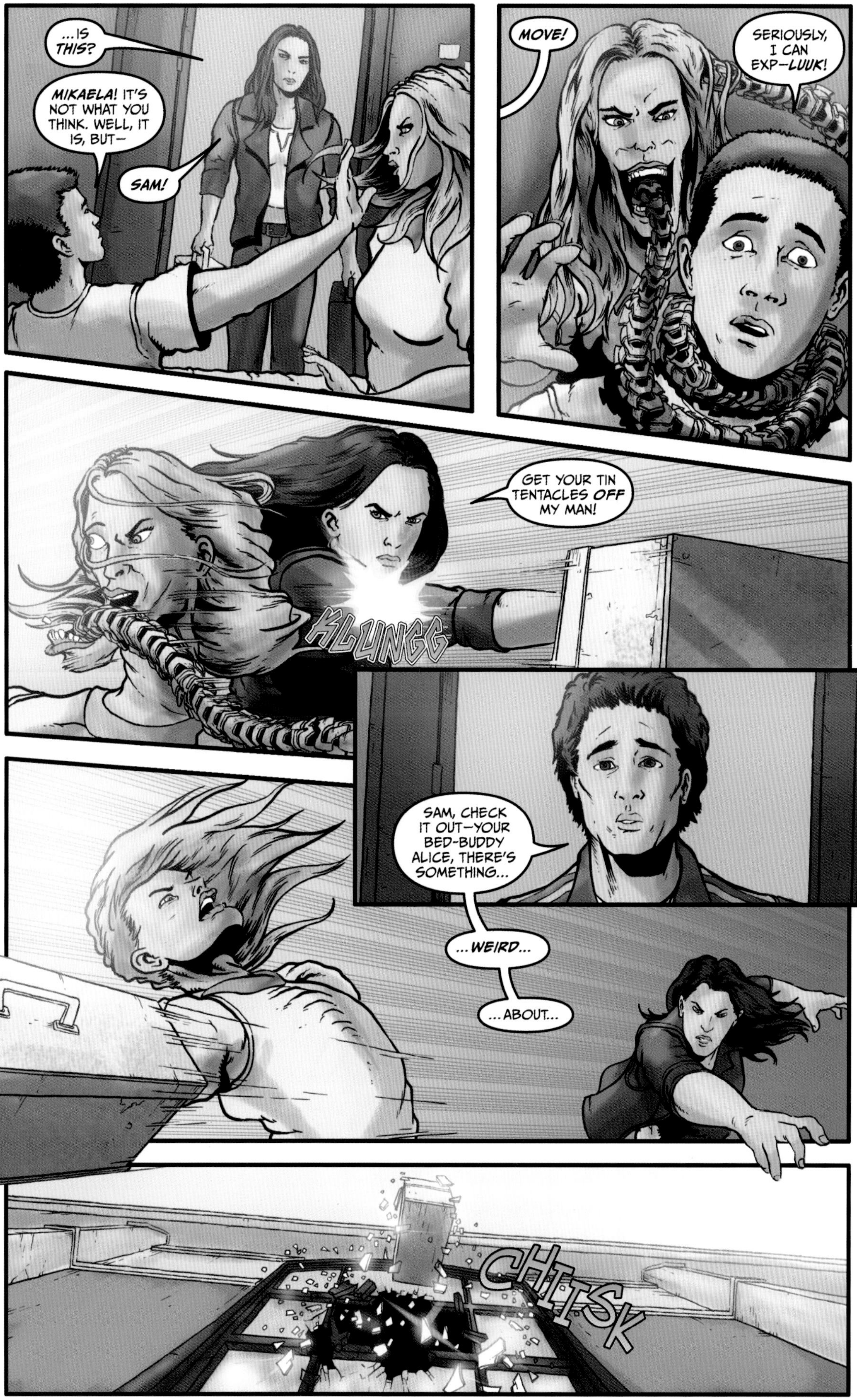
...IS THIS?
MIKAELA! IT'S NOT WHAT YOU THINK. WELL, IT IS, BUT—
SAM!
MOVE!
SERIOUSLY, I CAN EXP—LUUK!
GET YOUR TIN TENTACLES OFF MY MAN!
KLUNGG
SAM, CHECK IT OUT—YOUR BED-BUDDY ALICE, THERE'S SOMETHING...
...WEIRD...
...ABOUT...
CHISK

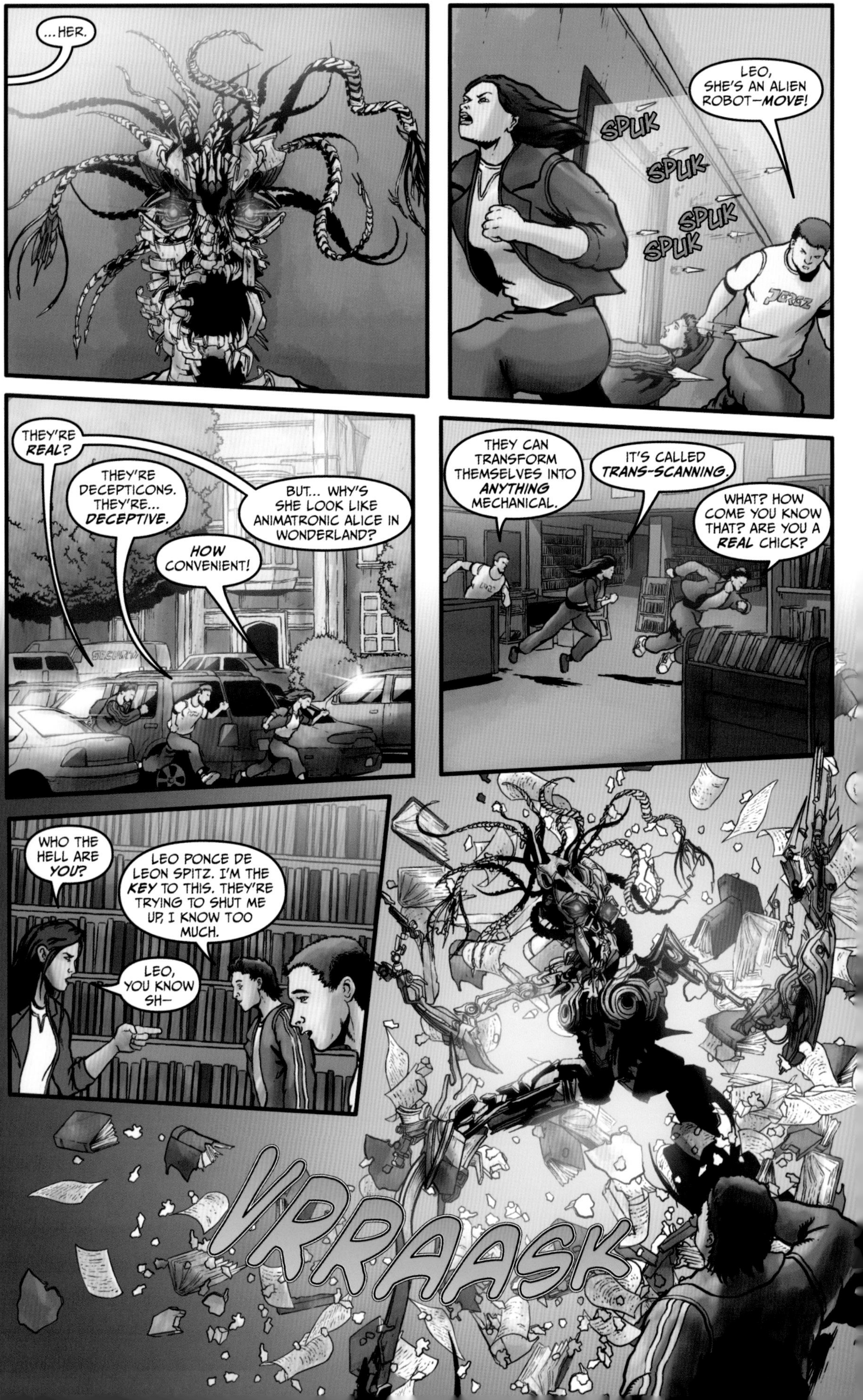
...HER.
LEO, SHE'S AN ALIEN ROBOT—MOVE!
SPUK
SPUK
SPUK
SPUK
THEY'RE REAL?
THEY'RE DECEPTICONS. THEY'RE... DECEPTIVE.
BUT... WHY'S SHE LOOK LIKE ANIMATRONIC ALICE IN WONDERLAND?
HOW CONVENIENT!
THEY CAN TRANSFORM THEMSELVES INTO ANYTHING MECHANICAL.
IT'S CALLED TRANS-SCANNING.
WHAT? HOW COME YOU KNOW THAT? ARE YOU A REAL CHICK?
WHO THE HELL ARE YOU?
LEO PONCE DE LEON SPITZ. I'M THE KEY TO THIS. THEY'RE TRYING TO SHUT ME UP, I KNOW TOO MUCH.
LEO, YOU KNOW SH—
VRRAASK

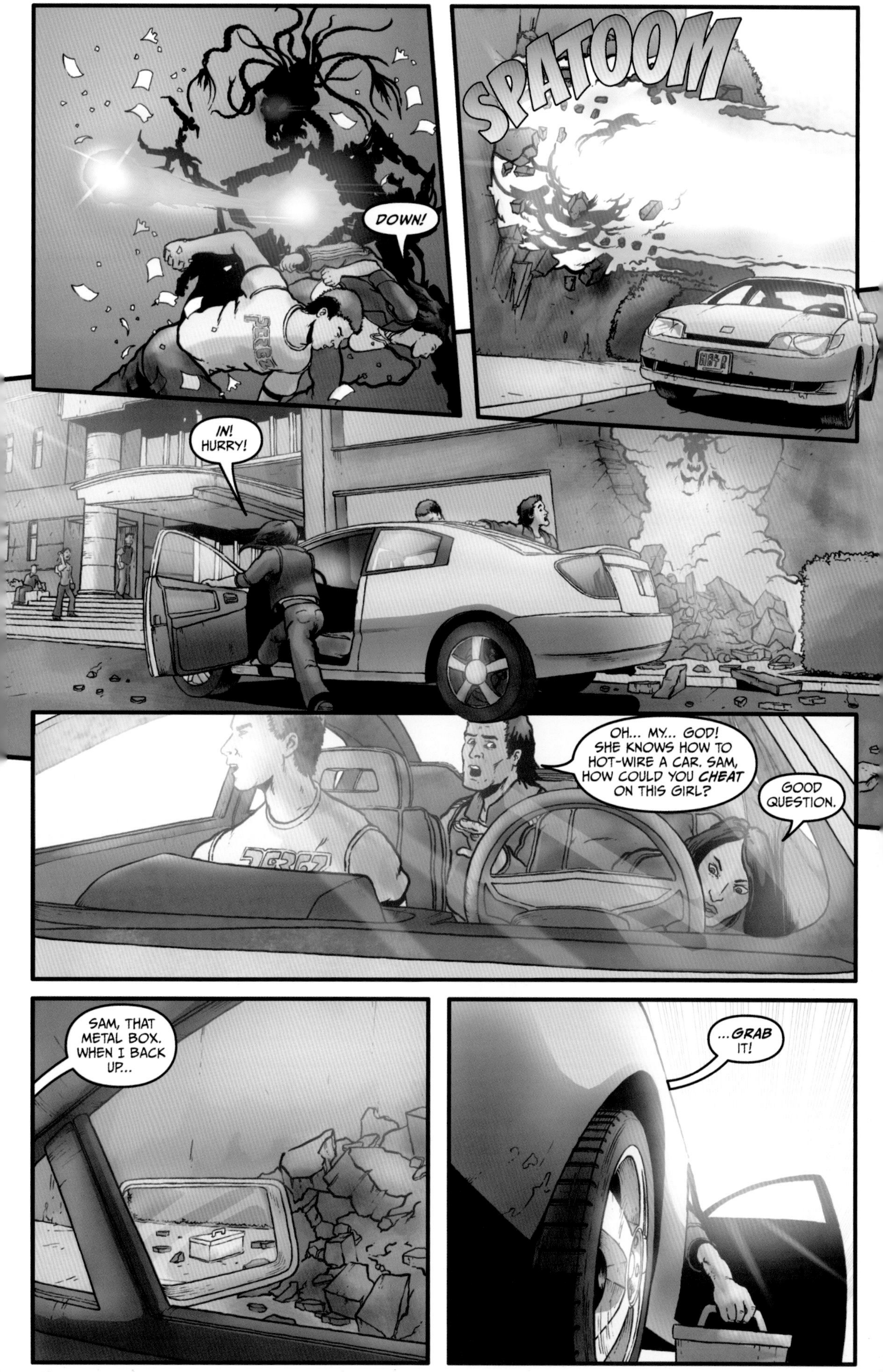
DOWN!
SPATOOM
IN! HURRY!
OH... MY... GOD! SHE KNOWS HOW TO HOT-WIRE A CAR. SAM, HOW COULD YOU *CHEAT* ON THIS GIRL?
GOOD QUESTION.
SAM, THAT METAL BOX. WHEN I BACK UP...
...*GRAB* IT!

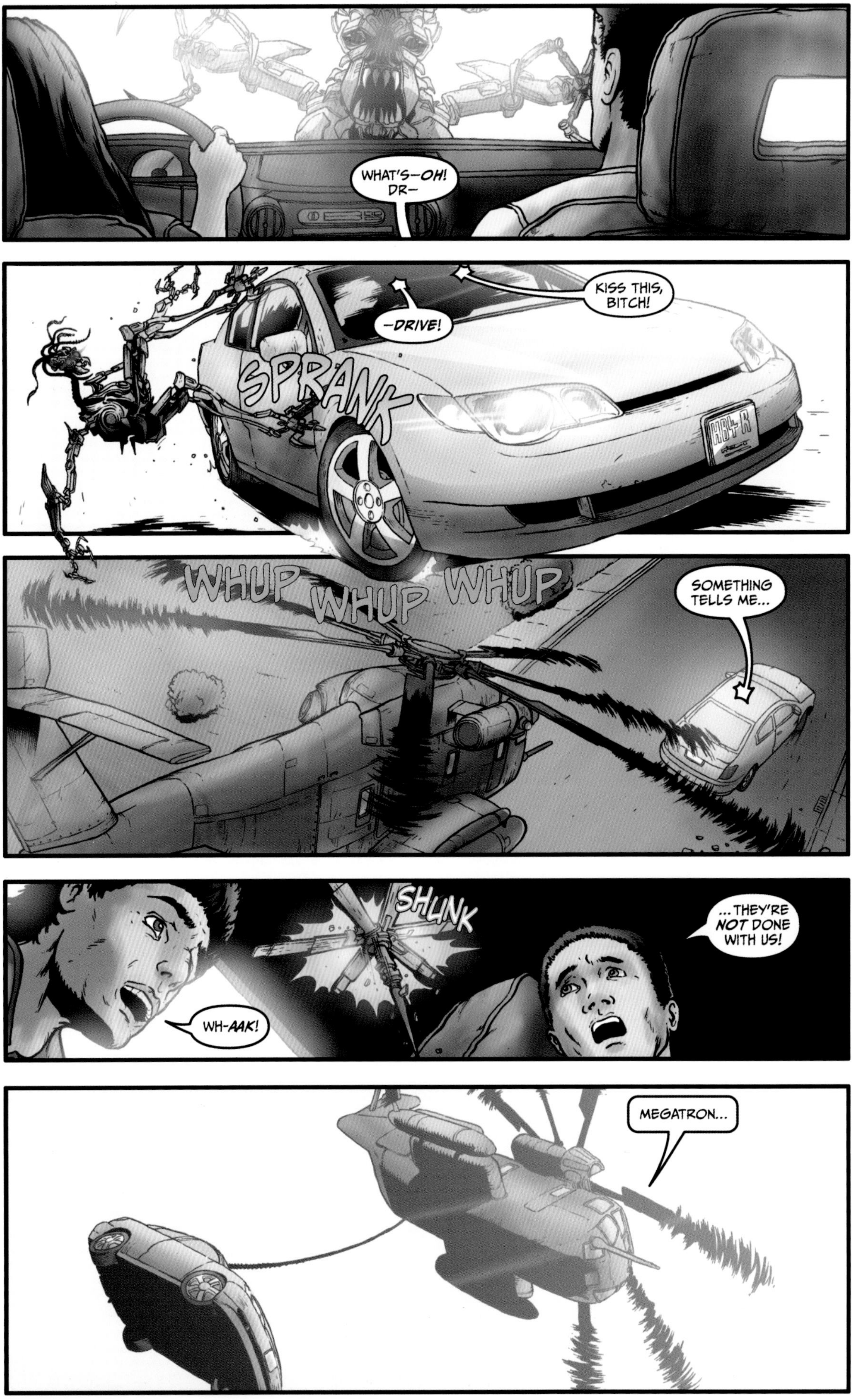
WHAT'S—OH! DR—
—DRIVE!
KISS THIS, BITCH!
SPRANK
HB4R
WHUP WHUP WHUP
SOMETHING TELLS ME...
SHUNK
WH-AAK!
...THEY'RE NOT DONE WITH US!
MEGATRON...

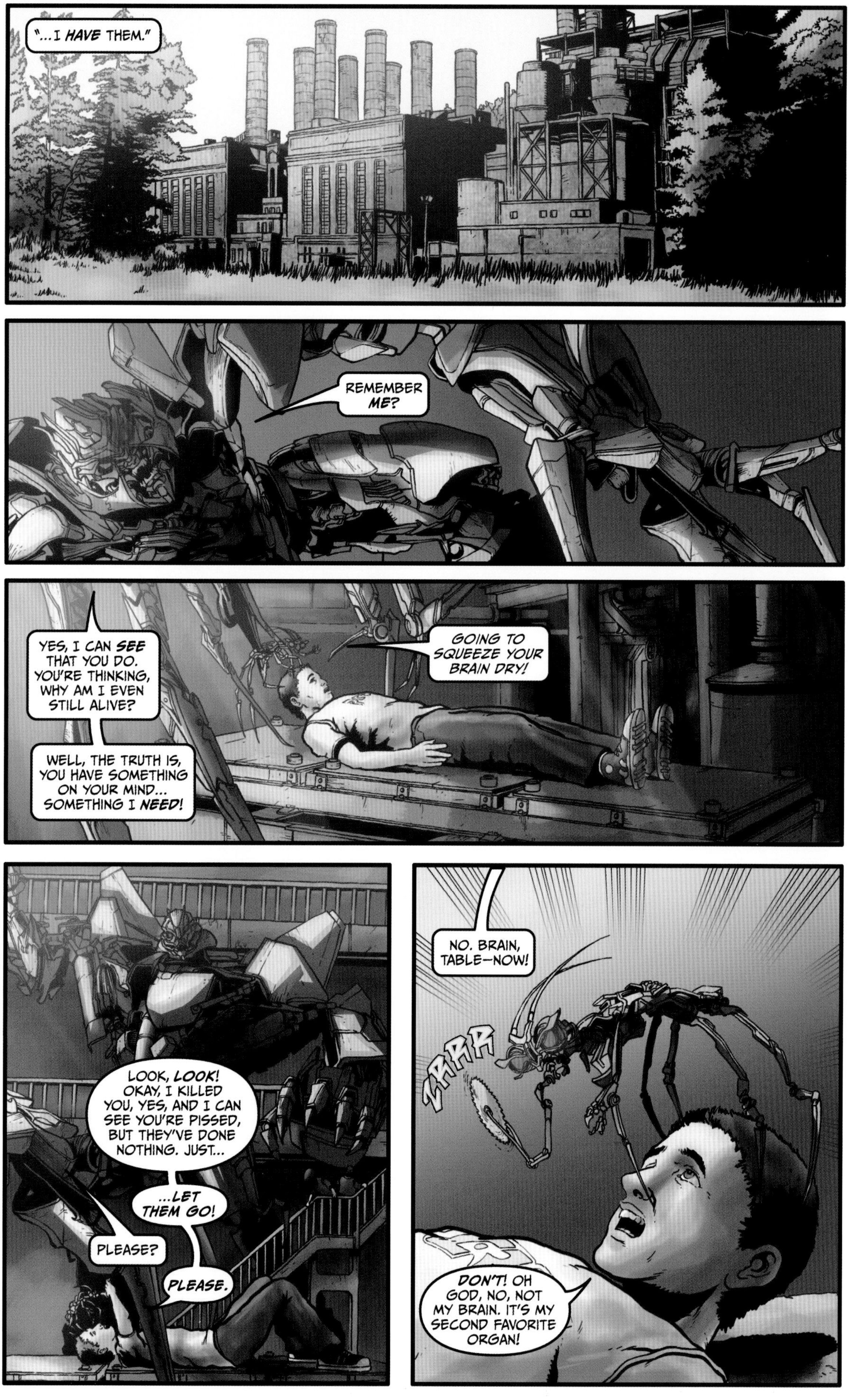
"...I *HAVE* THEM."
REMEMBER *ME*?
YES, I CAN *SEE* THAT YOU DO. YOU'RE THINKING, WHY AM I EVEN STILL ALIVE?
GOING TO SQUEEZE YOUR BRAIN DRY!
WELL, THE TRUTH IS, YOU HAVE SOMETHING ON YOUR MIND... SOMETHING I *NEED*!
LOOK, *LOOK*! OKAY, I KILLED YOU, YES, AND I CAN SEE YOU'RE PISSED, BUT THEY'VE DONE NOTHING. JUST...
...LET THEM GO!
PLEASE?
PLEASE.
NO. BRAIN, TABLE—NOW!
ZRRR
DON'T! OH GOD, NO, NOT MY BRAIN. IT'S MY SECOND FAVORITE ORGAN!

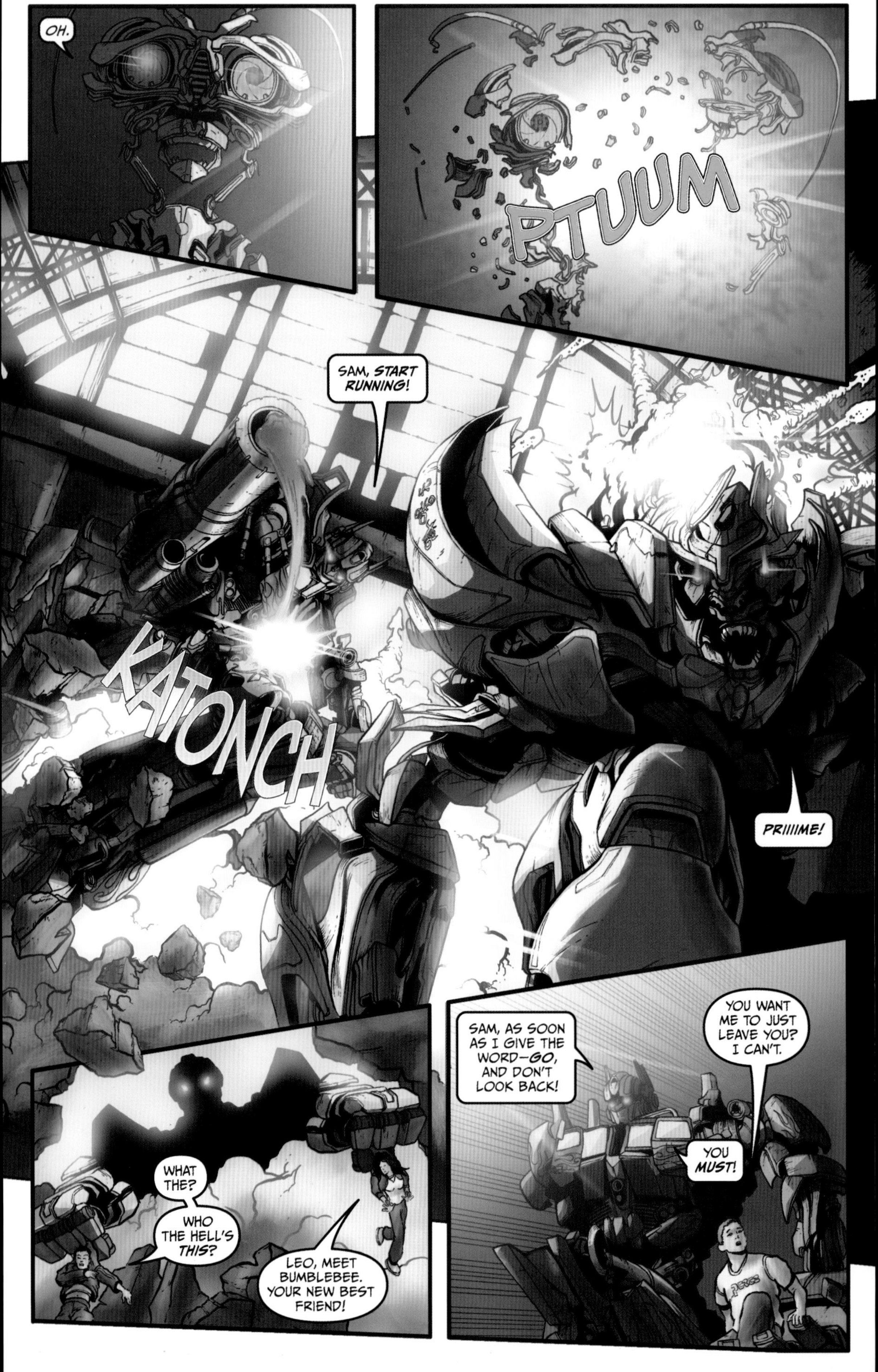
OH.
PTUUM
SAM, START RUNNING!
KATONCH
PRIIIIME!
WHAT THE?
WHO THE HELL'S THIS?
LEO, MEET BUMBLEBEE. YOUR NEW BEST FRIEND!
SAM, AS SOON AS I GIVE THE WORD—GO, AND DON'T LOOK BACK!
YOU WANT ME TO JUST LEAVE YOU? I CAN'T.
YOU MUST!

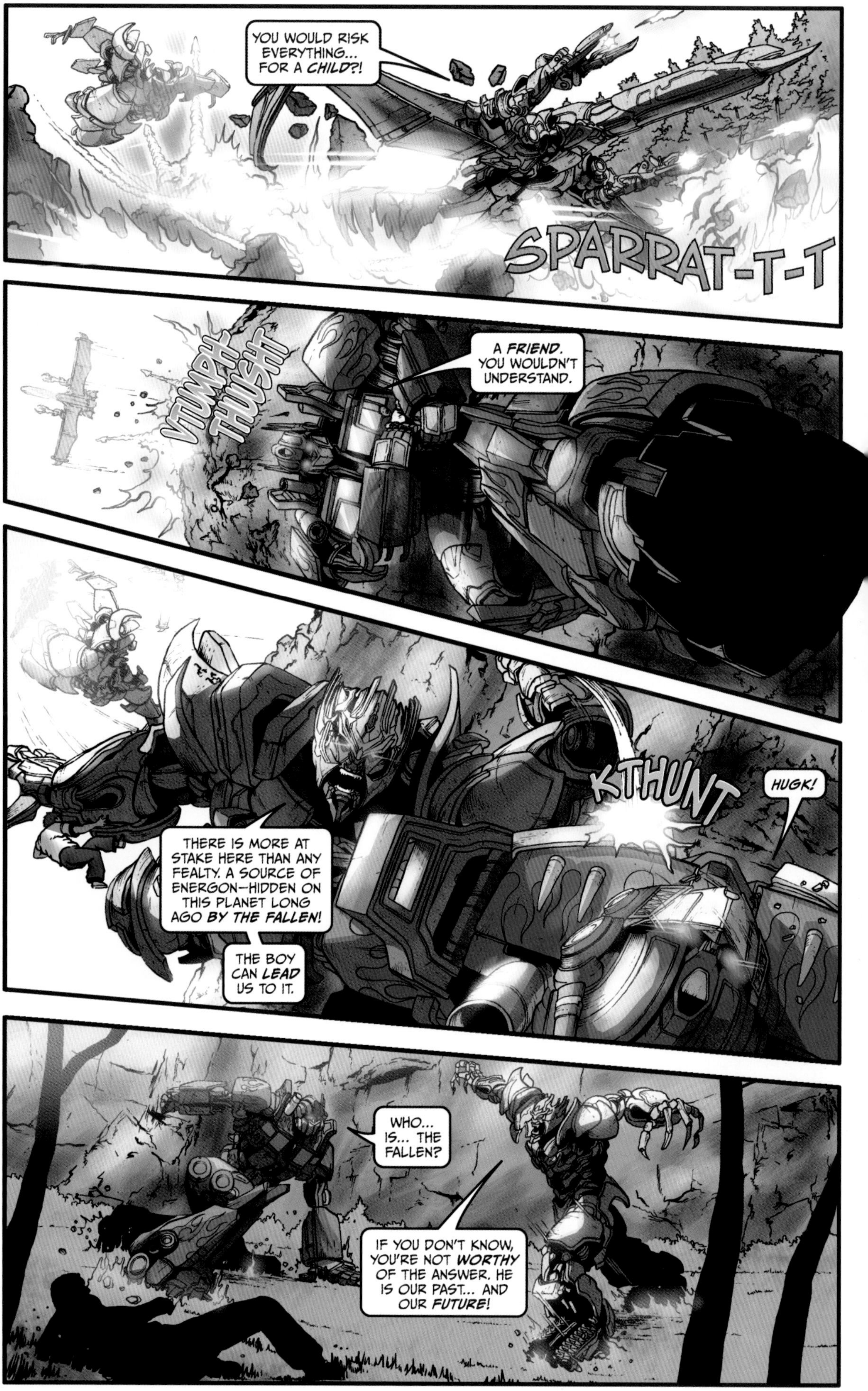
YOU WOULD RISK EVERYTHING... FOR A CHILD?!
SPARRAT-T-T
VTUMPH- THUSHT
A FRIEND. YOU WOULDN'T UNDERSTAND.
KTHUNT
HUGK!
THERE IS MORE AT STAKE HERE THAN ANY FEALTY. A SOURCE OF ENERGON--HIDDEN ON THIS PLANET LONG AGO BY THE FALLEN!
THE BOY CAN LEAD US TO IT.
WHO... IS... THE FALLEN?
IF YOU DON'T KNOW, YOU'RE NOT WORTHY OF THE ANSWER. HE IS OUR PAST... AND OUR FUTURE!

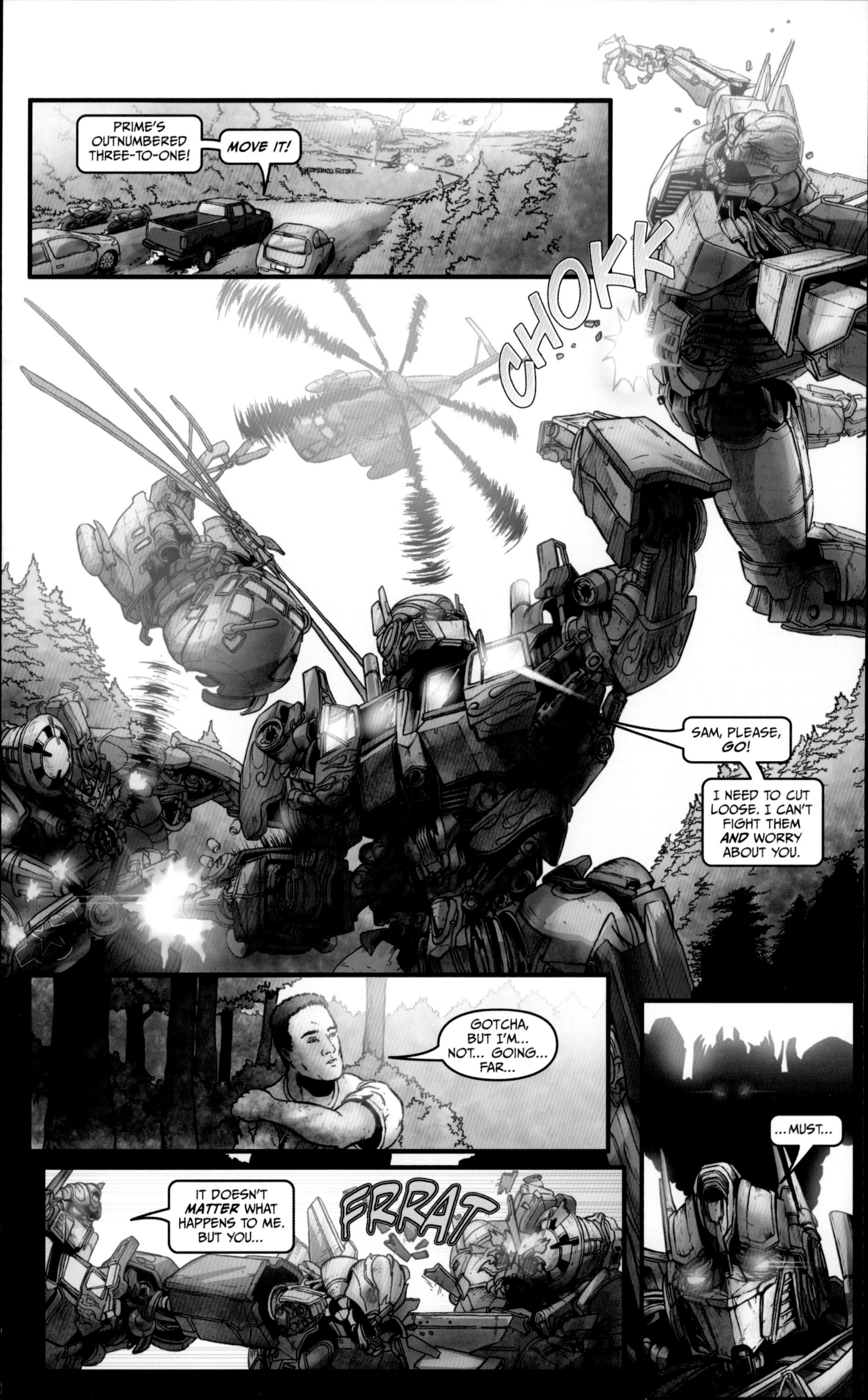
PRIME'S OUTNUMBERED THREE-TO-ONE!
MOVE IT!
CHOKK
SAM, PLEASE, GO!
I NEED TO CUT LOOSE. I CAN'T FIGHT THEM AND WORRY ABOUT YOU.
GOTCHA, BUT I'M... NOT... GOING... FAR...
IT DOESN'T MATTER WHAT HAPPENS TO ME. BUT YOU...
FRRAT
...MUST...

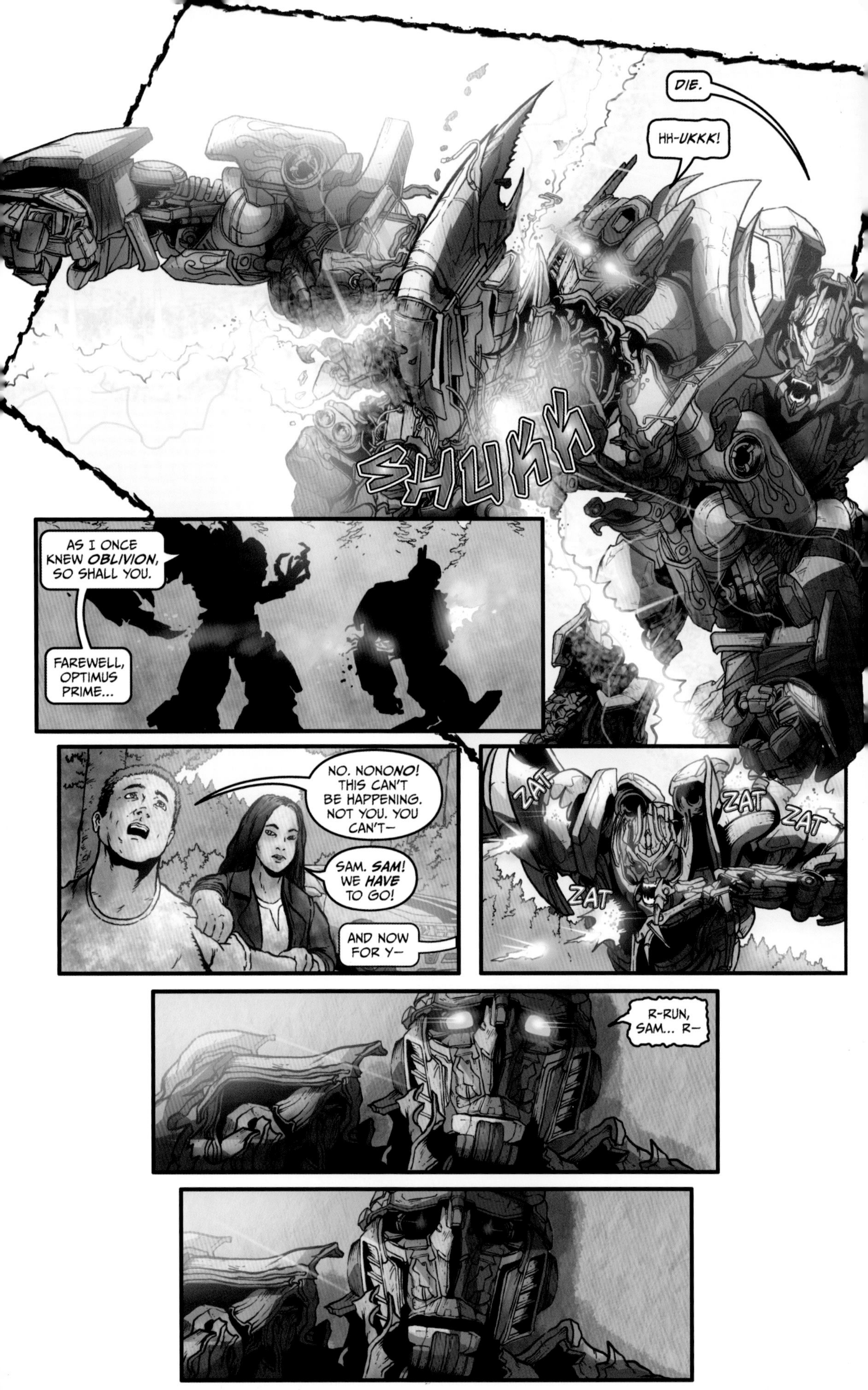
DIE.
HH-UKKK!
SHUKK
AS I ONCE KNEW OBLIVION, SO SHALL YOU.
FAREWELL, OPTIMUS PRIME...
NO. NONONO! THIS CAN'T BE HAPPENING. NOT YOU. YOU CAN'T—
SAM. SAM! WE HAVE TO GO!
AND NOW FOR Y—
ZAT
ZAT
ZAT
ZAT
R-RUN, SAM... R—

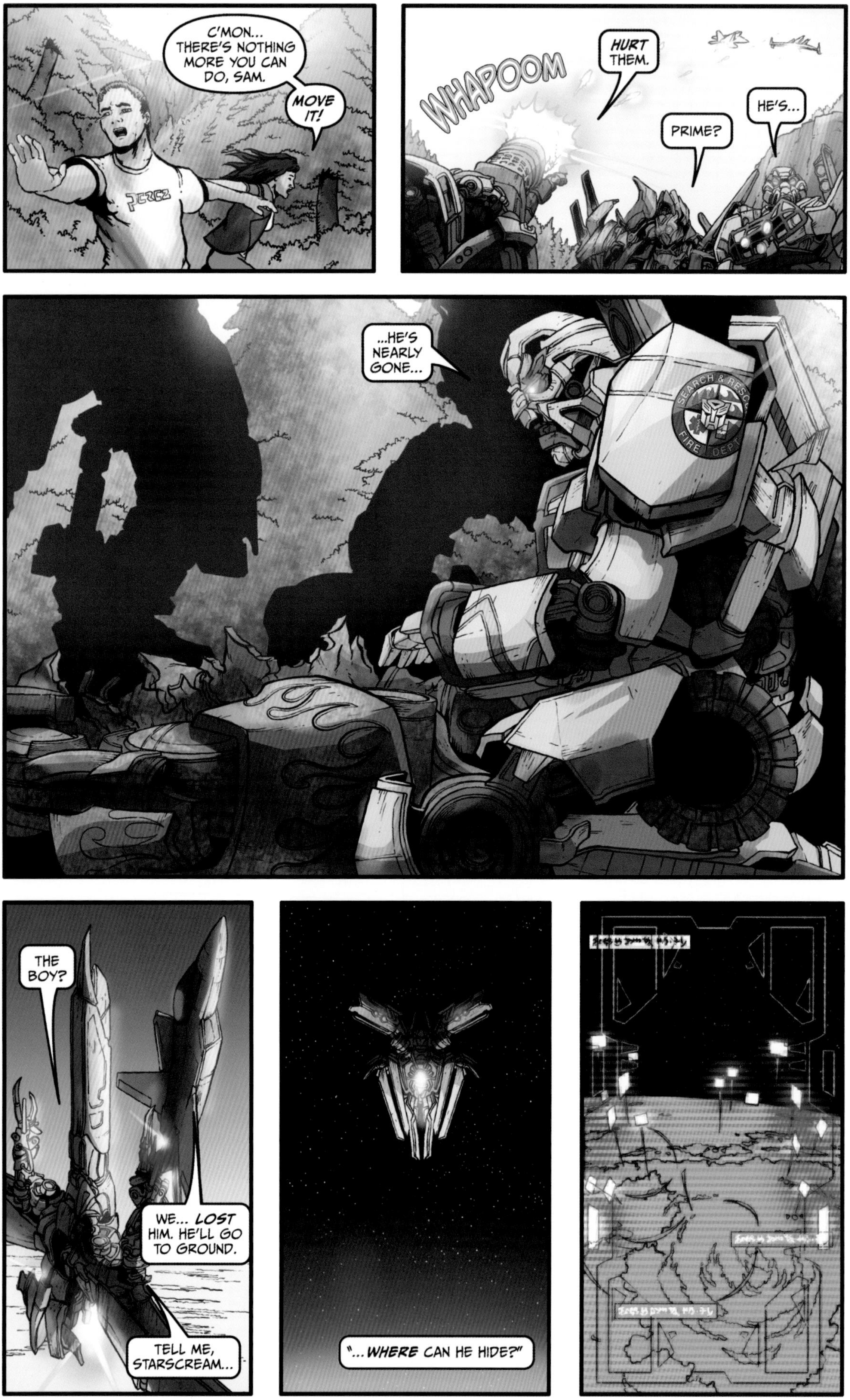
C'MON... THERE'S NOTHING MORE YOU CAN DO, SAM.
MOVE IT!
WHAPOOM
HURT THEM.
PRIME?
HE'S...
...HE'S NEARLY GONE...
SEARCH & RESCUE
FIRE DEPT
THE BOY?
WE... LOST HIM. HE'LL GO TO GROUND.
TELL ME, STARSCREAM...
"...WHERE CAN HE HIDE?"

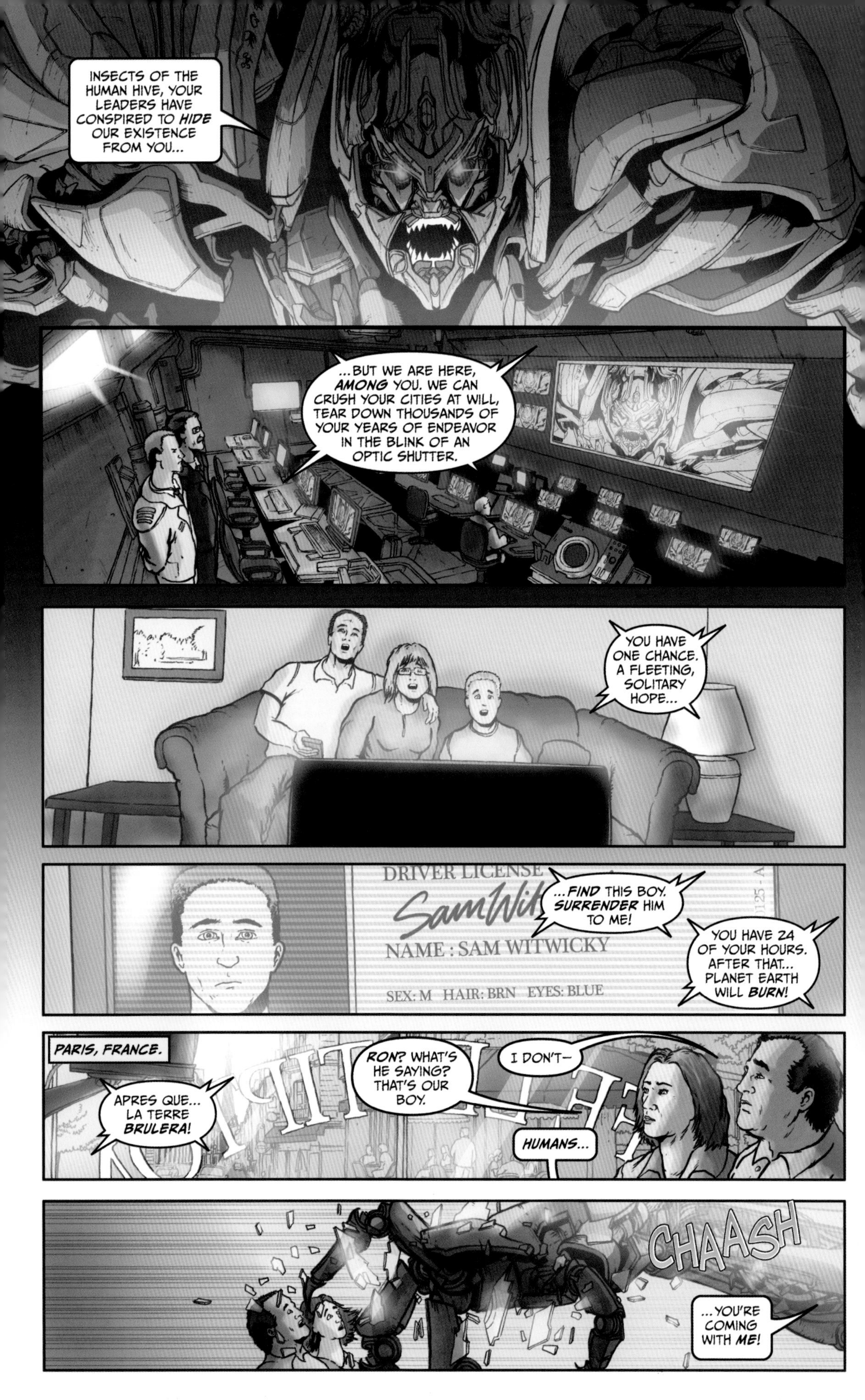
INSECTS OF THE HUMAN HIVE, YOUR LEADERS HAVE CONSPIRED TO *HIDE* OUR EXISTENCE FROM YOU...
...BUT WE ARE HERE, *AMONG* YOU. WE CAN CRUSH YOUR CITIES AT WILL, TEAR DOWN THOUSANDS OF YOUR YEARS OF ENDEAVOR IN THE BLINK OF AN OPTIC SHUTTER.
YOU HAVE ONE CHANCE. A FLEETING, SOLITARY HOPE...
DRIVER LICENSE
NAME : SAM WITWICKY
SEX: M HAIR: BRN EYES: BLUE
...*FIND* THIS BOY. *SURRENDER* HIM TO ME!
YOU HAVE 24 OF YOUR HOURS. AFTER THAT... PLANET EARTH WILL *BURN*!
PARIS, FRANCE.
APRES QUE... LA TERRE *BRULERA*!
RON? WHAT'S HE SAYING? THAT'S OUR BOY.
I DON'T—
HUMANS...
CHAASH
...YOU'RE COMING WITH *ME*!

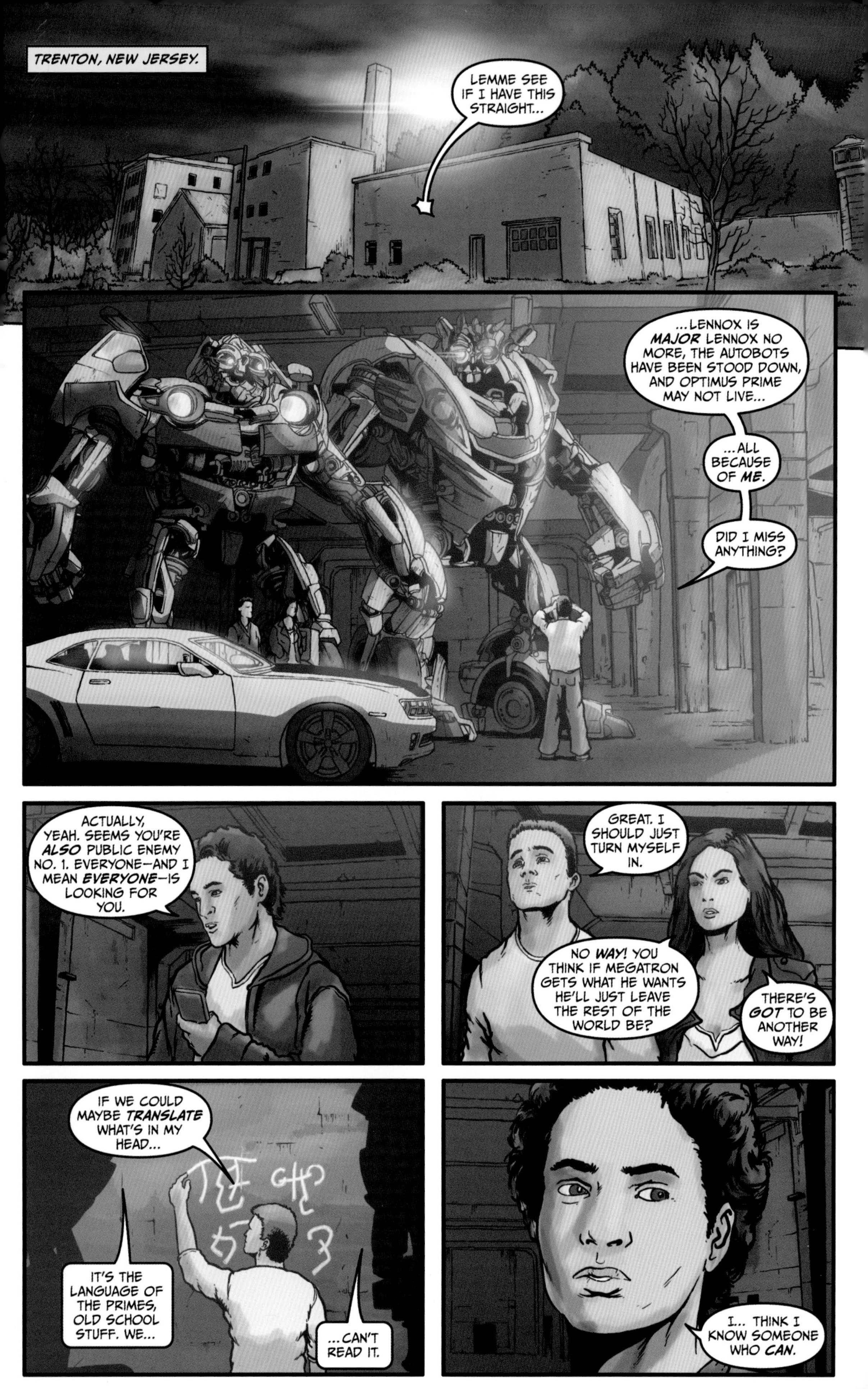
TRENTON, NEW JERSEY.
LEMME SEE IF I HAVE THIS STRAIGHT...
...LENNOX IS MAJOR LENNOX NO MORE, THE AUTOBOTS HAVE BEEN STOOD DOWN, AND OPTIMUS PRIME MAY NOT LIVE...
...ALL BECAUSE OF ME.
DID I MISS ANYTHING?
ACTUALLY, YEAH. SEEMS YOU'RE ALSO PUBLIC ENEMY NO. 1. EVERYONE—AND I MEAN EVERYONE—IS LOOKING FOR YOU.
GREAT. I SHOULD JUST TURN MYSELF IN.
NO WAY! YOU THINK IF MEGATRON GETS WHAT HE WANTS HE'LL JUST LEAVE THE REST OF THE WORLD BE?
THERE'S GOT TO BE ANOTHER WAY!
IF WE COULD MAYBE TRANSLATE WHAT'S IN MY HEAD...
IT'S THE LANGUAGE OF THE PRIMES, OLD SCHOOL STUFF. WE...
...CAN'T READ IT.
I... THINK I KNOW SOMEONE WHO CAN.

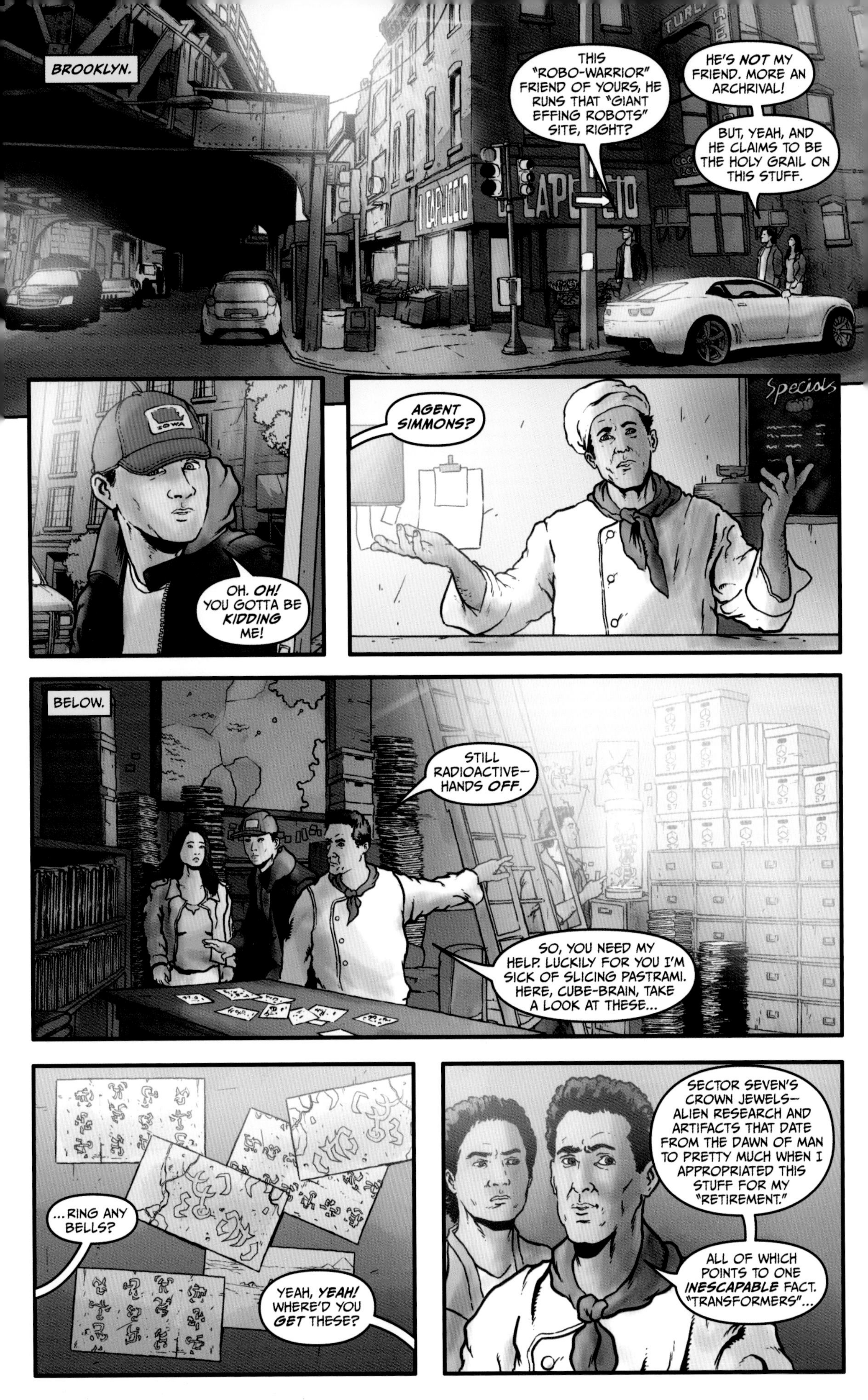
BROOKLYN.
THIS "ROBO-WARRIOR" FRIEND OF YOURS, HE RUNS THAT "GIANT EFFING ROBOTS" SITE, RIGHT?
HE'S NOT MY FRIEND. MORE AN ARCHRIVAL!
BUT, YEAH, AND HE CLAIMS TO BE THE HOLY GRAIL ON THIS STUFF.
I CAPUCCIO
OH. OH! YOU GOTTA BE KIDDING ME!
Specials
AGENT SIMMONS?
BELOW.
STILL RADIOACTIVE— HANDS OFF.
SO, YOU NEED MY HELP. LUCKILY FOR YOU I'M SICK OF SLICING PASTRAMI. HERE, CUBE-BRAIN, TAKE A LOOK AT THESE...
...RING ANY BELLS?
YEAH, YEAH! WHERE'D YOU GET THESE?
SECTOR SEVEN'S CROWN JEWELS— ALIEN RESEARCH AND ARTIFACTS THAT DATE FROM THE DAWN OF MAN TO PRETTY MUCH WHEN I APPROPRIATED THIS STUFF FOR MY "RETIREMENT."
ALL OF WHICH POINTS TO ONE INESCAPABLE FACT. "TRANSFORMERS"...

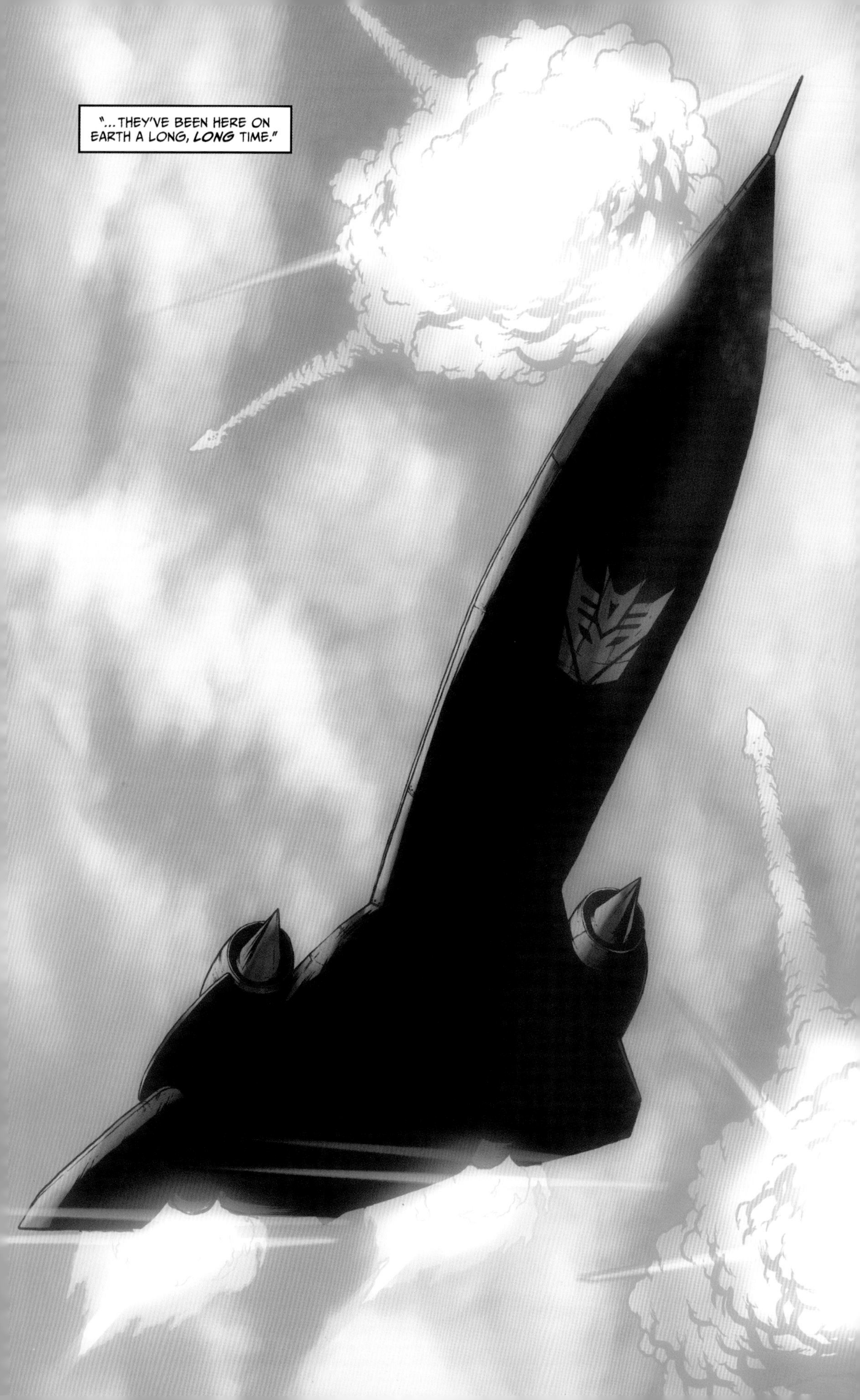
"...THEY'VE BEEN HERE ON EARTH A LONG, LONG TIME."

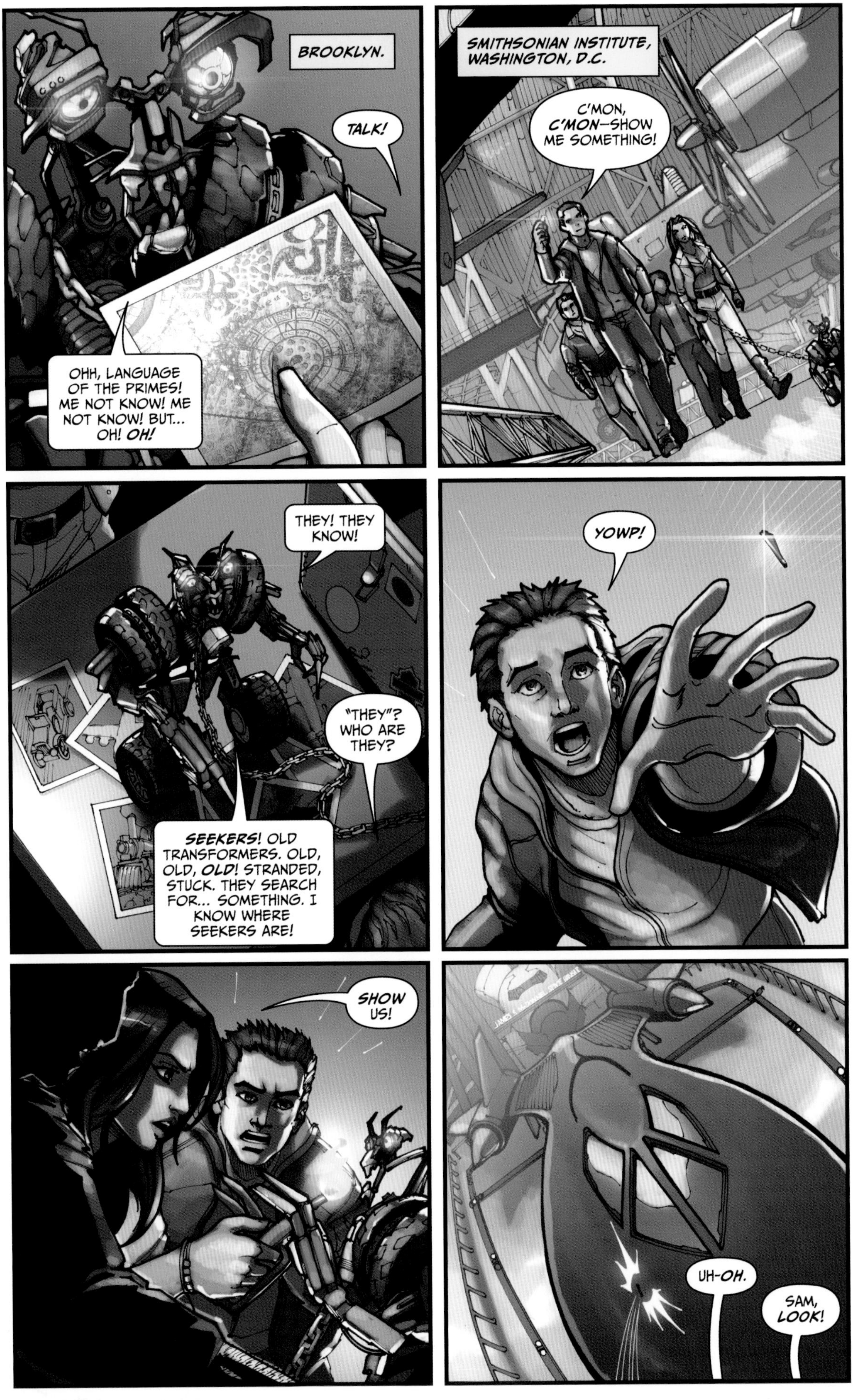
BROOKLYN.
TALK!
OHH, LANGUAGE OF THE PRIMES! ME NOT KNOW! ME NOT KNOW! BUT... OH! OH!
SMITHSONIAN INSTITUTE, WASHINGTON, D.C.
C'MON, C'MON—SHOW ME SOMETHING!
THEY! THEY KNOW!
"THEY"? WHO ARE THEY?
SEEKERS! OLD TRANSFORMERS. OLD, OLD, OLD! STRANDED, STUCK. THEY SEARCH FOR... SOMETHING. I KNOW WHERE SEEKERS ARE!
YOWP!
SHOW US!
UH-OH.
SAM, LOOK!

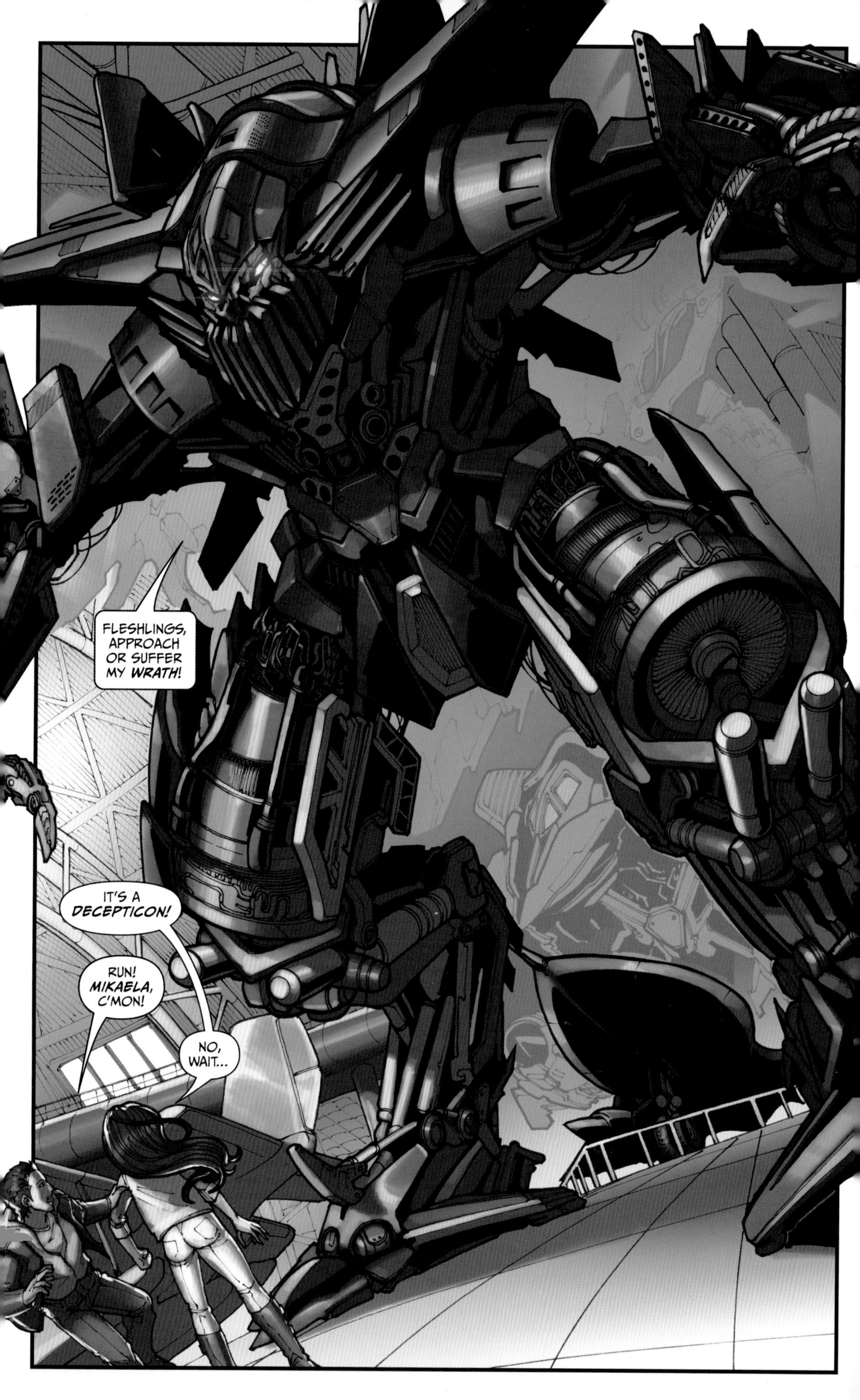
FLESHLINGS, APPROACH OR SUFFER MY WRATH!
IT'S A DECEPTICON!
RUN! MIKAELA, C'MON!
NO, WAIT...

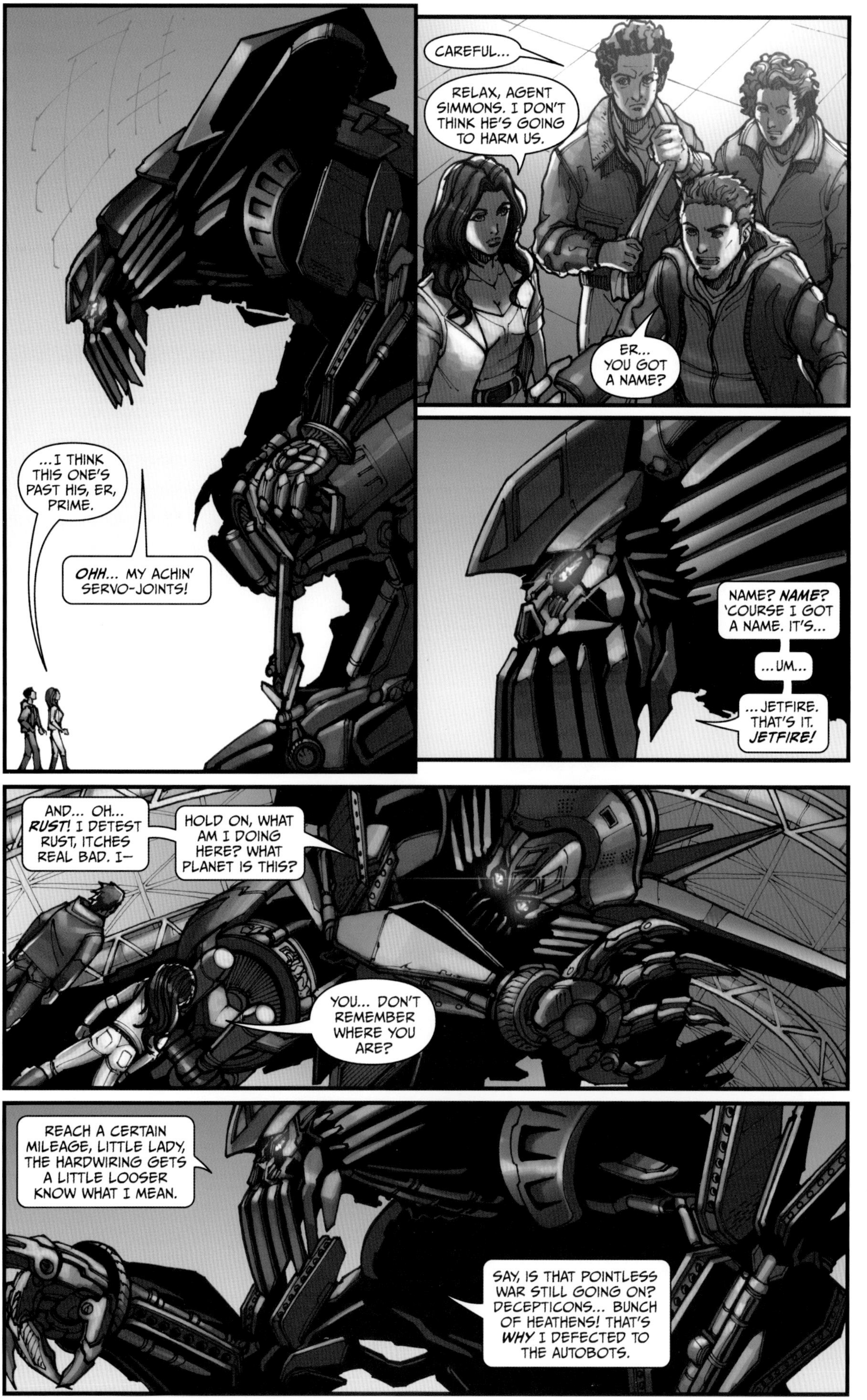
...I THINK THIS ONE'S PAST HIS, ER, PRIME.
OHH... MY ACHIN' SERVO-JOINTS!
CAREFUL...
RELAX, AGENT SIMMONS. I DON'T THINK HE'S GOING TO HARM US.
ER... YOU GOT A NAME?
NAME? *NAME?* 'COURSE I GOT A NAME. IT'S...
...UM...
...JETFIRE. THAT'S IT. *JETFIRE!*
AND... OH... *RUST!* I DETEST RUST, ITCHES REAL BAD. I—
HOLD ON, WHAT AM I DOING HERE? WHAT PLANET IS THIS?
YOU... DON'T REMEMBER WHERE YOU ARE?
REACH A CERTAIN MILEAGE, LITTLE LADY, THE HARDWIRING GETS A LITTLE LOOSER KNOW WHAT I MEAN.
SAY, IS THAT POINTLESS WAR STILL GOING ON? DECEPTICONS... BUNCH OF HEATHENS! THAT'S *WHY* I DEFECTED TO THE AUTOBOTS.

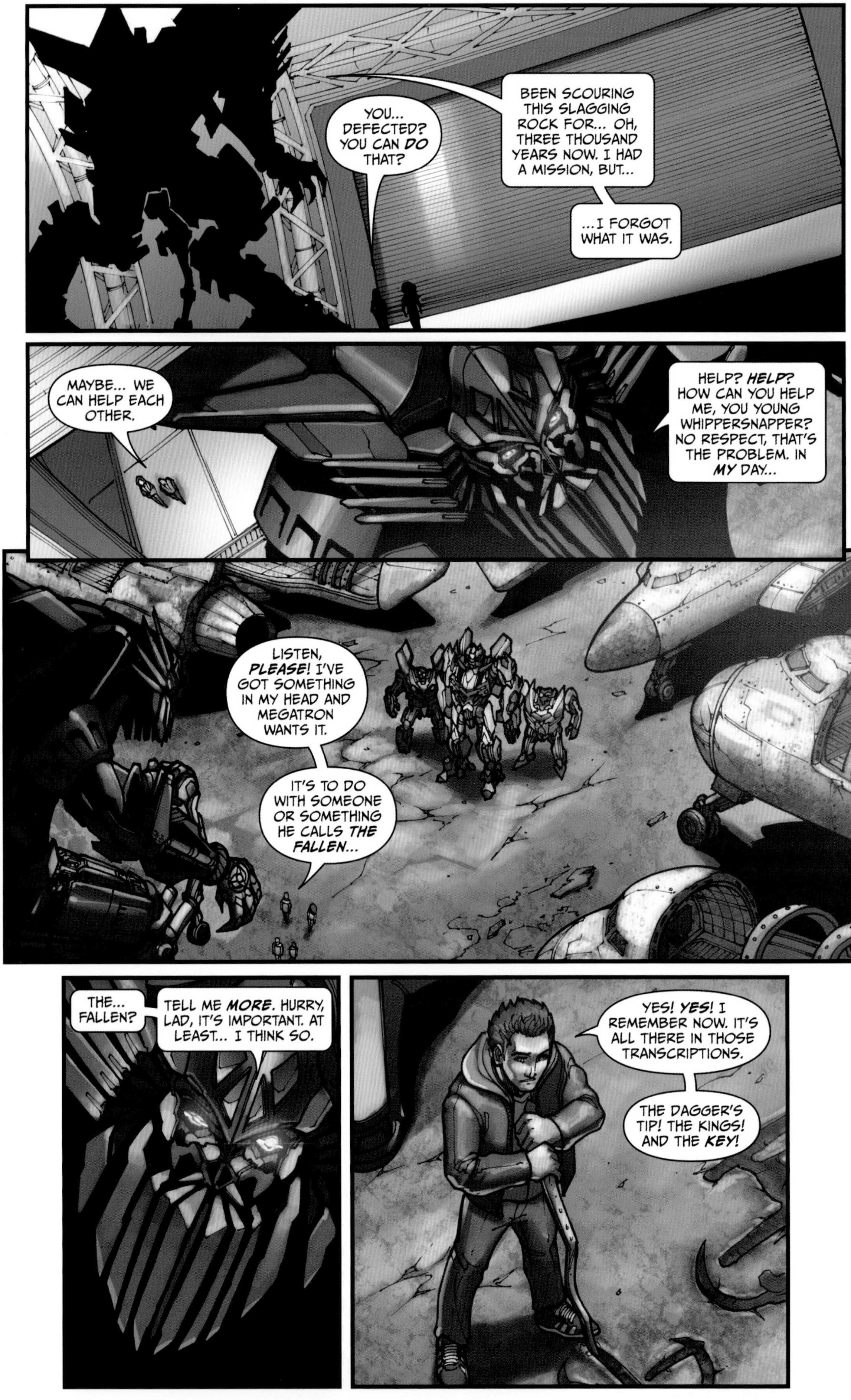
YOU... DEFECTED? YOU CAN DO THAT?
BEEN SCOURING THIS SLAGGING ROCK FOR... OH, THREE THOUSAND YEARS NOW. I HAD A MISSION, BUT...
...I FORGOT WHAT IT WAS.
MAYBE... WE CAN HELP EACH OTHER.
HELP? HELP? HOW CAN YOU HELP ME, YOU YOUNG WHIPPERSNAPPER? NO RESPECT, THAT'S THE PROBLEM. IN MY DAY...
LISTEN, PLEASE! I'VE GOT SOMETHING IN MY HEAD AND MEGATRON WANTS IT.
IT'S TO DO WITH SOMEONE OR SOMETHING HE CALLS THE FALLEN...
THE... FALLEN?
TELL ME MORE. HURRY, LAD, IT'S IMPORTANT. AT LEAST... I THINK SO.
YES! YES! I REMEMBER NOW. IT'S ALL THERE IN THOSE TRANSCRIPTIONS.
THE DAGGER'S TIP! THE KINGS! AND THE KEY!

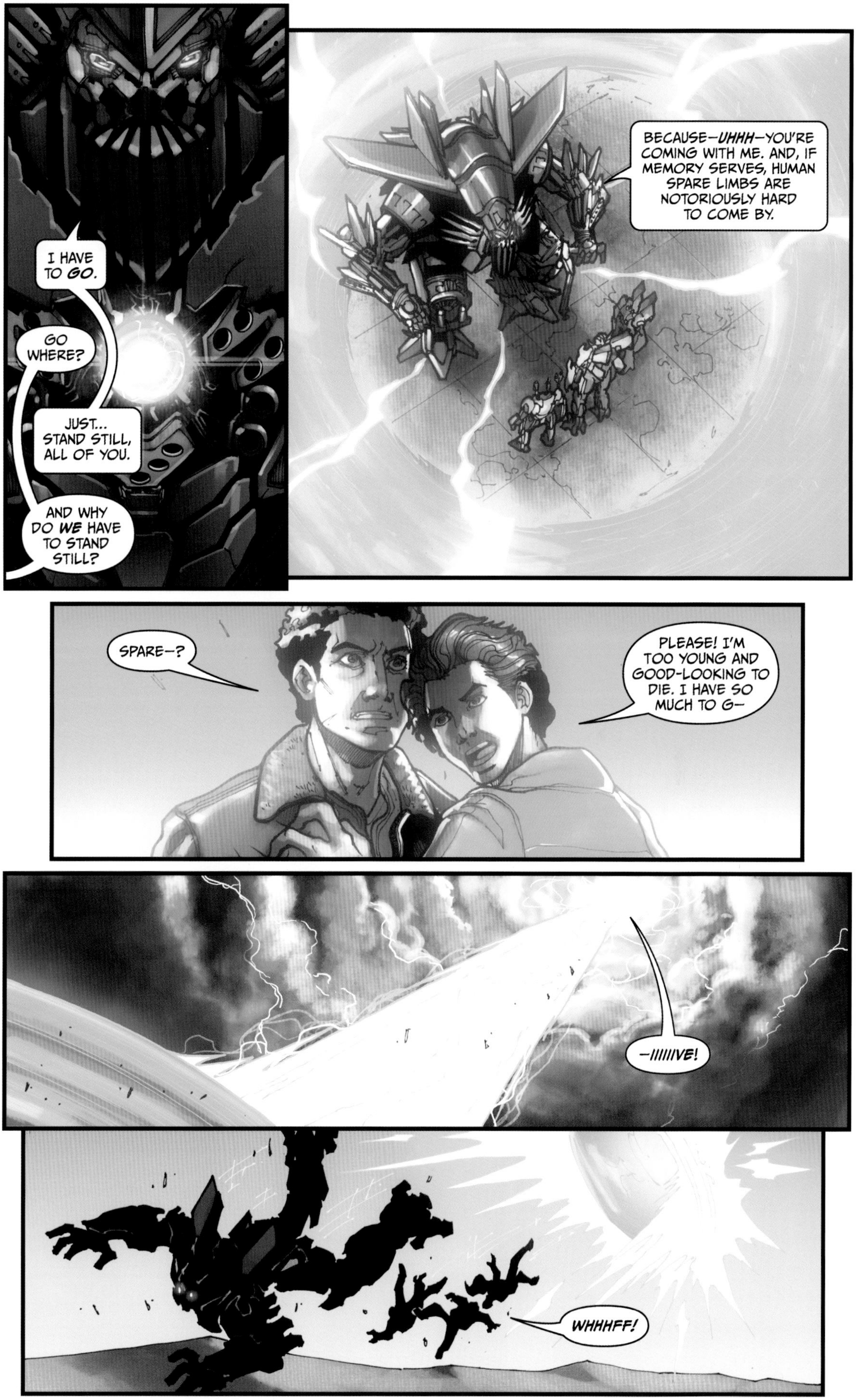
I HAVE TO GO.
GO WHERE?
JUST... STAND STILL, ALL OF YOU.
AND WHY DO WE HAVE TO STAND STILL?
BECAUSE—UHHH—YOU'RE COMING WITH ME. AND, IF MEMORY SERVES, HUMAN SPARE LIMBS ARE NOTORIOUSLY HARD TO COME BY.
SPARE—?
PLEASE! I'M TOO YOUNG AND GOOD-LOOKING TO DIE. I HAVE SO MUCH TO G—
—IIIIIIVE!
WHHHFF!

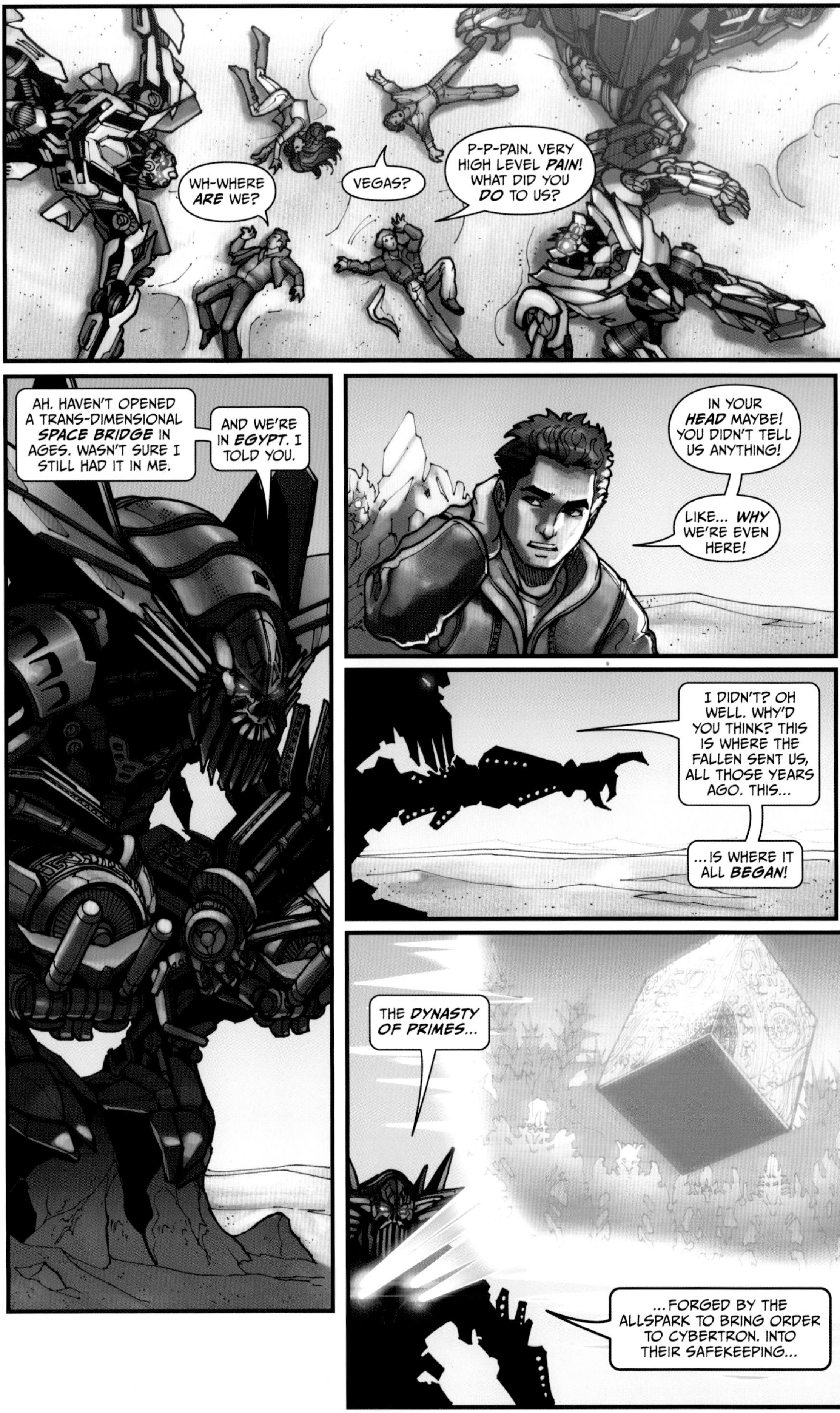
WH-WHERE ARE WE?
VEGAS?
P-P-PAIN. VERY HIGH LEVEL PAIN! WHAT DID YOU DO TO US?
AH. HAVEN'T OPENED A TRANS-DIMENSIONAL SPACE BRIDGE IN AGES. WASN'T SURE I STILL HAD IT IN ME.
AND WE'RE IN EGYPT. I TOLD YOU.
IN YOUR HEAD MAYBE! YOU DIDN'T TELL US ANYTHING!
LIKE... WHY WE'RE EVEN HERE!
I DIDN'T? OH WELL. WHY'D YOU THINK? THIS IS WHERE THE FALLEN SENT US, ALL THOSE YEARS AGO. THIS...
...IS WHERE IT ALL BEGAN!
THE DYNASTY OF PRIMES...
...FORGED BY THE ALLSPARK TO BRING ORDER TO CYBERTRON. INTO THEIR SAFEKEEPING...

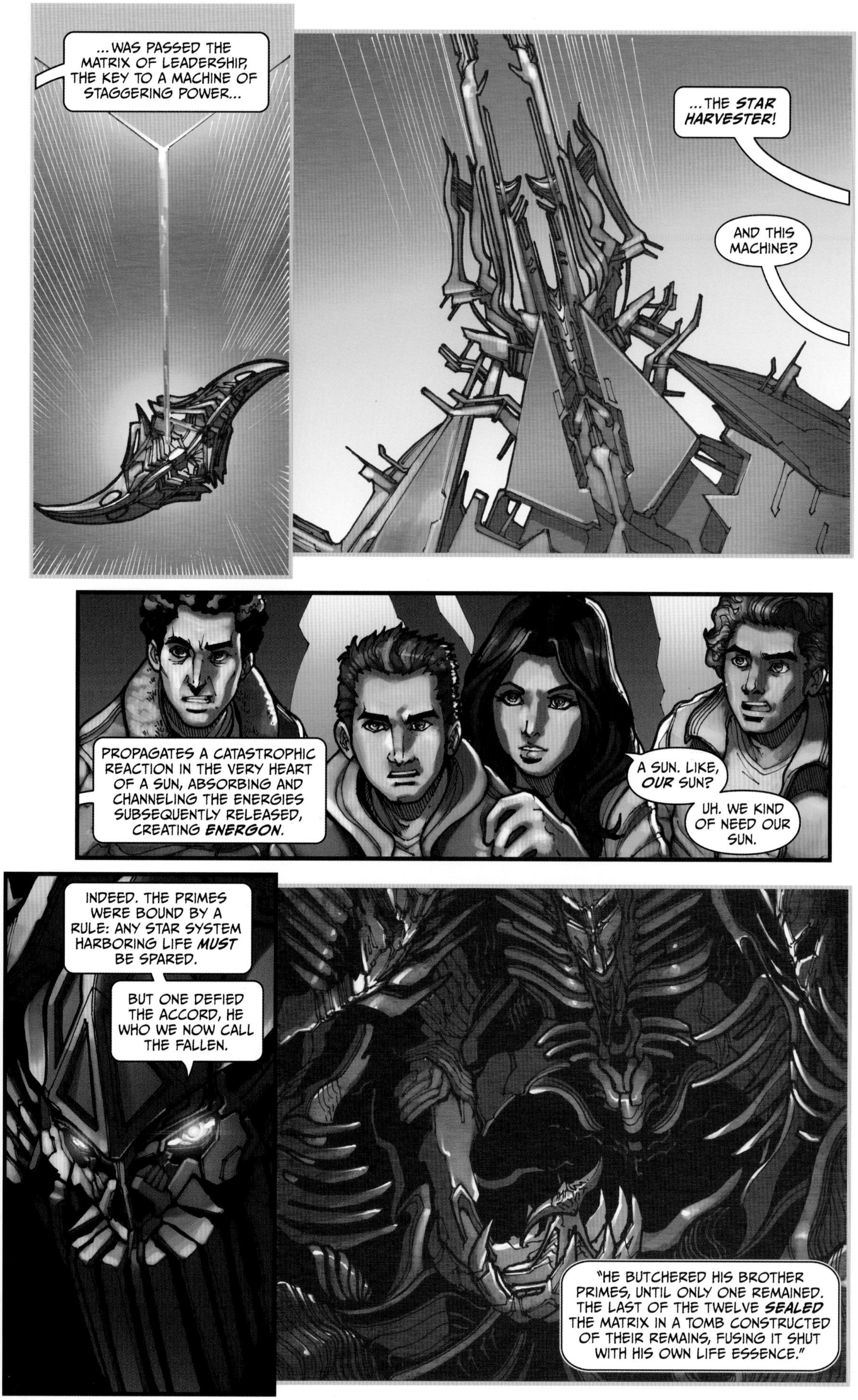
...WAS PASSED THE MATRIX OF LEADERSHIP, THE KEY TO A MACHINE OF STAGGERING POWER...
...THE STAR HARVESTER!
AND THIS MACHINE?
PROPAGATES A CATASTROPHIC REACTION IN THE VERY HEART OF A SUN, ABSORBING AND CHANNELING THE ENERGIES SUBSEQUENTLY RELEASED, CREATING ENERGON.
A SUN. LIKE, OUR SUN?
UH. WE KIND OF NEED OUR SUN.
INDEED. THE PRIMES WERE BOUND BY A RULE: ANY STAR SYSTEM HARBORING LIFE MUST BE SPARED.
BUT ONE DEFIED THE ACCORD, HE WHO WE NOW CALL THE FALLEN.
"HE BUTCHERED HIS BROTHER PRIMES, UNTIL ONLY ONE REMAINED. THE LAST OF THE TWELVE SEALED THE MATRIX IN A TOMB CONSTRUCTED OF THEIR REMAINS, FUSING IT SHUT WITH HIS OWN LIFE ESSENCE."

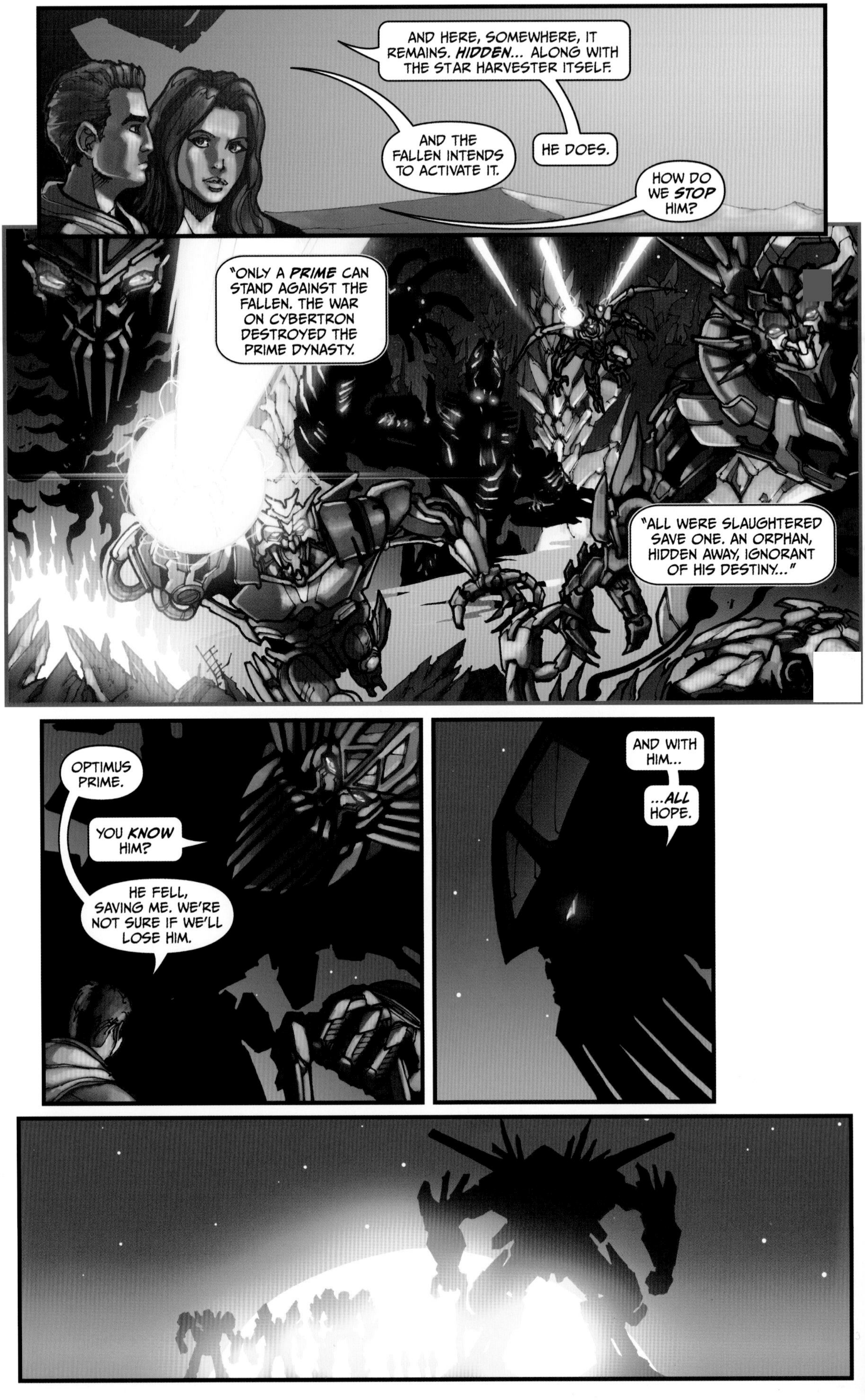
AND HERE, SOMEWHERE, IT REMAINS. HIDDEN... ALONG WITH THE STAR HARVESTER ITSELF.
AND THE FALLEN INTENDS TO ACTIVATE IT.
HE DOES.
HOW DO WE STOP HIM?
"ONLY A PRIME CAN STAND AGAINST THE FALLEN. THE WAR ON CYBERTRON DESTROYED THE PRIME DYNASTY.
"ALL WERE SLAUGHTERED SAVE ONE. AN ORPHAN, HIDDEN AWAY, IGNORANT OF HIS DESTINY..."
OPTIMUS PRIME.
YOU KNOW HIM?
HE FELL, SAVING ME. WE'RE NOT SURE IF WE'LL LOSE HIM.
AND WITH HIM...
...ALL HOPE.

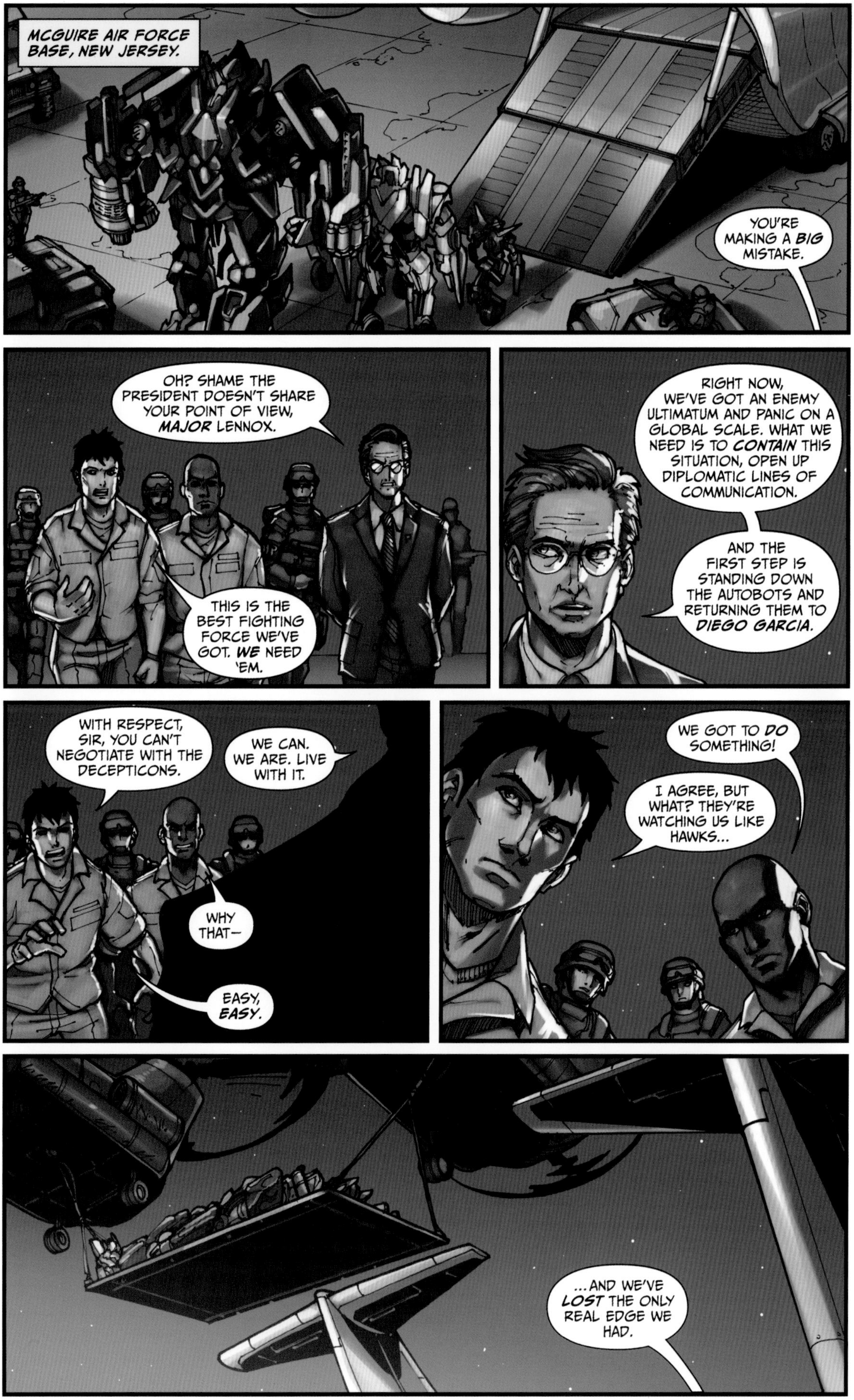
MCGUIRE AIR FORCE BASE, NEW JERSEY.
YOU'RE MAKING A BIG MISTAKE.
OH? SHAME THE PRESIDENT DOESN'T SHARE YOUR POINT OF VIEW, MAJOR LENNOX.
THIS IS THE BEST FIGHTING FORCE WE'VE GOT. WE NEED 'EM.
RIGHT NOW, WE'VE GOT AN ENEMY ULTIMATUM AND PANIC ON A GLOBAL SCALE. WHAT WE NEED IS TO CONTAIN THIS SITUATION, OPEN UP DIPLOMATIC LINES OF COMMUNICATION.
AND THE FIRST STEP IS STANDING DOWN THE AUTOBOTS AND RETURNING THEM TO DIEGO GARCIA.
WITH RESPECT, SIR, YOU CAN'T NEGOTIATE WITH THE DECEPTICONS.
WE CAN. WE ARE. LIVE WITH IT.
WHY THAT—
EASY, EASY.
WE GOT TO DO SOMETHING!
I AGREE, BUT WHAT? THEY'RE WATCHING US LIKE HAWKS...
...AND WE'VE LOST THE ONLY REAL EDGE WE HAD.

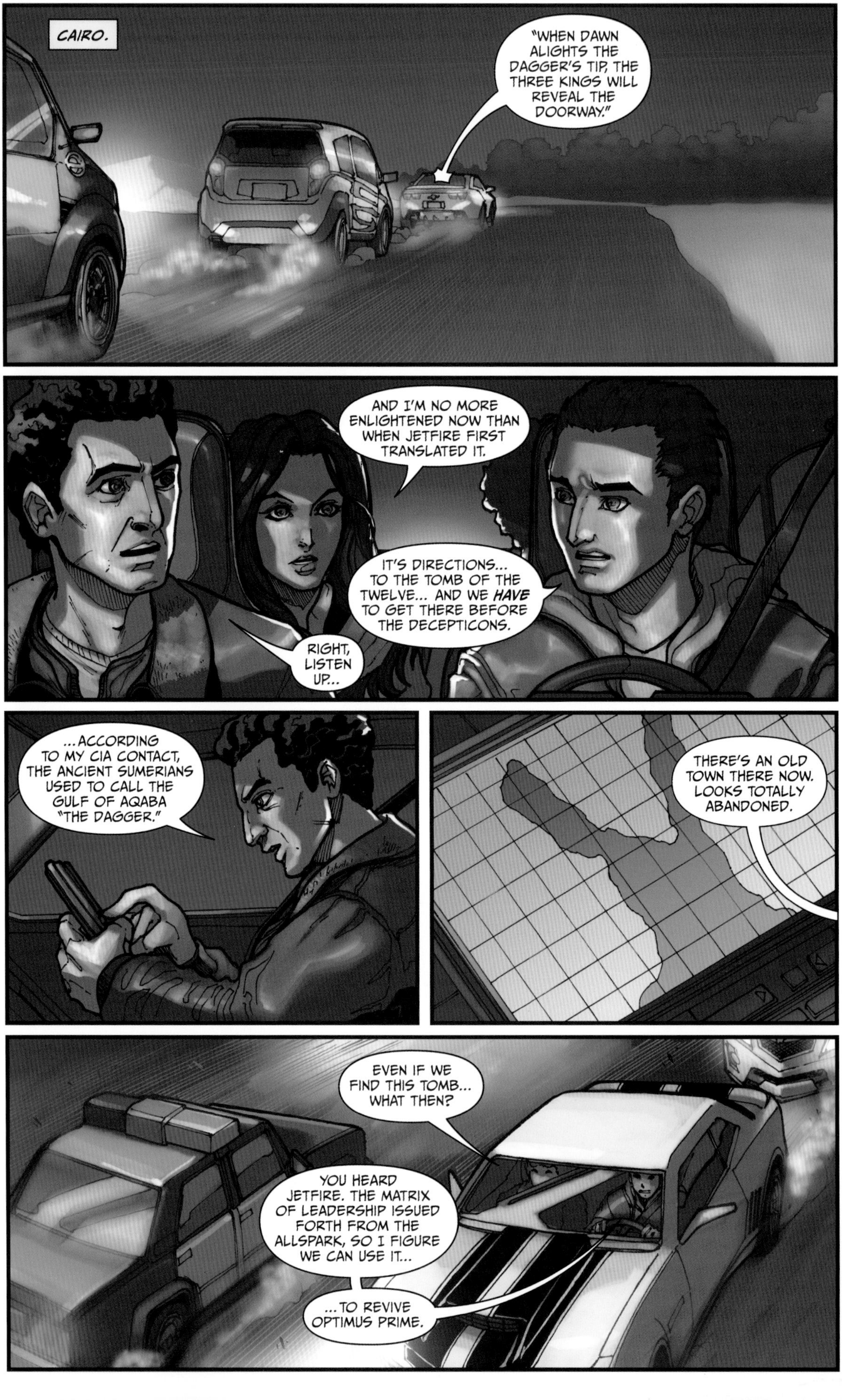
CAIRO.
"WHEN DAWN ALIGHTS THE DAGGER'S TIP, THE THREE KINGS WILL REVEAL THE DOORWAY."
AND I'M NO MORE ENLIGHTENED NOW THAN WHEN JETFIRE FIRST TRANSLATED IT.
IT'S DIRECTIONS... TO THE TOMB OF THE TWELVE... AND WE *HAVE* TO GET THERE BEFORE THE DECEPTICONS.
RIGHT, LISTEN UP...
...ACCORDING TO MY CIA CONTACT, THE ANCIENT SUMERIANS USED TO CALL THE GULF OF AQABA "THE DAGGER."
THERE'S AN OLD TOWN THERE NOW. LOOKS TOTALLY ABANDONED.
EVEN IF WE FIND THIS TOMB... WHAT THEN?
YOU HEARD JETFIRE. THE MATRIX OF LEADERSHIP ISSUED FORTH FROM THE ALLSPARK, SO I FIGURE WE CAN USE IT...
...TO REVIVE OPTIMUS PRIME.

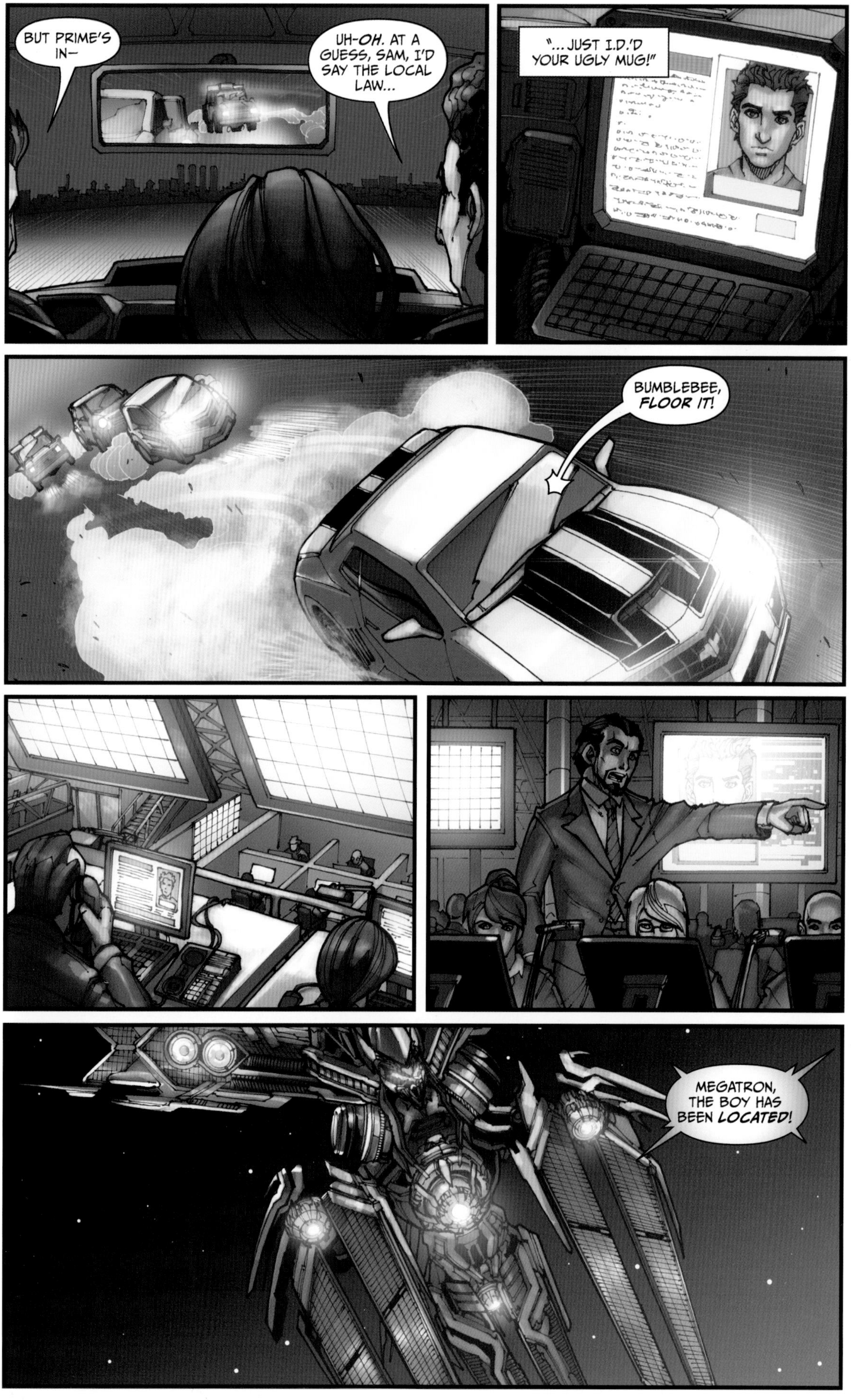
BUT PRIME'S IN—
UH-OH. AT A GUESS, SAM, I'D SAY THE LOCAL LAW...
"...JUST I.D.'D YOUR UGLY MUG!"
BUMBLEBEE, FLOOR IT!
MEGATRON, THE BOY HAS BEEN LOCATED!

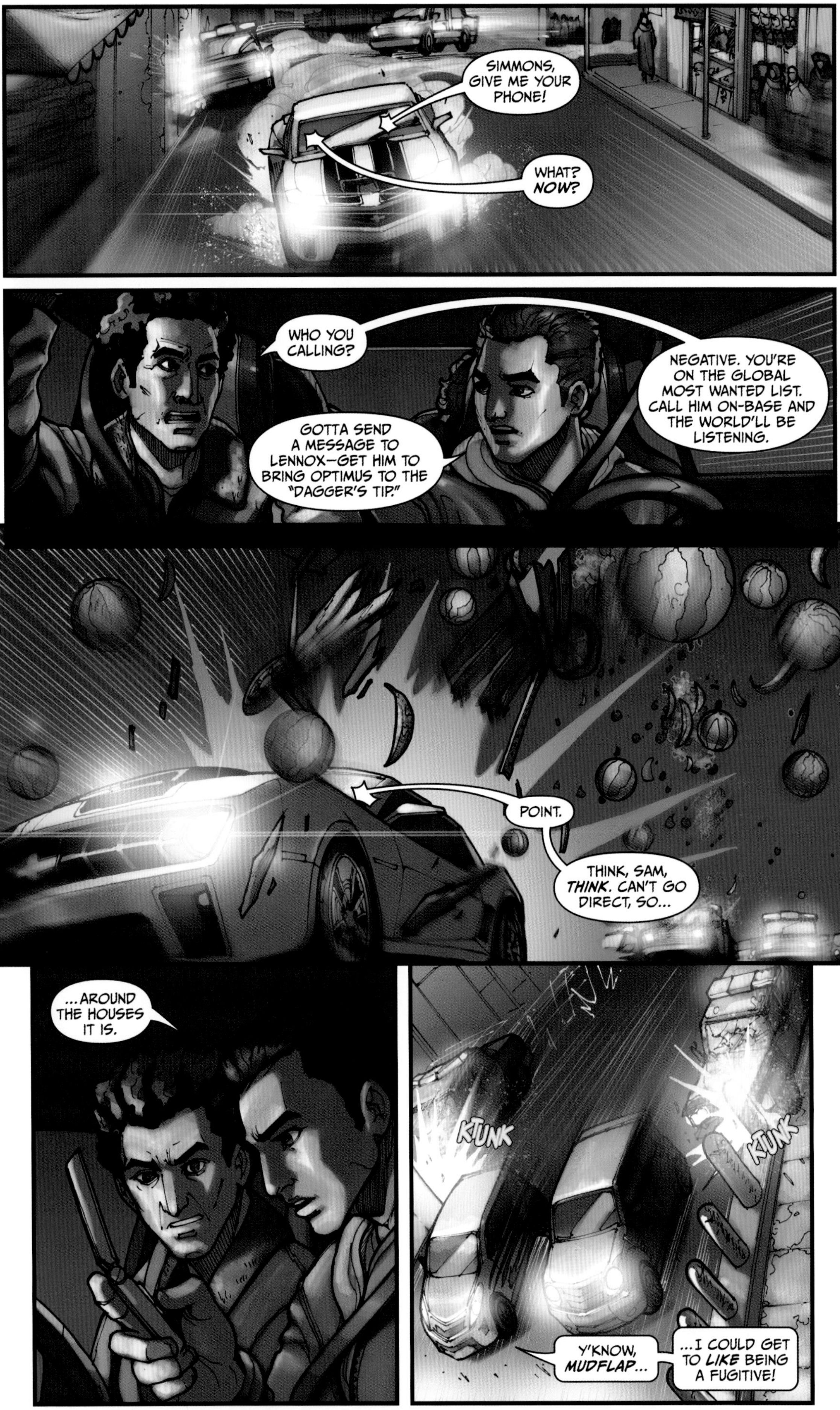
SIMMONS, GIVE ME YOUR PHONE!
WHAT? *NOW?*
WHO YOU CALLING?
GOTTA SEND A MESSAGE TO LENNOX—GET HIM TO BRING OPTIMUS TO THE "DAGGER'S TIP."
NEGATIVE. YOU'RE ON THE GLOBAL MOST WANTED LIST. CALL HIM ON-BASE AND THE WORLD'LL BE LISTENING.
POINT.
THINK, SAM, *THINK*. CAN'T GO DIRECT, SO...
...AROUND THE HOUSES IT IS.
KTUNK
KTUNK
Y'KNOW, *MUDFLAP*...
...I COULD GET TO *LIKE* BEING A FUGITIVE!

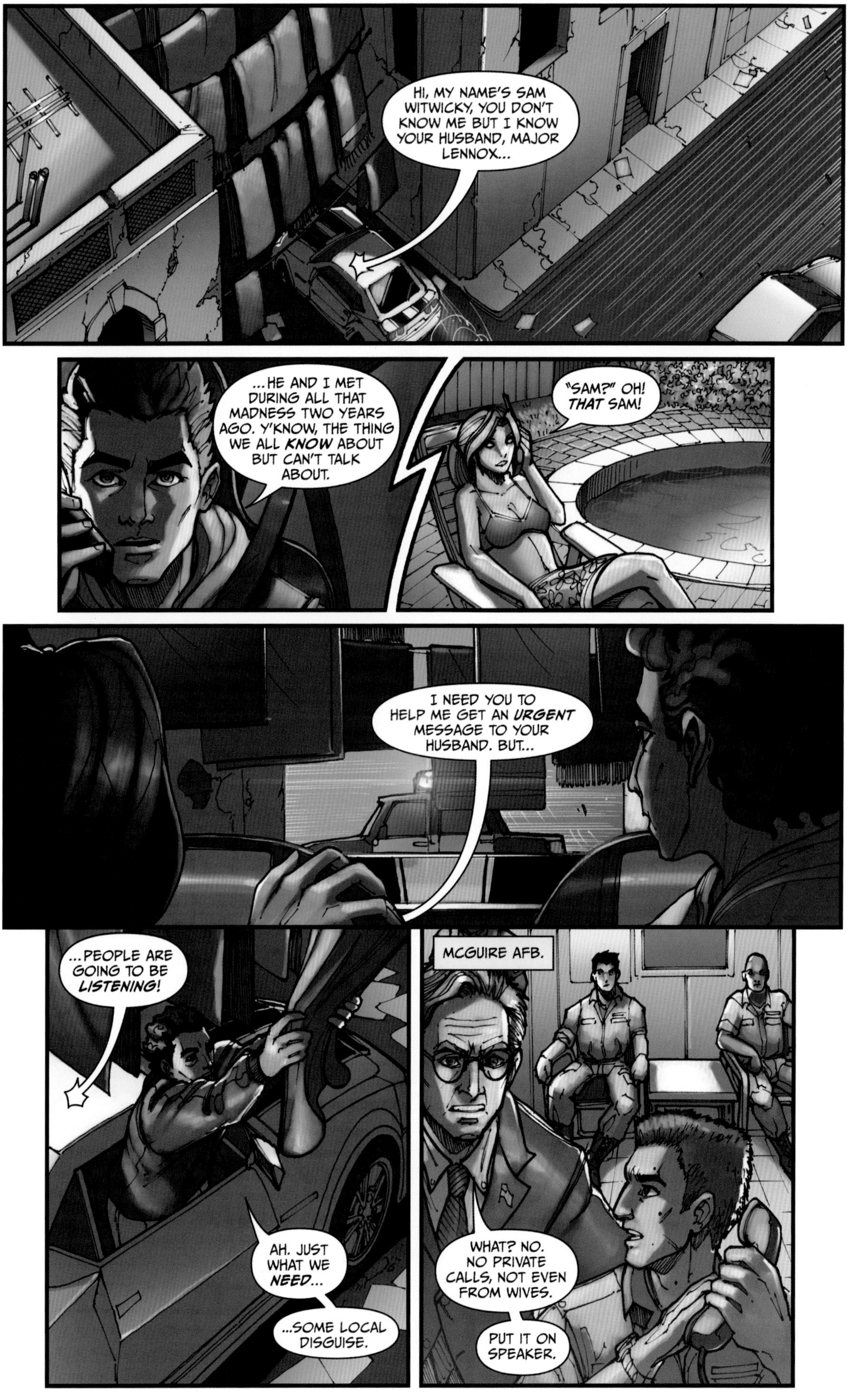
HI, MY NAME'S SAM WITWICKY, YOU DON'T KNOW ME BUT I KNOW YOUR HUSBAND, MAJOR LENNOX...
...HE AND I MET DURING ALL THAT MADNESS TWO YEARS AGO. Y'KNOW, THE THING WE ALL KNOW ABOUT BUT CAN'T TALK ABOUT.
"SAM?" OH! THAT SAM!
I NEED YOU TO HELP ME GET AN URGENT MESSAGE TO YOUR HUSBAND. BUT...
...PEOPLE ARE GOING TO BE LISTENING!
AH. JUST WHAT WE NEED...
...SOME LOCAL DISGUISE.
MCGUIRE AFB.
WHAT? NO. NO PRIVATE CALLS, NOT EVEN FROM WIVES.
PUT IT ON SPEAKER.

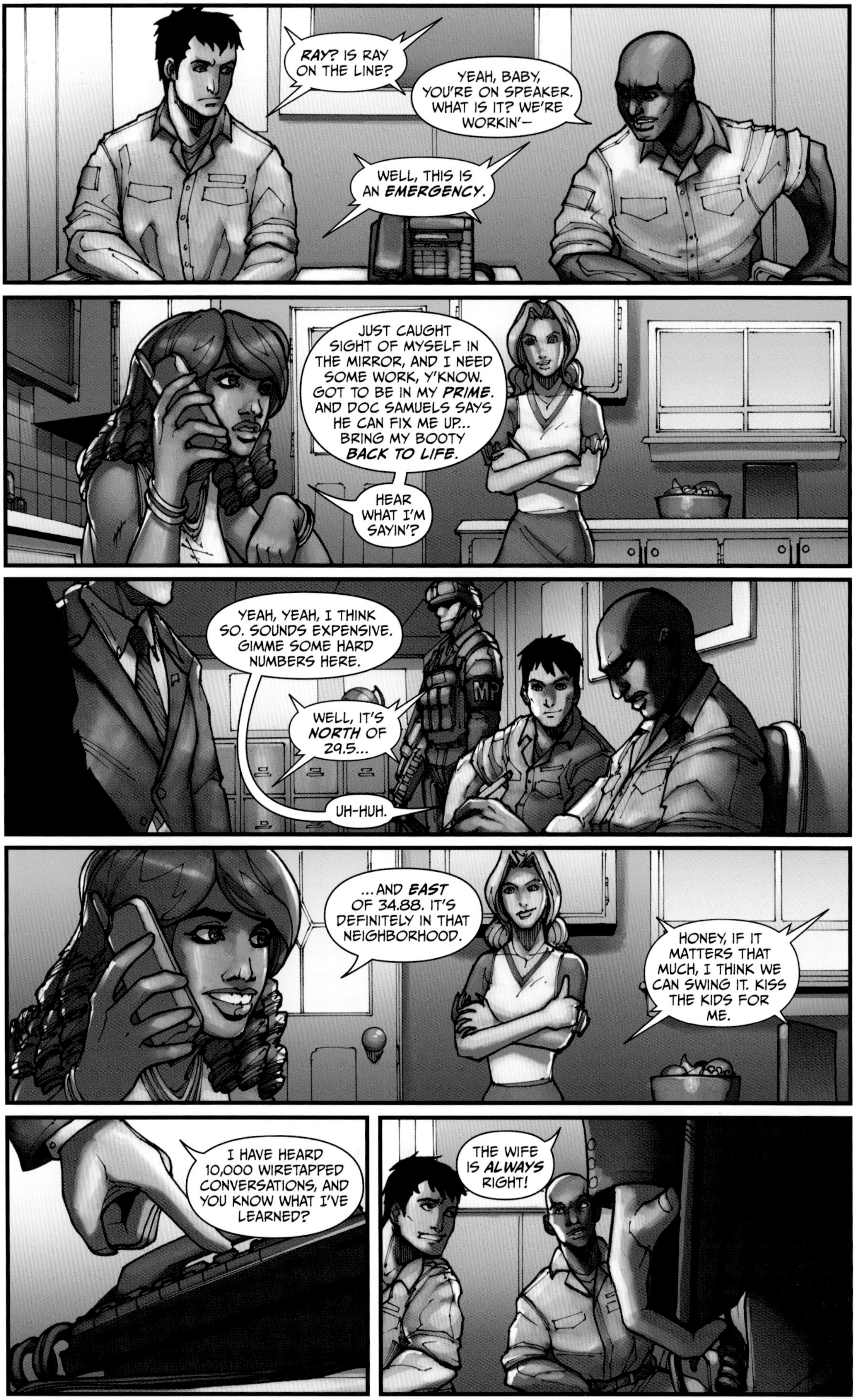
RAY? IS RAY ON THE LINE?
YEAH, BABY, YOU'RE ON SPEAKER. WHAT IS IT? WE'RE WORKIN'—
WELL, THIS IS AN EMERGENCY.
JUST CAUGHT SIGHT OF MYSELF IN THE MIRROR, AND I NEED SOME WORK, Y'KNOW. GOT TO BE IN MY PRIME. AND DOC SAMUELS SAYS HE CAN FIX ME UP... BRING MY BOOTY BACK TO LIFE.
HEAR WHAT I'M SAYIN'?
YEAH, YEAH, I THINK SO. SOUNDS EXPENSIVE. GIMME SOME HARD NUMBERS HERE.
WELL, IT'S NORTH OF 29.5...
UH-HUH.
...AND EAST OF 34.88. IT'S DEFINITELY IN THAT NEIGHBORHOOD.
HONEY, IF IT MATTERS THAT MUCH, I THINK WE CAN SWING IT. KISS THE KIDS FOR ME.
I HAVE HEARD 10,000 WIRETAPPED CONVERSATIONS, AND YOU KNOW WHAT I'VE LEARNED?
THE WIFE IS ALWAYS RIGHT!
MP

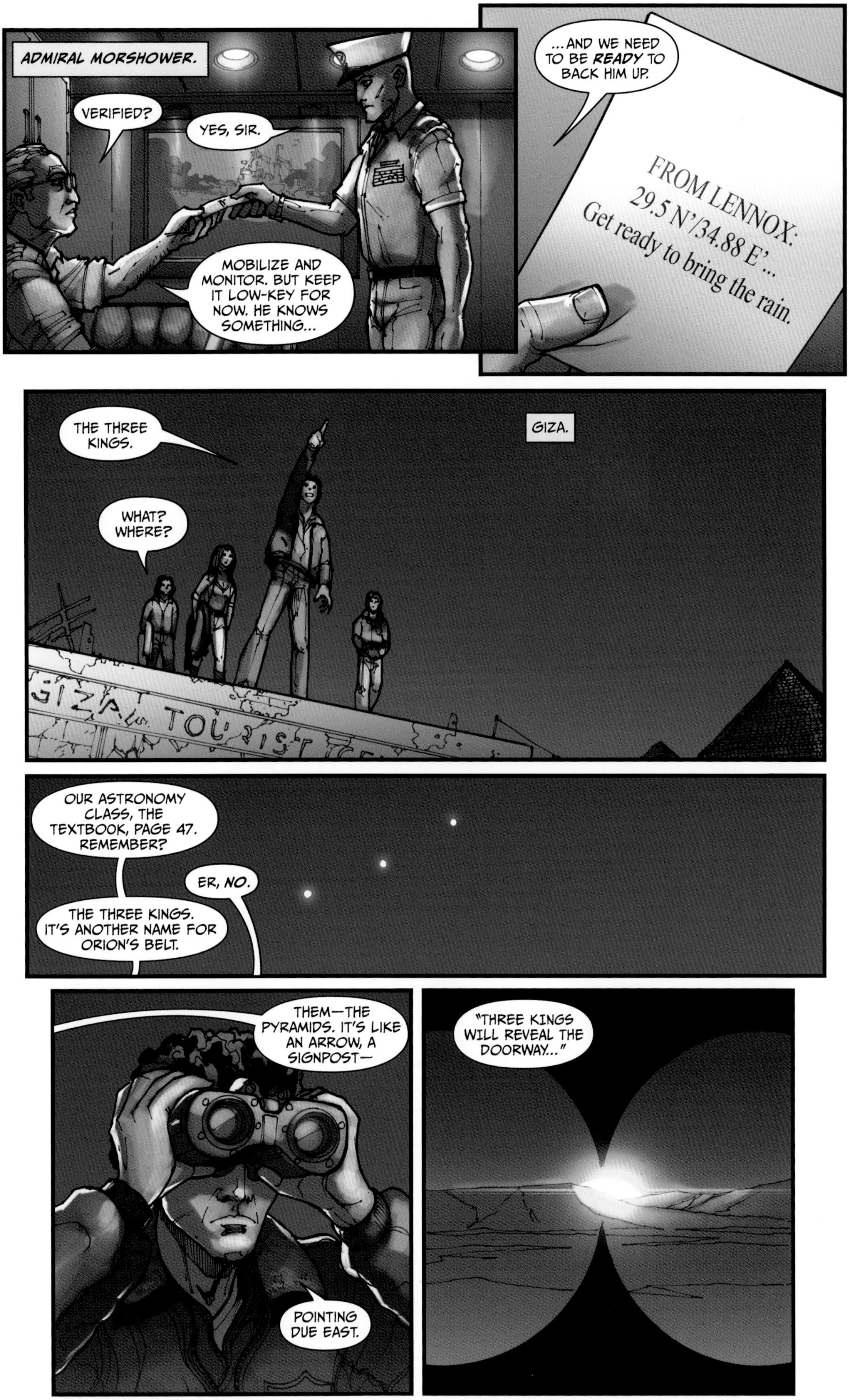
ADMIRAL MORSHOWER.
VERIFIED?
YES, SIR.
MOBILIZE AND MONITOR. BUT KEEP IT LOW-KEY FOR NOW. HE KNOWS SOMETHING...
...AND WE NEED TO BE READY TO BACK HIM UP.
FROM LENNOX:
29.5 N'/34.88 E'...
Get ready to bring the rain.
GIZA.
THE THREE KINGS.
WHAT? WHERE?
GIZA TOURIST
OUR ASTRONOMY CLASS, THE TEXTBOOK, PAGE 47. REMEMBER?
ER, NO.
THE THREE KINGS. IT'S ANOTHER NAME FOR ORION'S BELT.
THEM—THE PYRAMIDS. IT'S LIKE AN ARROW, A SIGNPOST—
POINTING DUE EAST.
"THREE KINGS WILL REVEAL THE DOORWAY..."

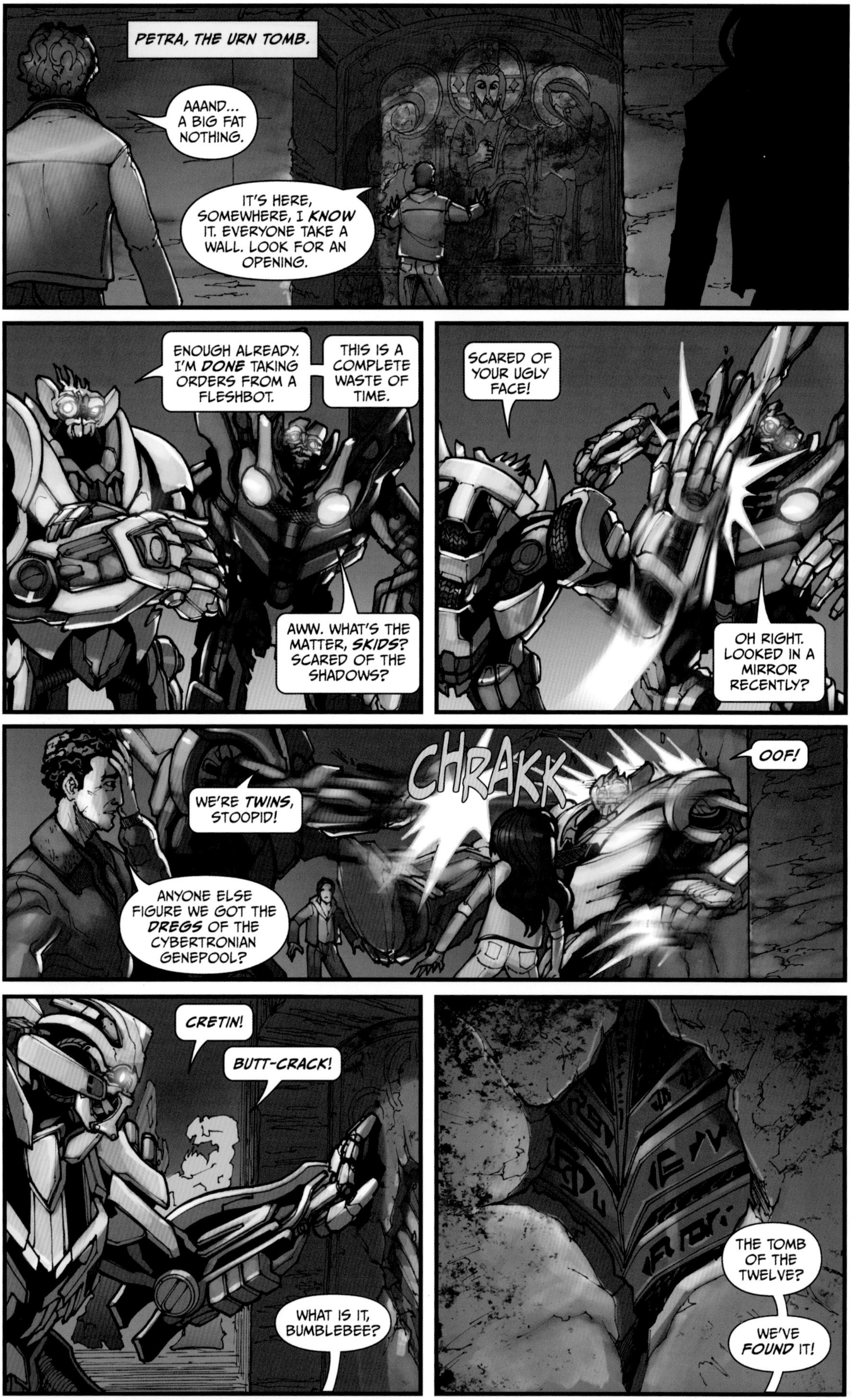
PETRA, THE URN TOMB.
AAAND... A BIG FAT NOTHING.
IT'S HERE, SOMEWHERE, I *KNOW* IT. EVERYONE TAKE A WALL. LOOK FOR AN OPENING.
ENOUGH ALREADY. I'M *DONE* TAKING ORDERS FROM A FLESHBOT.
THIS IS A COMPLETE WASTE OF TIME.
AWW. WHAT'S THE MATTER, *SKIDS*? SCARED OF THE SHADOWS?
SCARED OF YOUR UGLY FACE!
OH RIGHT. LOOKED IN A MIRROR RECENTLY?
WE'RE *TWINS*, STOOPID!
CHRAKK
OOF!
ANYONE ELSE FIGURE WE GOT THE *DREGS* OF THE CYBERTRONIAN GENEPOOL?
CRETIN!
BUTT-CRACK!
WHAT IS IT, BUMBLEBEE?
THE TOMB OF THE TWELVE?
WE'VE *FOUND* IT!

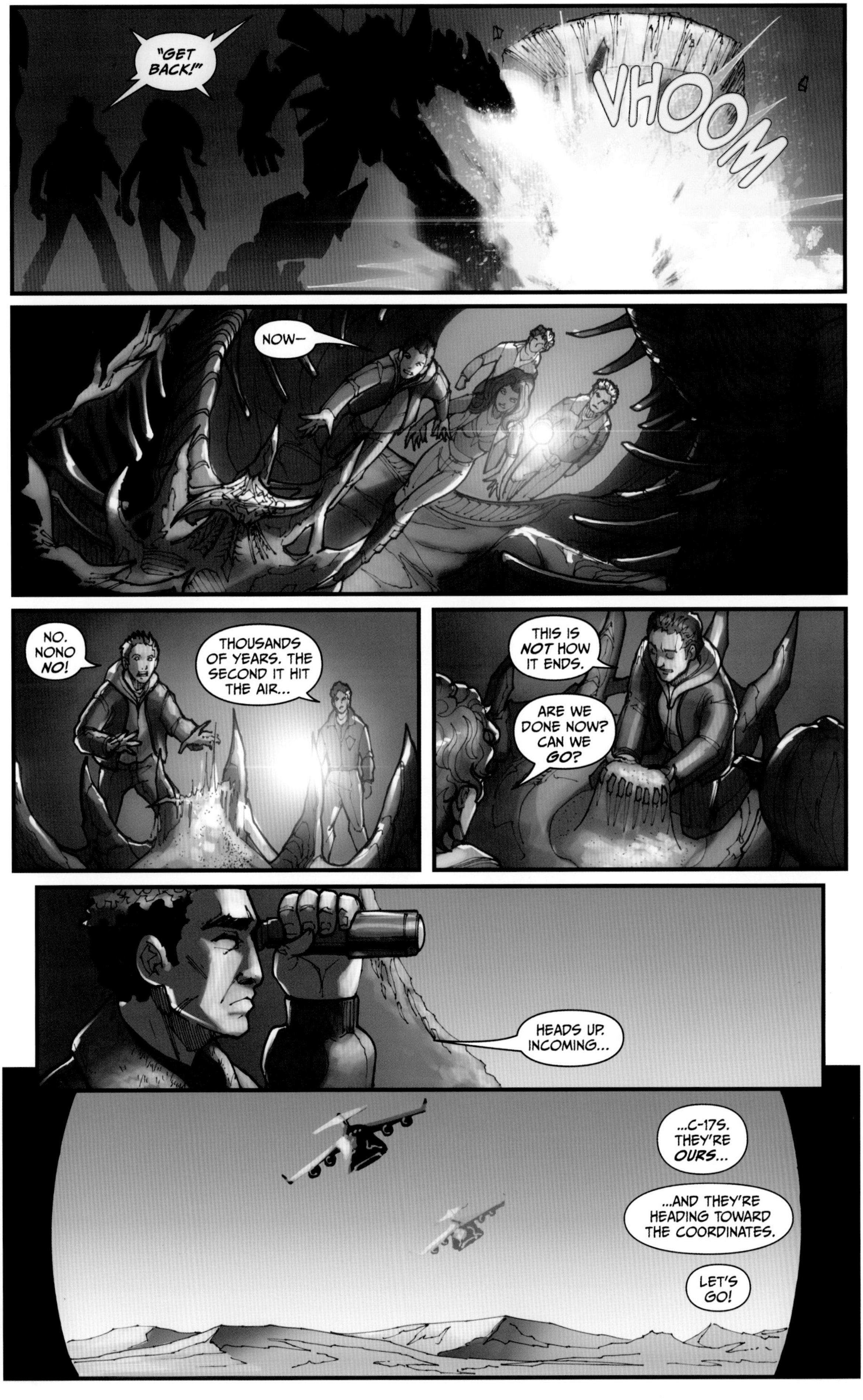
"GET BACK!"
VHOOM
NOW–
NO. NONO NO!
THOUSANDS OF YEARS. THE SECOND IT HIT THE AIR...
THIS IS NOT HOW IT ENDS.
ARE WE DONE NOW? CAN WE GO?
HEADS UP. INCOMING...
...C-17S. THEY'RE OURS...
...AND THEY'RE HEADING TOWARD THE COORDINATES.
LET'S GO!

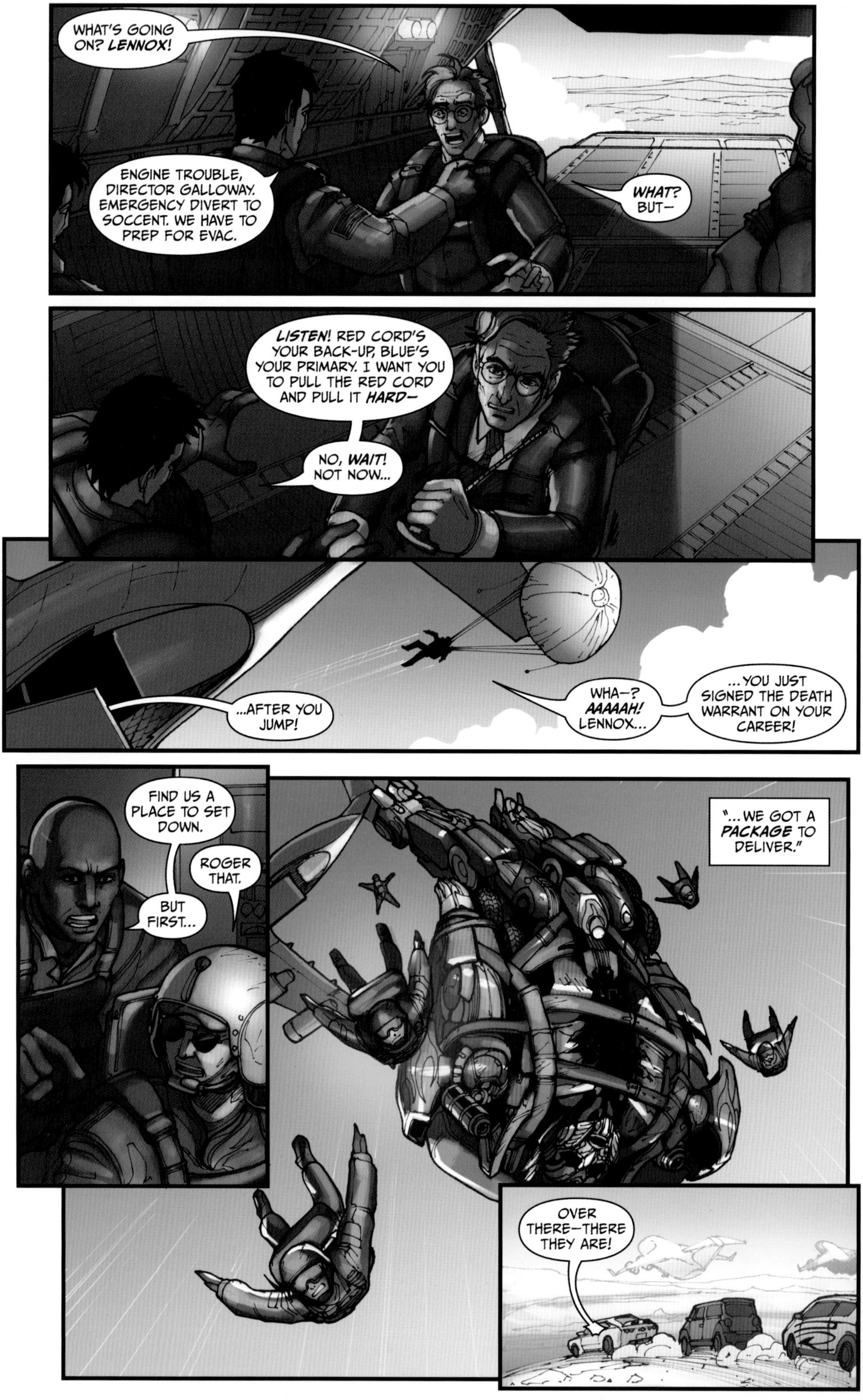
WHAT'S GOING ON? LENNOX!
ENGINE TROUBLE, DIRECTOR GALLOWAY. EMERGENCY DIVERT TO SOCCENT. WE HAVE TO PREP FOR EVAC.
WHAT? BUT—
LISTEN! RED CORD'S YOUR BACK-UP, BLUE'S YOUR PRIMARY. I WANT YOU TO PULL THE RED CORD AND PULL IT HARD—
NO, WAIT! NOT NOW...
...AFTER YOU JUMP!
WHA—? AAAAAH! LENNOX...
...YOU JUST SIGNED THE DEATH WARRANT ON YOUR CAREER!
FIND US A PLACE TO SET DOWN.
ROGER THAT.
BUT FIRST...
"...WE GOT A PACKAGE TO DELIVER."
OVER THERE—THERE THEY ARE!

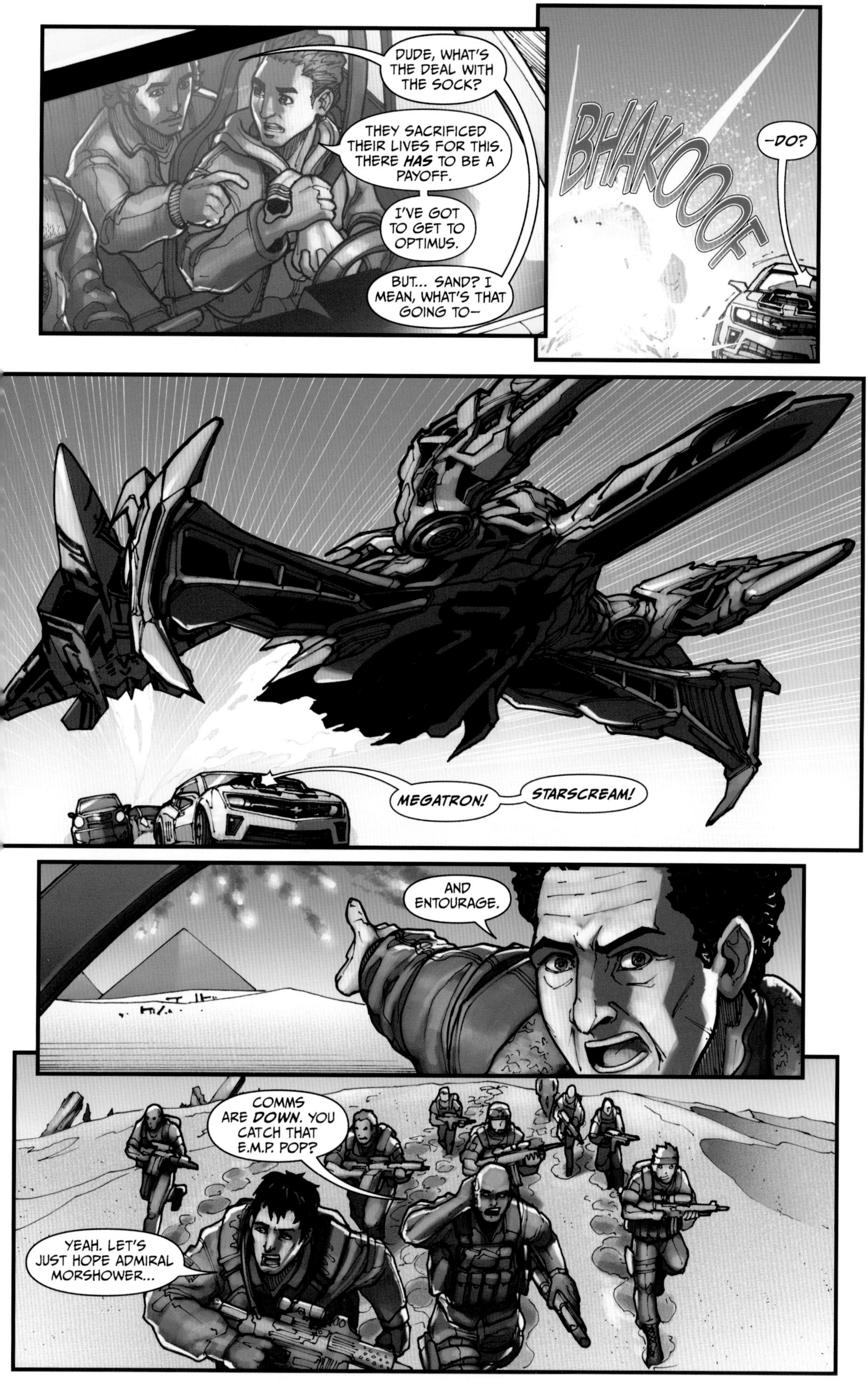
DUDE, WHAT'S THE DEAL WITH THE SOCK?
THEY SACRIFICED THEIR LIVES FOR THIS. THERE HAS TO BE A PAYOFF.
I'VE GOT TO GET TO OPTIMUS.
BUT... SAND? I MEAN, WHAT'S THAT GOING TO–
BHAKOOOF
–DO?
MEGATRON!
STARSCREAM!
AND ENTOURAGE.
COMMS ARE DOWN. YOU CATCH THAT E.M.P. POP?
YEAH. LET'S JUST HOPE ADMIRAL MORSHOWER...

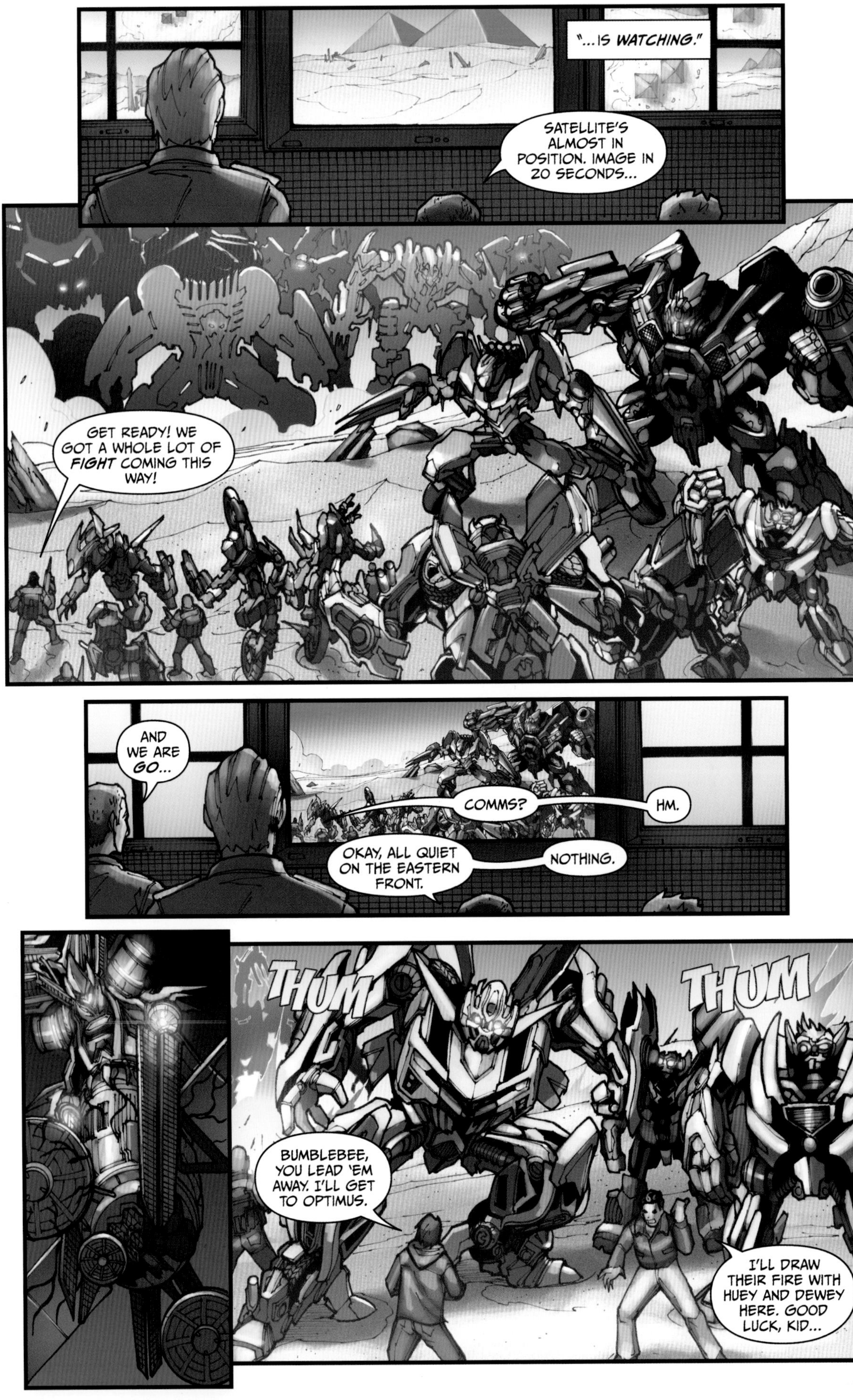
"...IS WATCHING."
SATELLITE'S ALMOST IN POSITION. IMAGE IN 20 SECONDS...
GET READY! WE GOT A WHOLE LOT OF FIGHT COMING THIS WAY!
AND WE ARE GO...
COMMS?
HM.
OKAY, ALL QUIET ON THE EASTERN FRONT.
NOTHING.
THUM
THUM
BUMBLEBEE, YOU LEAD 'EM AWAY. I'LL GET TO OPTIMUS.
I'LL DRAW THEIR FIRE WITH HUEY AND DEWEY HERE. GOOD LUCK, KID...

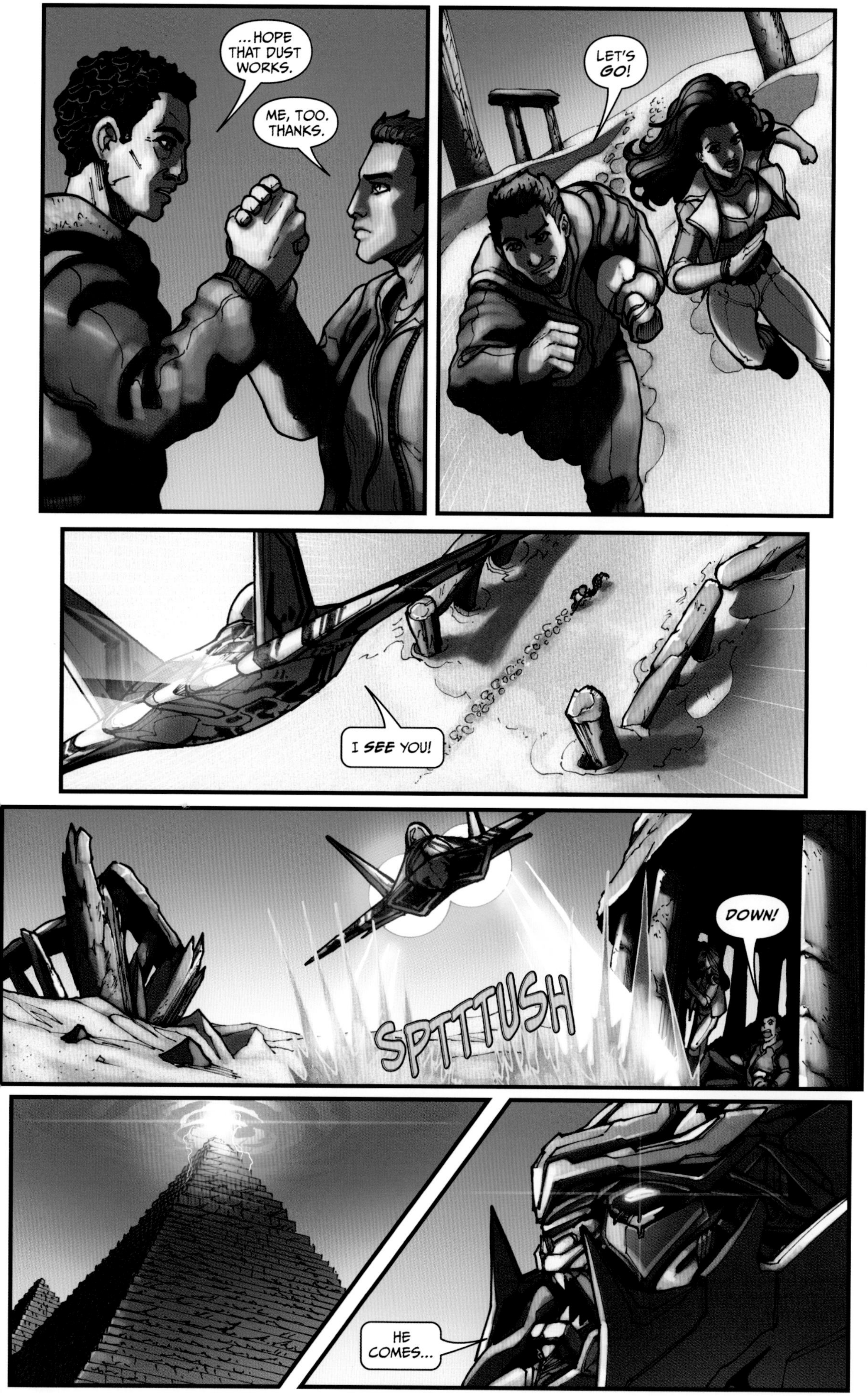
...HOPE THAT DUST WORKS.
ME, TOO. THANKS.
LET'S GO!
I SEE YOU!
DOWN!
SPTTTUSH
HE COMES...

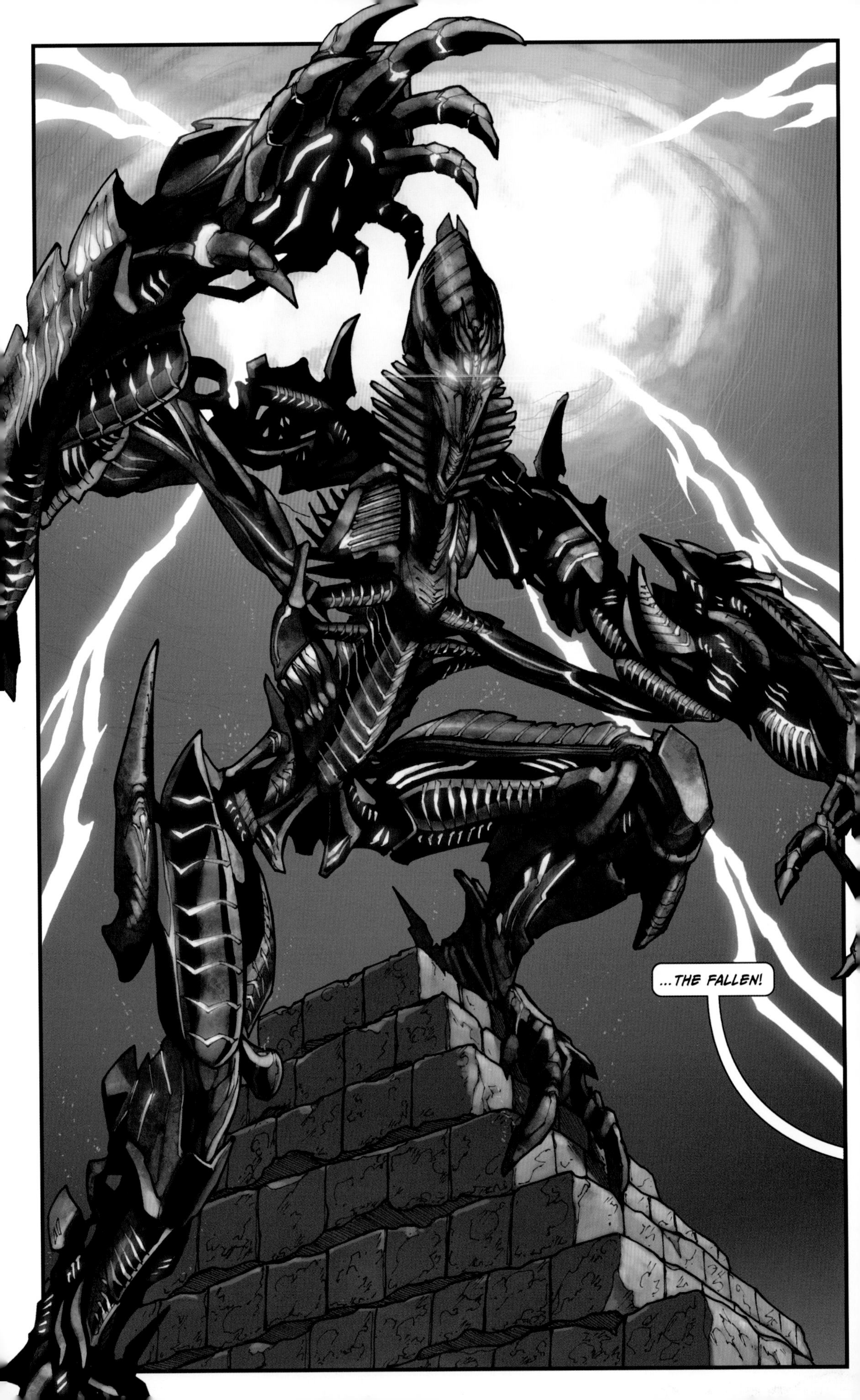
...THE FALLEN!

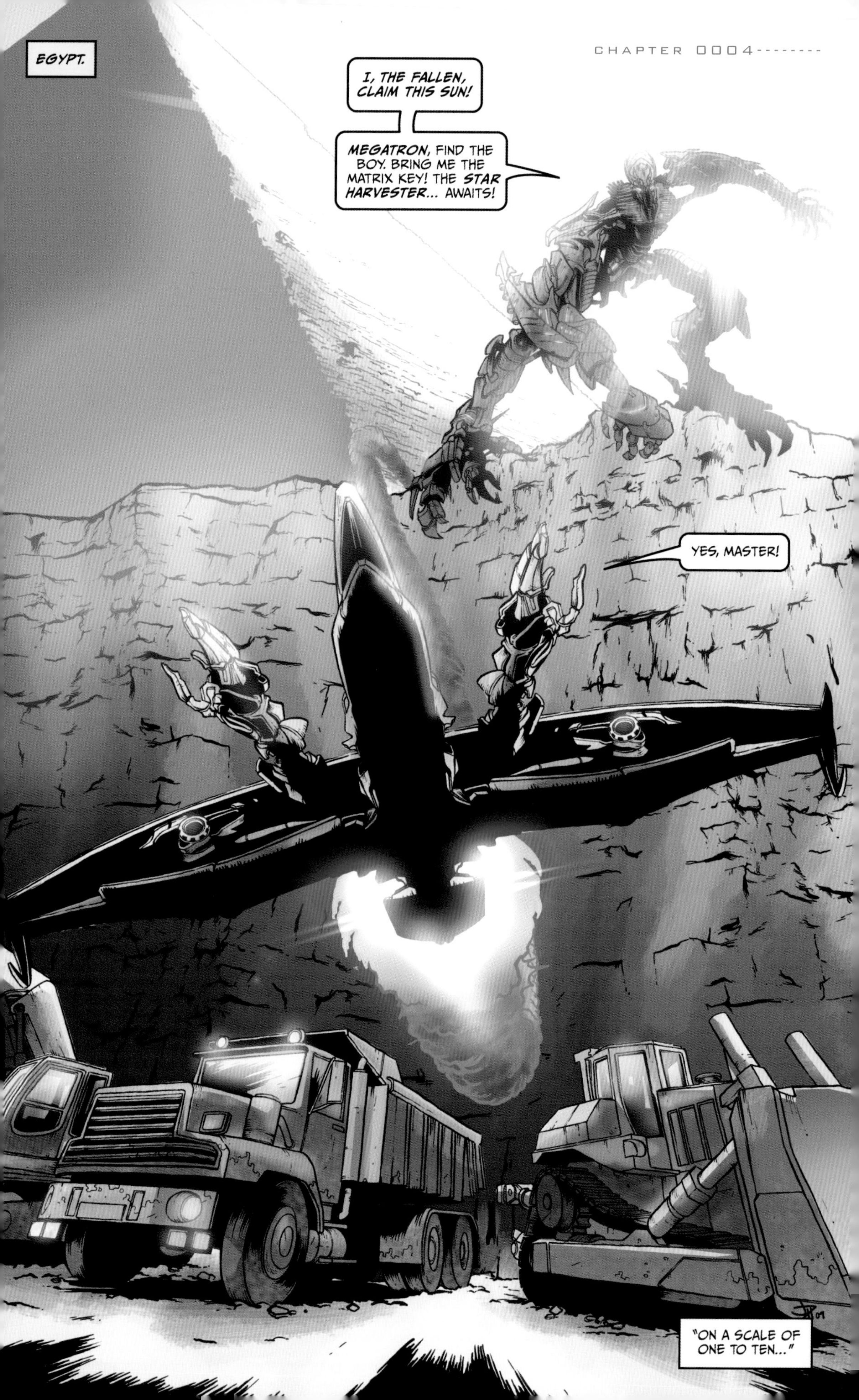
EGYPT.
I, THE FALLEN, CLAIM THIS SUN!
MEGATRON, FIND THE BOY. BRING ME THE MATRIX KEY! THE STAR HARVESTER... AWAITS!
YES, MASTER!
"ON A SCALE OF ONE TO TEN..."

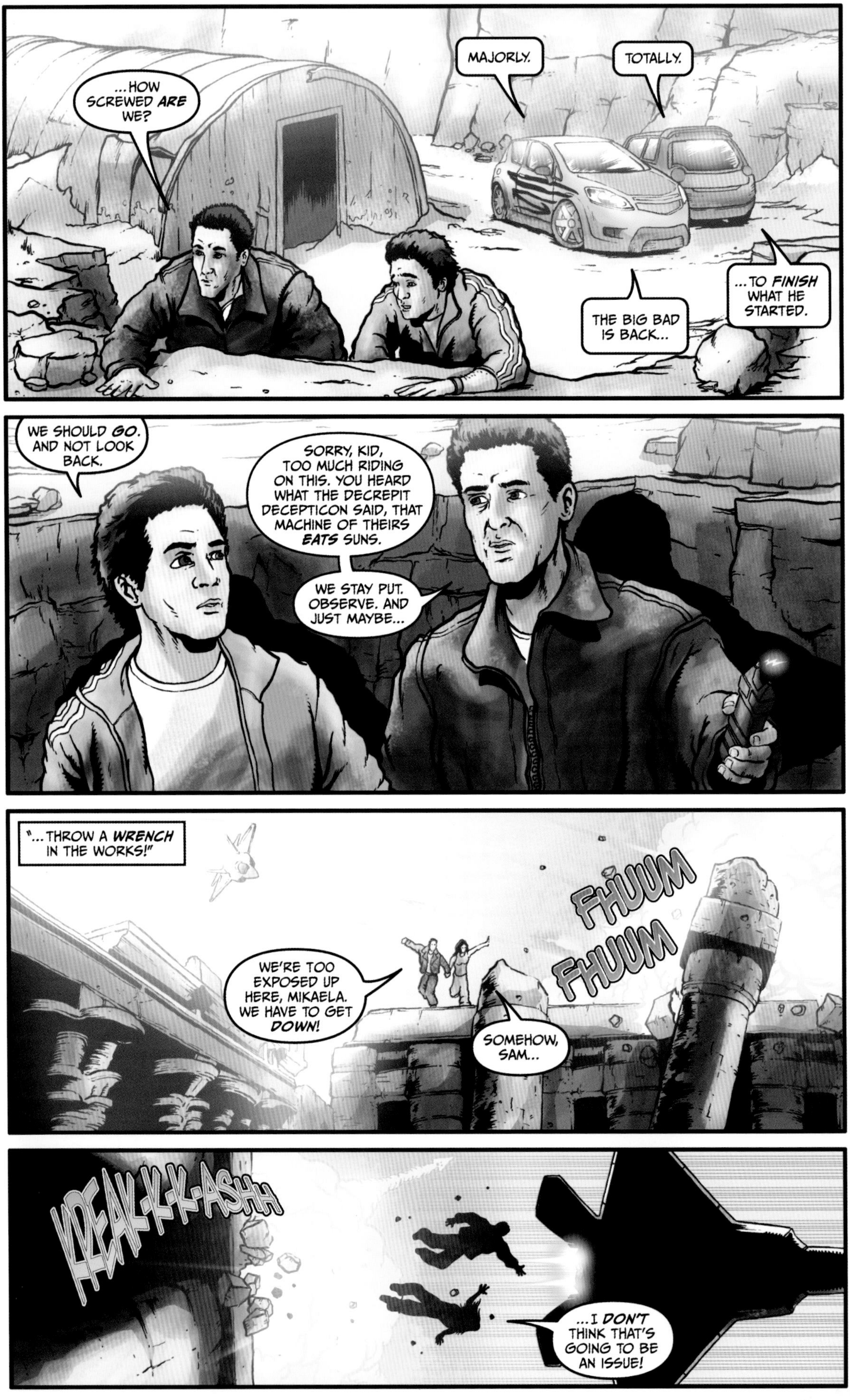
...HOW SCREWED ARE WE?
MAJORLY.
TOTALLY.
THE BIG BAD IS BACK...
...TO FINISH WHAT HE STARTED.
WE SHOULD GO. AND NOT LOOK BACK.
SORRY, KID, TOO MUCH RIDING ON THIS. YOU HEARD WHAT THE DECREPIT DECEPTICON SAID, THAT MACHINE OF THEIRS EATS SUNS.
WE STAY PUT. OBSERVE. AND JUST MAYBE...
"...THROW A WRENCH IN THE WORKS!"
FHUUM
FHUUM
WE'RE TOO EXPOSED UP HERE, MIKAELA. WE HAVE TO GET DOWN!
SOMEHOW, SAM...
KREAK-K-K-ASHH
...I DON'T THINK THAT'S GOING TO BE AN ISSUE!

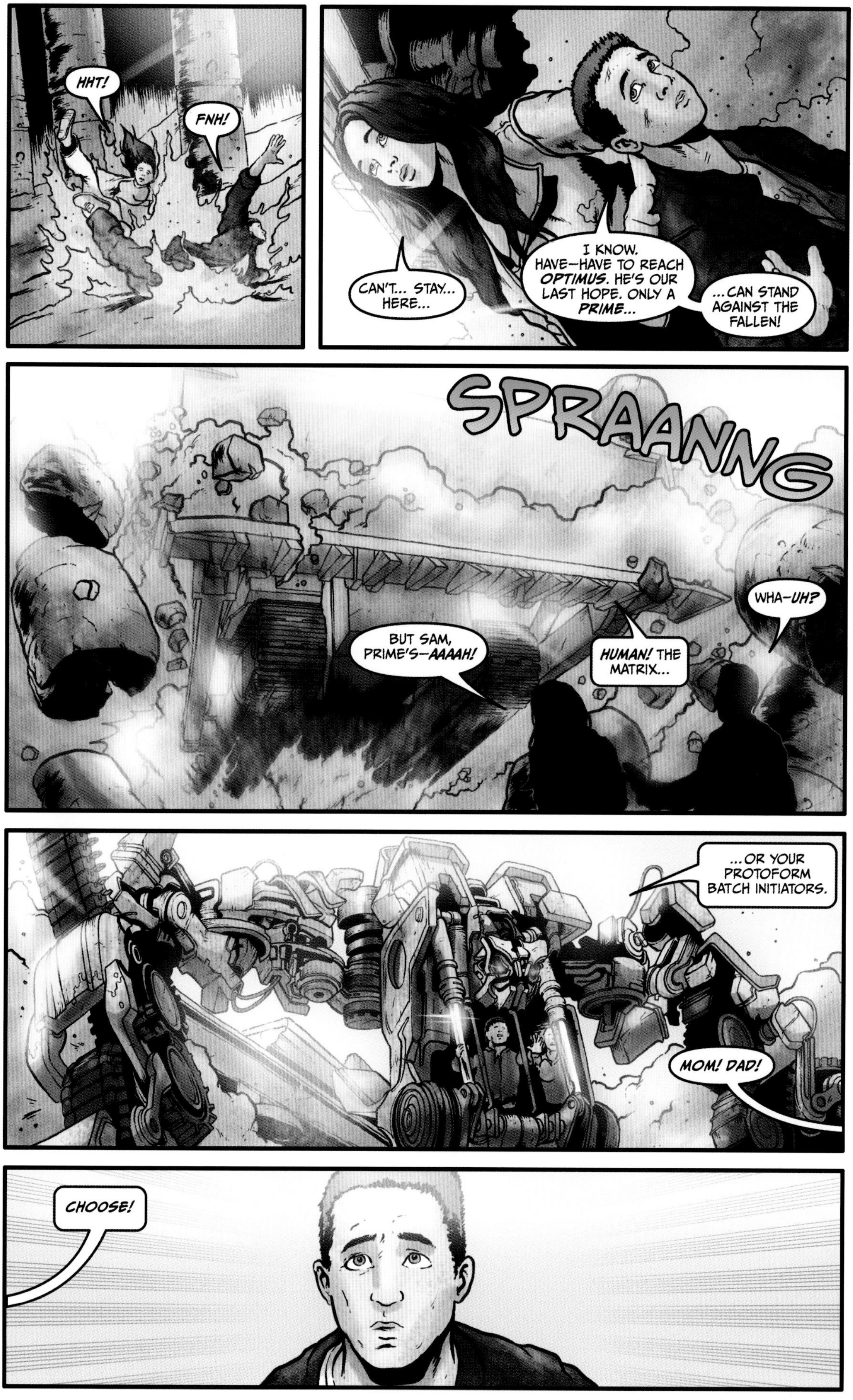
HHT!
FNH!
CAN'T... STAY... HERE...
I KNOW. HAVE—HAVE TO REACH *OPTIMUS*. HE'S OUR LAST HOPE. ONLY A *PRIME*...
...CAN STAND AGAINST THE FALLEN!
SPRAANNG
BUT SAM, PRIME'S—*AAAAH!*
HUMAN! THE MATRIX...
WHA-*UH?*
...OR YOUR PROTOFORM BATCH INITIATORS.
MOM! DAD!
CHOOSE!

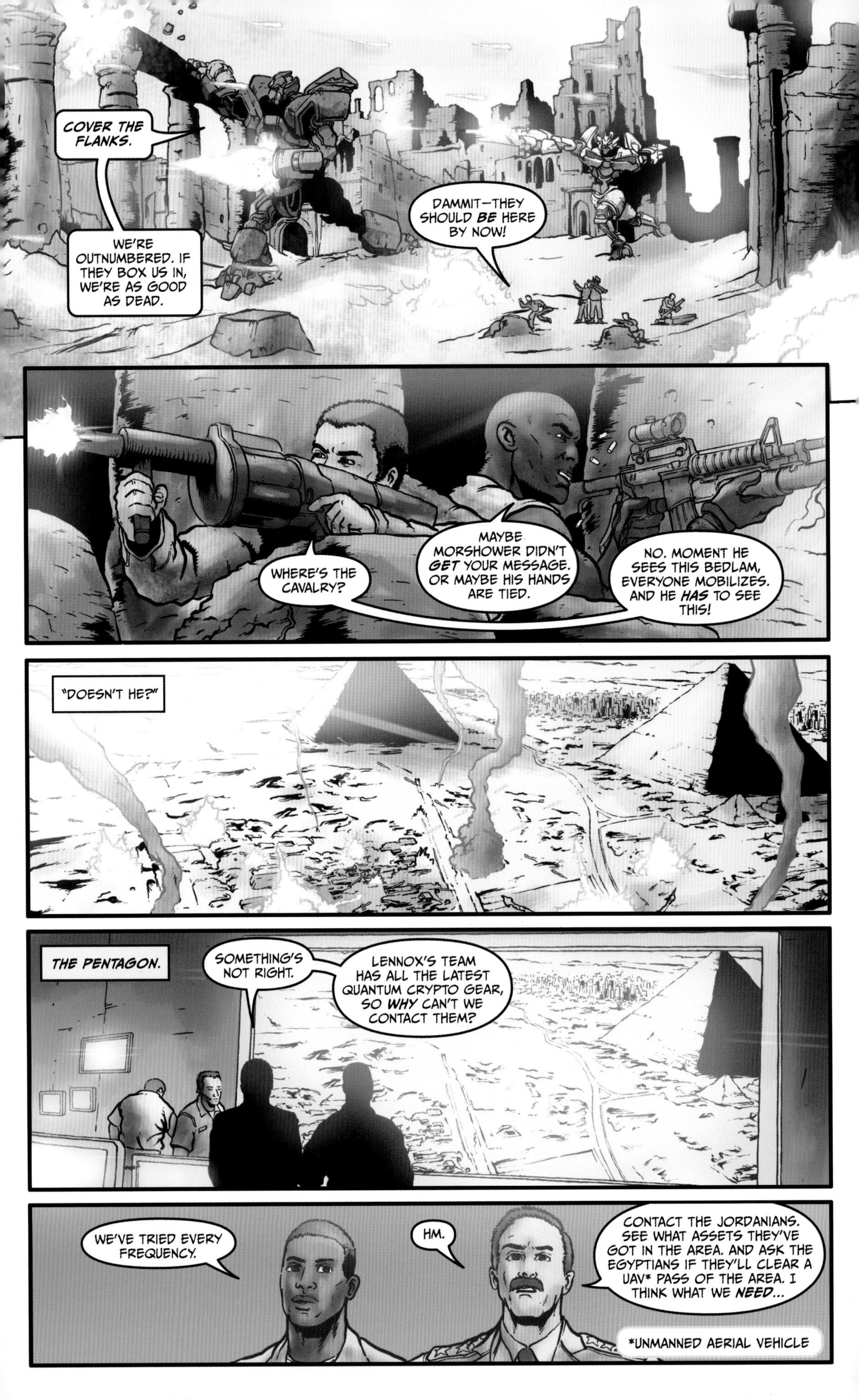
COVER THE FLANKS.
WE'RE OUTNUMBERED. IF THEY BOX US IN, WE'RE AS GOOD AS DEAD.
DAMMIT—THEY SHOULD BE HERE BY NOW!
WHERE'S THE CAVALRY?
MAYBE MORSHOWER DIDN'T GET YOUR MESSAGE. OR MAYBE HIS HANDS ARE TIED.
NO. MOMENT HE SEES THIS BEDLAM, EVERYONE MOBILIZES. AND HE HAS TO SEE THIS!
"DOESN'T HE?"
THE PENTAGON.
SOMETHING'S NOT RIGHT.
LENNOX'S TEAM HAS ALL THE LATEST QUANTUM CRYPTO GEAR, SO WHY CAN'T WE CONTACT THEM?
WE'VE TRIED EVERY FREQUENCY.
HM.
CONTACT THE JORDANIANS. SEE WHAT ASSETS THEY'VE GOT IN THE AREA. AND ASK THE EGYPTIANS IF THEY'LL CLEAR A UAV* PASS OF THE AREA. I THINK WHAT WE NEED...
*UNMANNED AERIAL VEHICLE

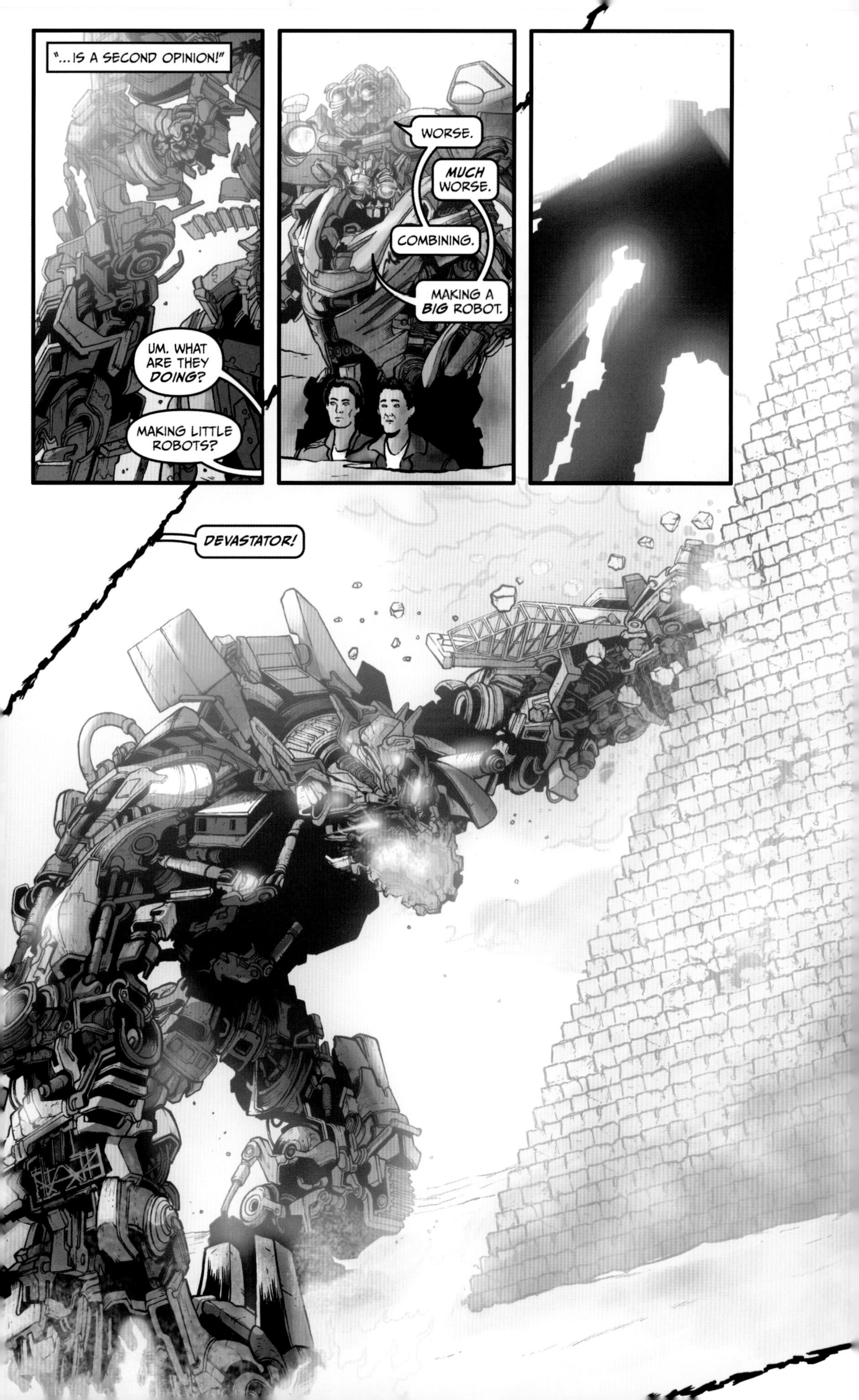
"...IS A SECOND OPINION!"
UM. WHAT ARE THEY DOING?
MAKING LITTLE ROBOTS?
WORSE.
MUCH WORSE.
COMBINING.
MAKING A BIG ROBOT.
DEVASTATOR!

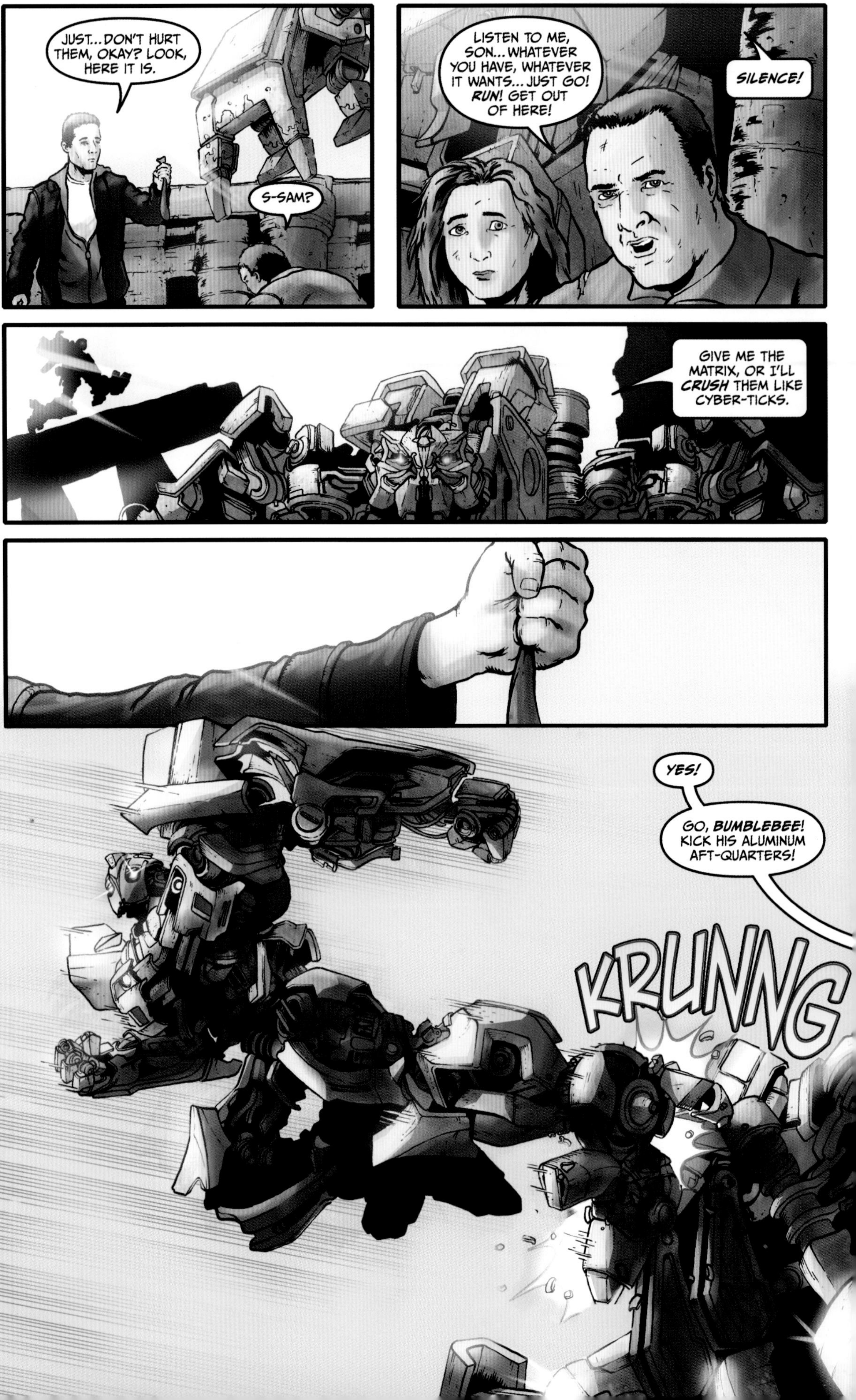
JUST...DON'T HURT THEM, OKAY? LOOK, HERE IT IS.
S-SAM?
LISTEN TO ME, SON...WHATEVER YOU HAVE, WHATEVER IT WANTS...JUST GO! RUN! GET OUT OF HERE!
SILENCE!
GIVE ME THE MATRIX, OR I'LL CRUSH THEM LIKE CYBER-TICKS.
YES!
GO, BUMBLEBEE! KICK HIS ALUMINUM AFT-QUARTERS!
KRUNNG

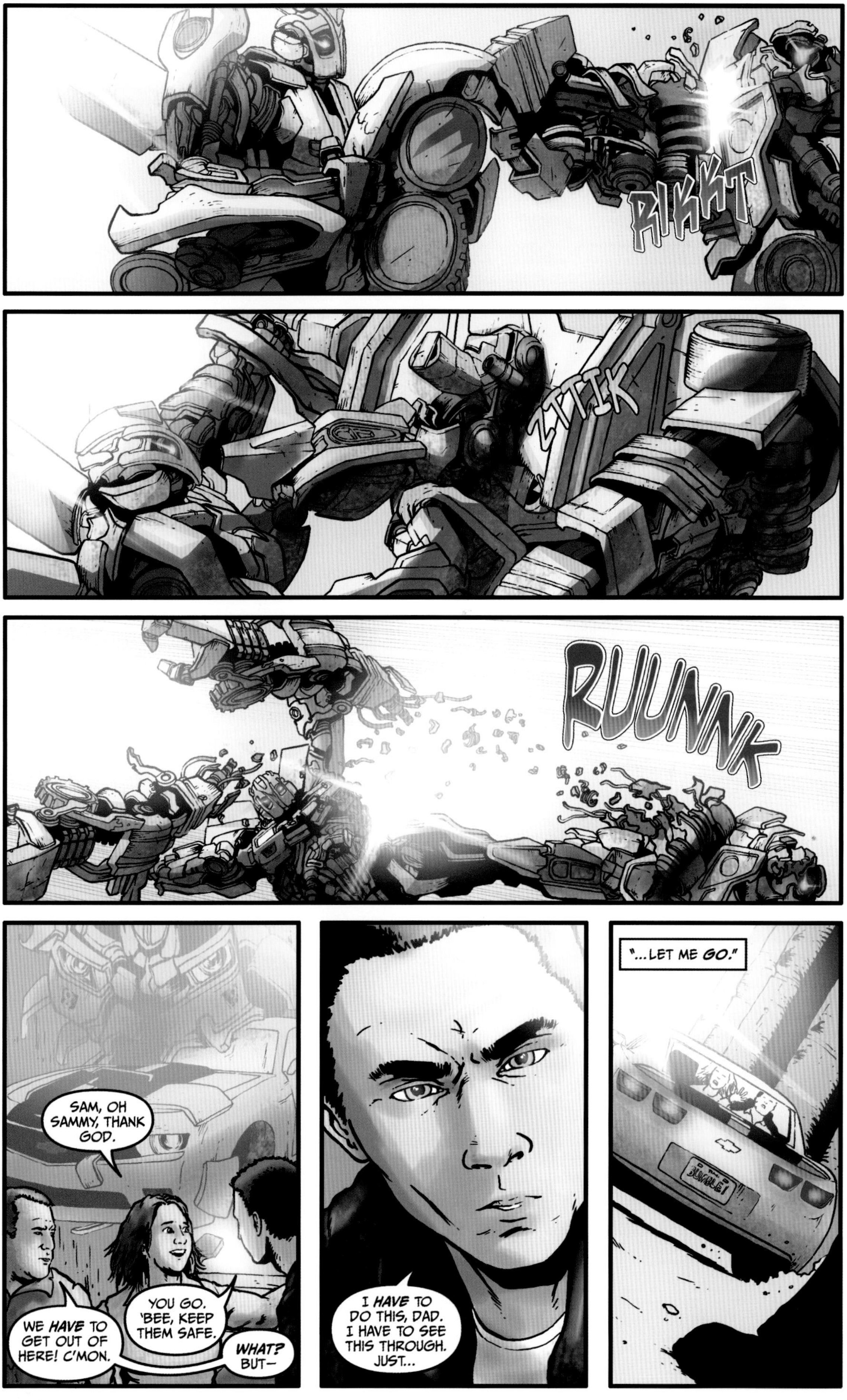
RIKKT
ZTTIK
RUUNNK
SAM, OH SAMMY, THANK GOD.
WE *HAVE* TO GET OUT OF HERE! C'MON.
YOU GO. 'BEE, KEEP THEM SAFE.
WHAT? BUT—
I *HAVE* TO DO THIS, DAD. I HAVE TO SEE THIS THROUGH. JUST...
"...LET ME *GO*."

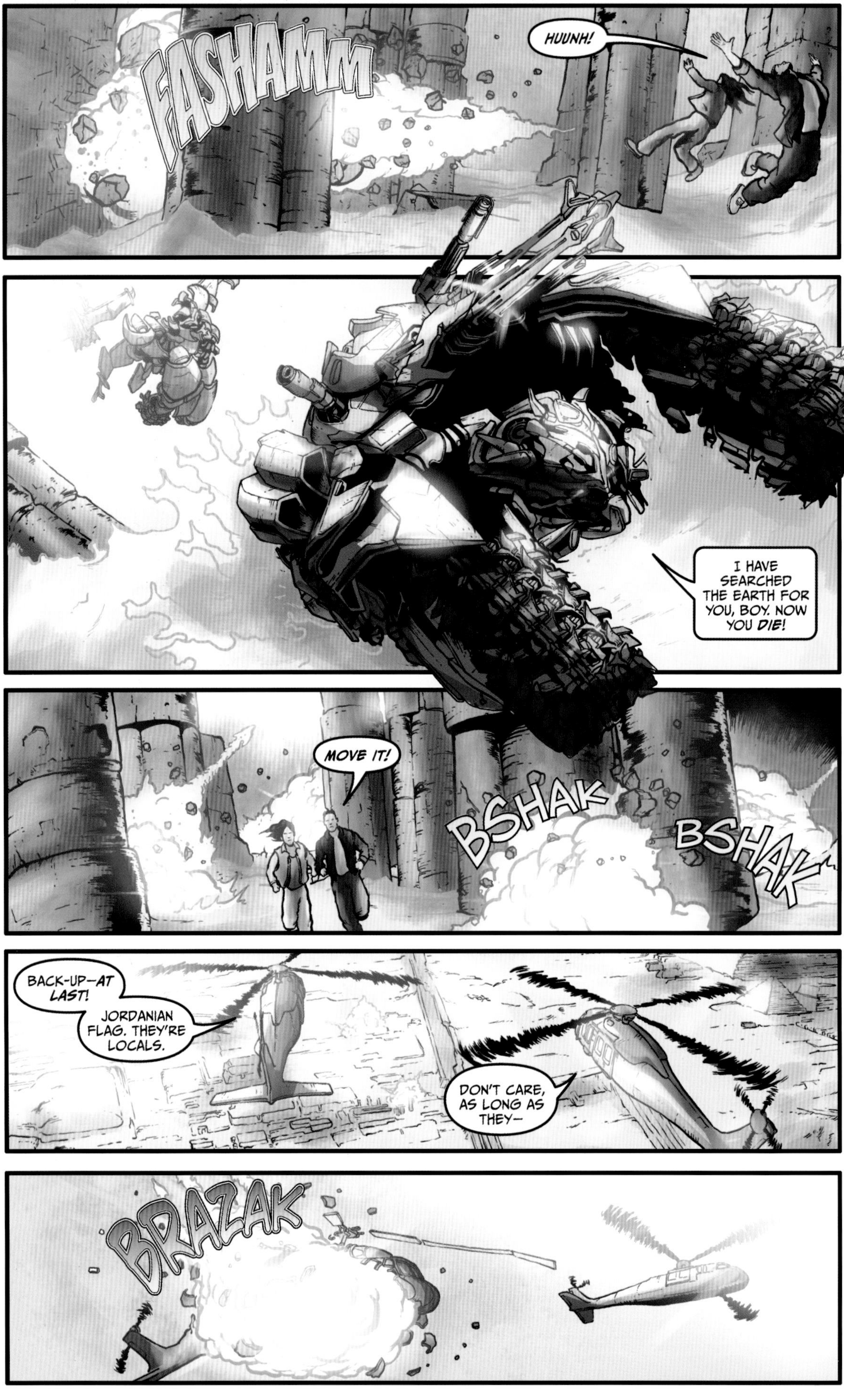
FASHAMM
HUUNH!
I HAVE SEARCHED THE EARTH FOR YOU, BOY. NOW YOU DIE!
MOVE IT!
BSHAK
BSHAK
BACK-UP—AT LAST!
JORDANIAN FLAG. THEY'RE LOCALS.
DON'T CARE, AS LONG AS THEY—
BRAZAK

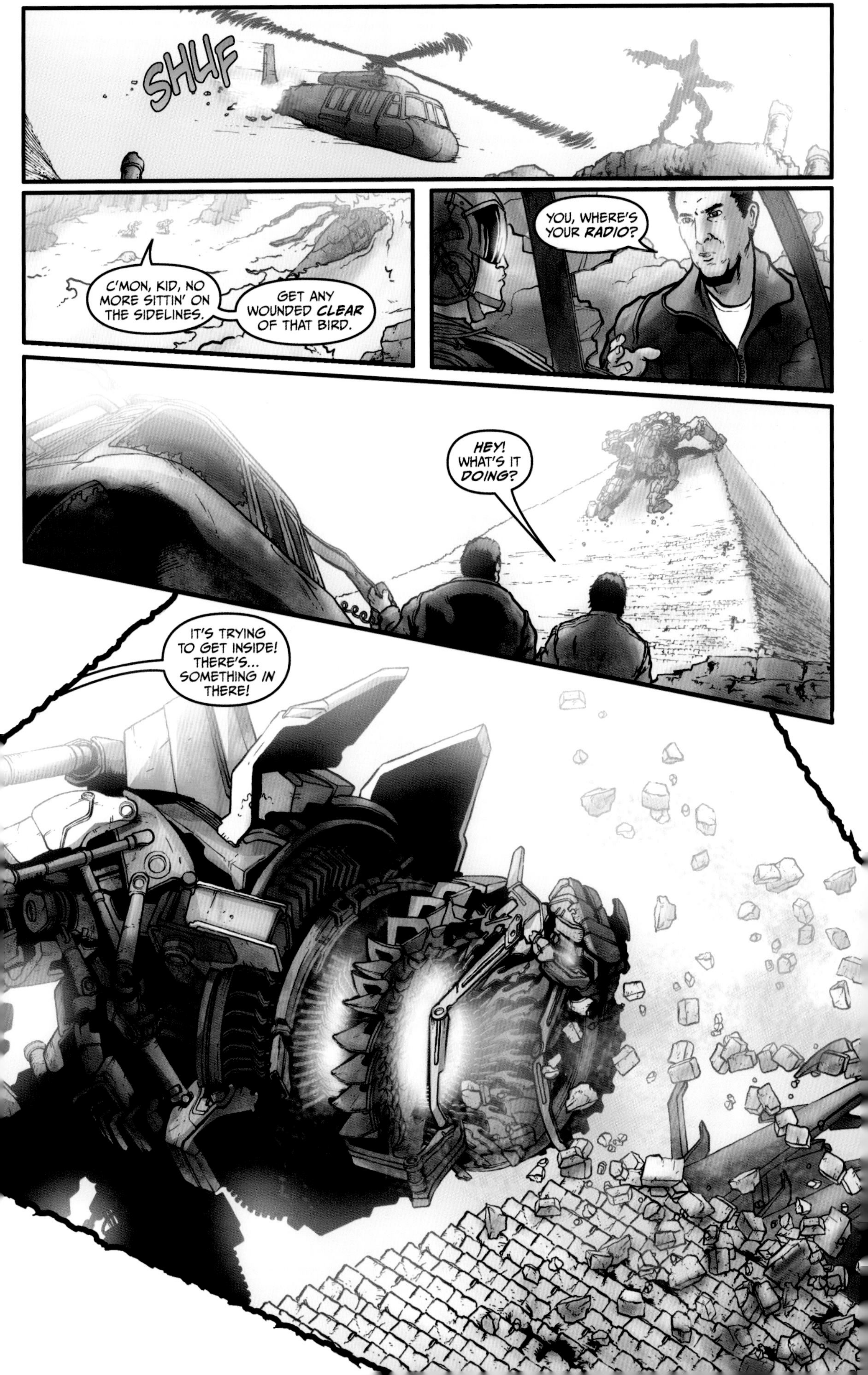
SHUF
C'MON, KID, NO MORE SITTIN' ON THE SIDELINES.
GET ANY WOUNDED CLEAR OF THAT BIRD.
YOU, WHERE'S YOUR RADIO?
HEY! WHAT'S IT DOING?
IT'S TRYING TO GET INSIDE! THERE'S... SOMETHING IN THERE!

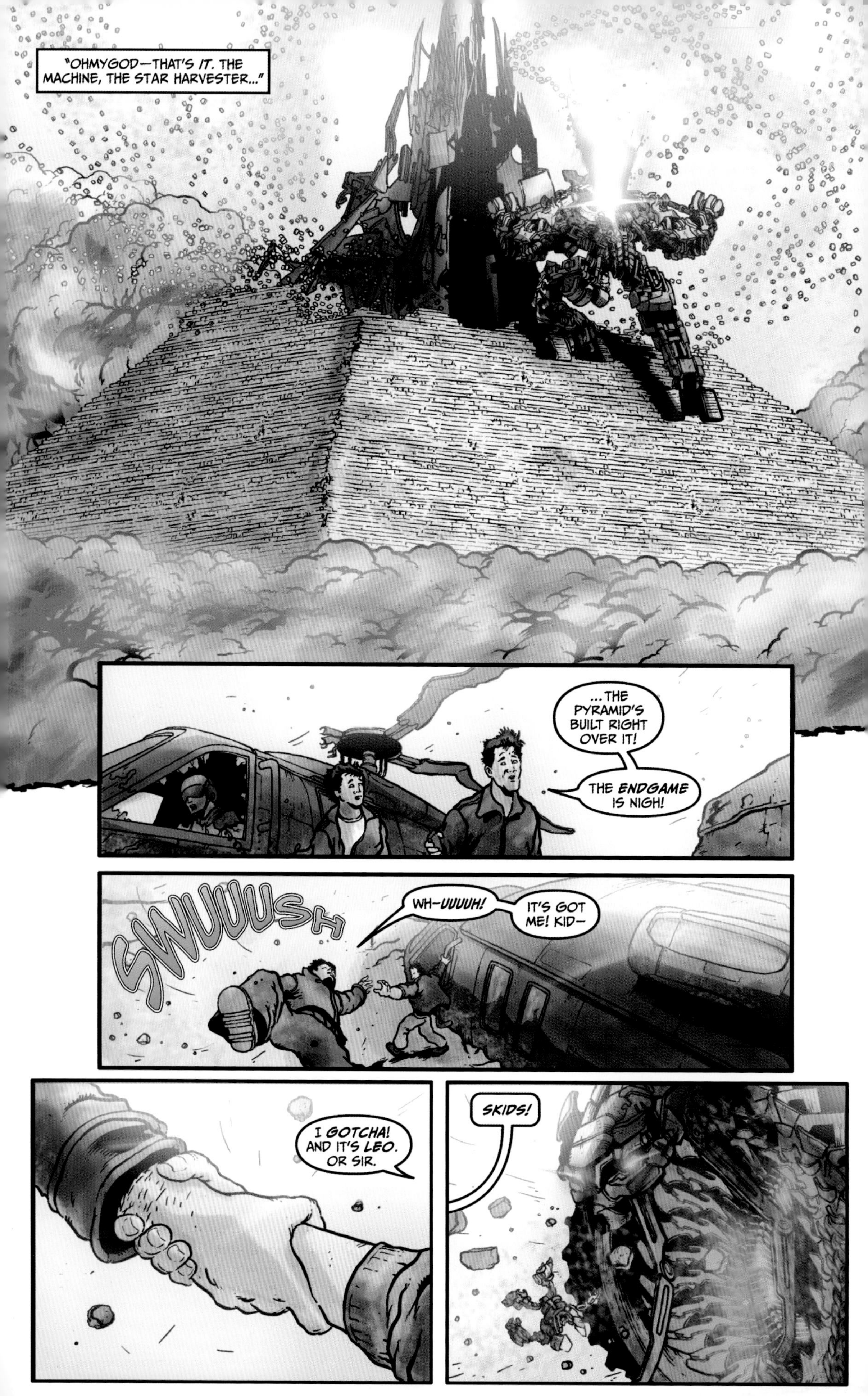
"OHMYGOD—THAT'S *IT*. THE MACHINE, THE STAR HARVESTER..."
...THE PYRAMID'S BUILT RIGHT OVER IT!
THE *ENDGAME* IS NIGH!
SWUUUSH
WH-*UUUUH!*
IT'S GOT ME! KID—
I *GOTCHA!* AND IT'S *LEO*. OR SIR.
SKIDS!

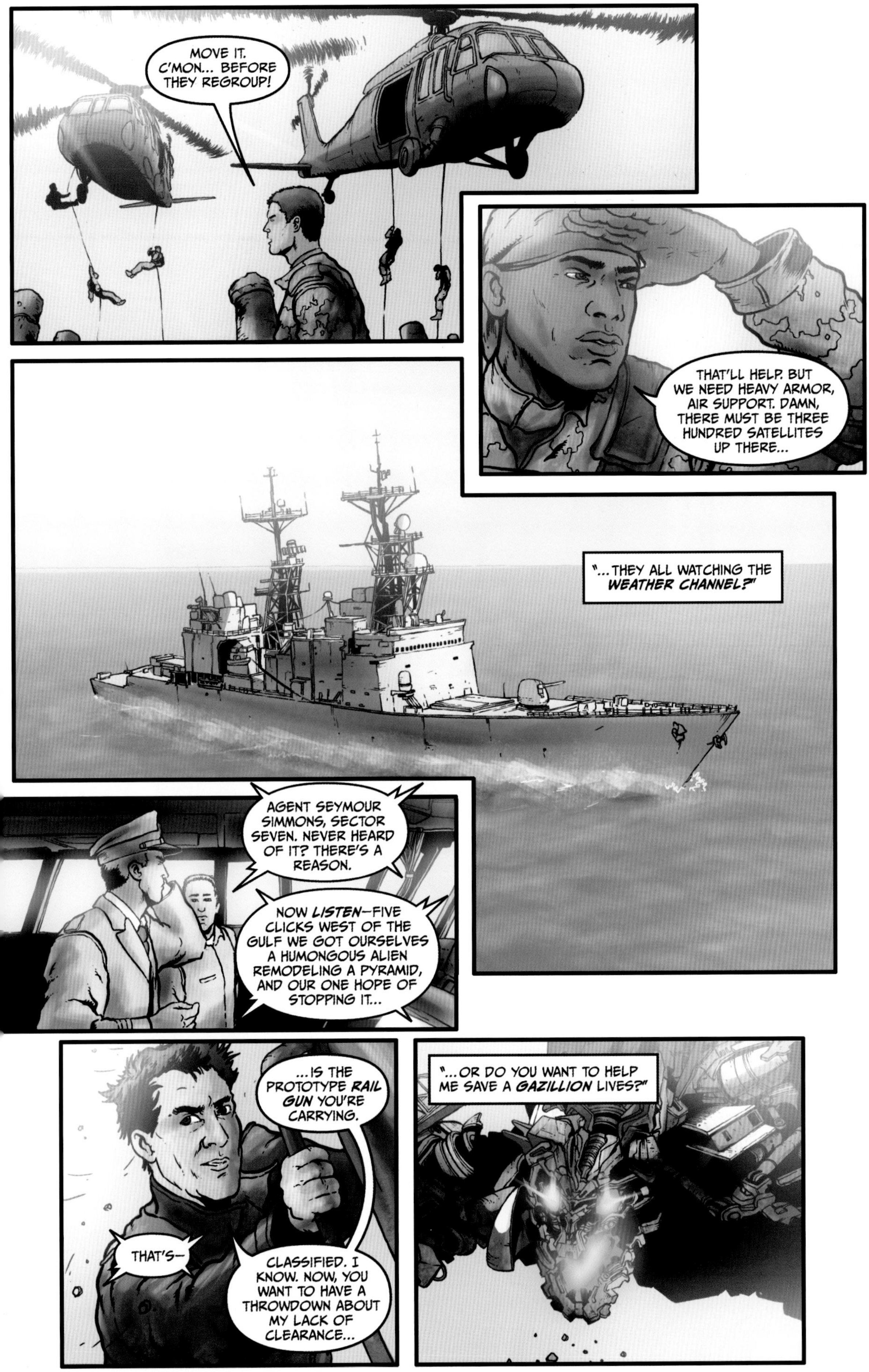
MOVE IT. C'MON... BEFORE THEY REGROUP!
THAT'LL HELP. BUT WE NEED HEAVY ARMOR, AIR SUPPORT. DAMN, THERE MUST BE THREE HUNDRED SATELLITES UP THERE...
"...THEY ALL WATCHING THE WEATHER CHANNEL?"
AGENT SEYMOUR SIMMONS, SECTOR SEVEN. NEVER HEARD OF IT? THERE'S A REASON.
NOW LISTEN—FIVE CLICKS WEST OF THE GULF WE GOT OURSELVES A HUMONGOUS ALIEN REMODELING A PYRAMID, AND OUR ONE HOPE OF STOPPING IT...
...IS THE PROTOTYPE RAIL GUN YOU'RE CARRYING.
THAT'S—
CLASSIFIED. I KNOW. NOW, YOU WANT TO HAVE A THROWDOWN ABOUT MY LACK OF CLEARANCE...
"...OR DO YOU WANT TO HELP ME SAVE A GAZILLION LIVES?"

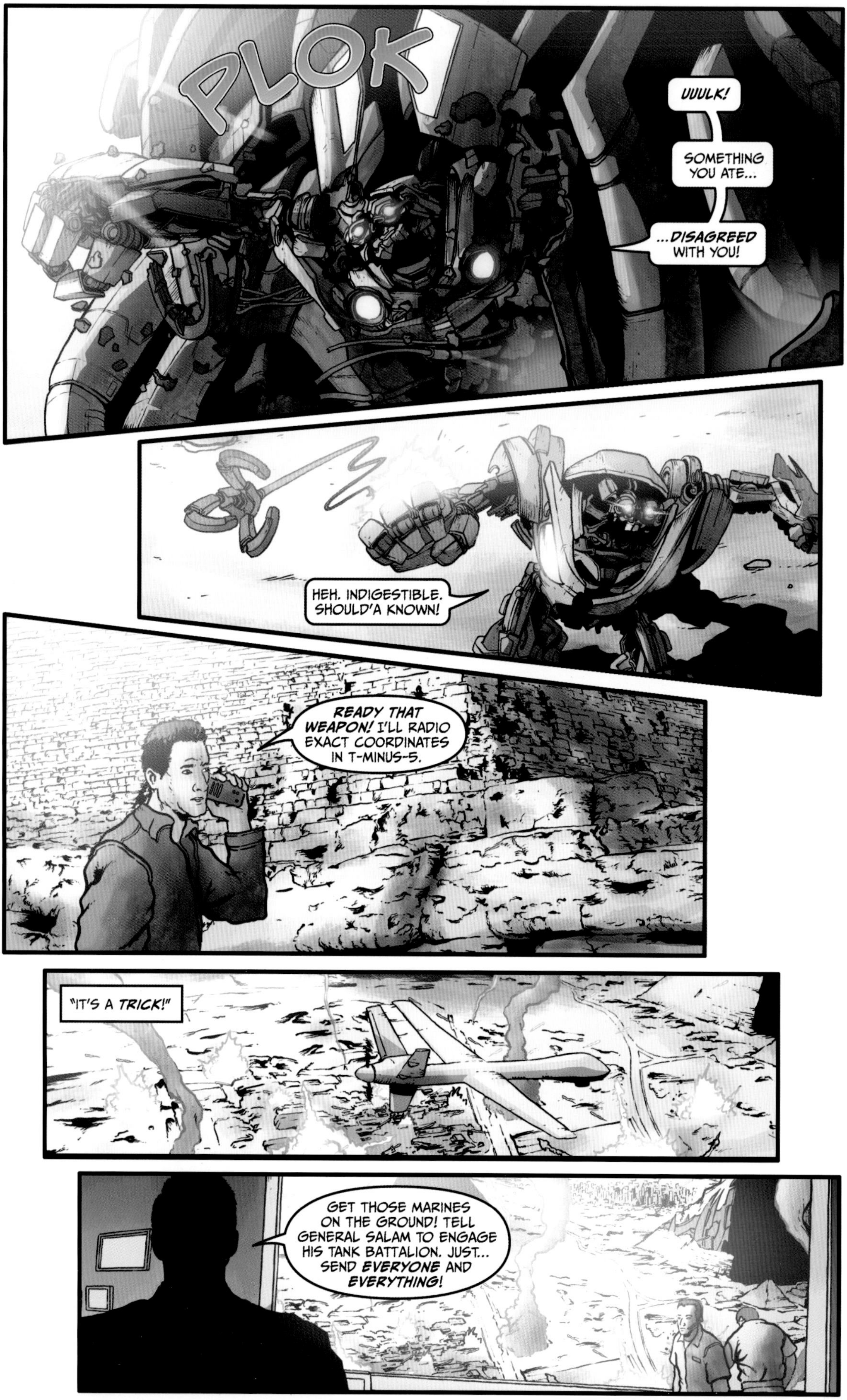
PLOK
UUULK!
SOMETHING YOU ATE...
...DISAGREED WITH YOU!
HEH. INDIGESTIBLE. SHOULD'A KNOWN!
READY THAT WEAPON! I'LL RADIO EXACT COORDINATES IN T-MINUS-5.
"IT'S A TRICK!"
GET THOSE MARINES ON THE GROUND! TELL GENERAL SALAM TO ENGAGE HIS TANK BATTALION. JUST... SEND EVERYONE AND EVERYTHING!

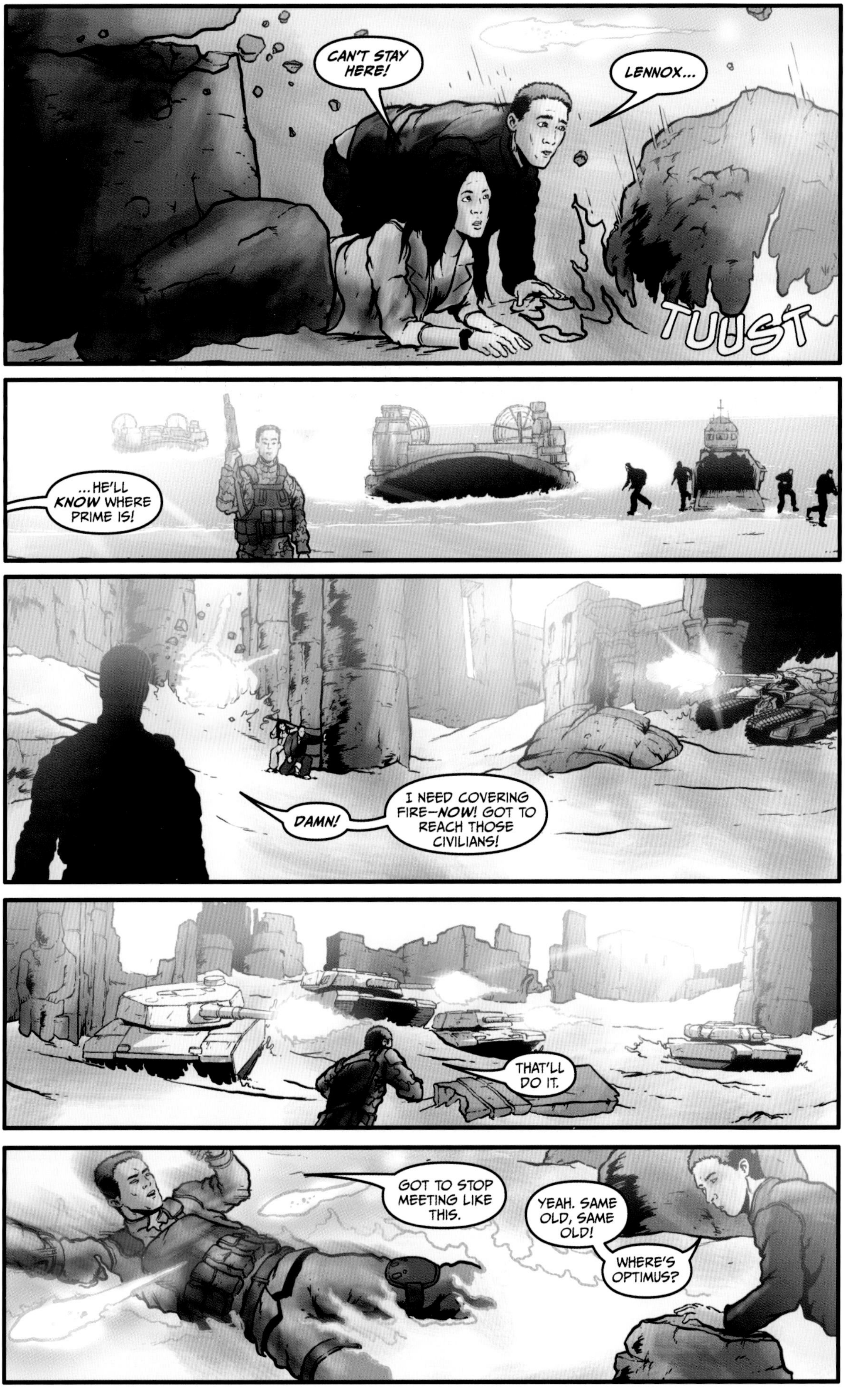
CAN'T STAY HERE!
LENNOX...
TUUST
...HE'LL KNOW WHERE PRIME IS!
DAMN!
I NEED COVERING FIRE—NOW! GOT TO REACH THOSE CIVILIANS!
THAT'LL DO IT.
GOT TO STOP MEETING LIKE THIS.
YEAH. SAME OLD, SAME OLD!
WHERE'S OPTIMUS?

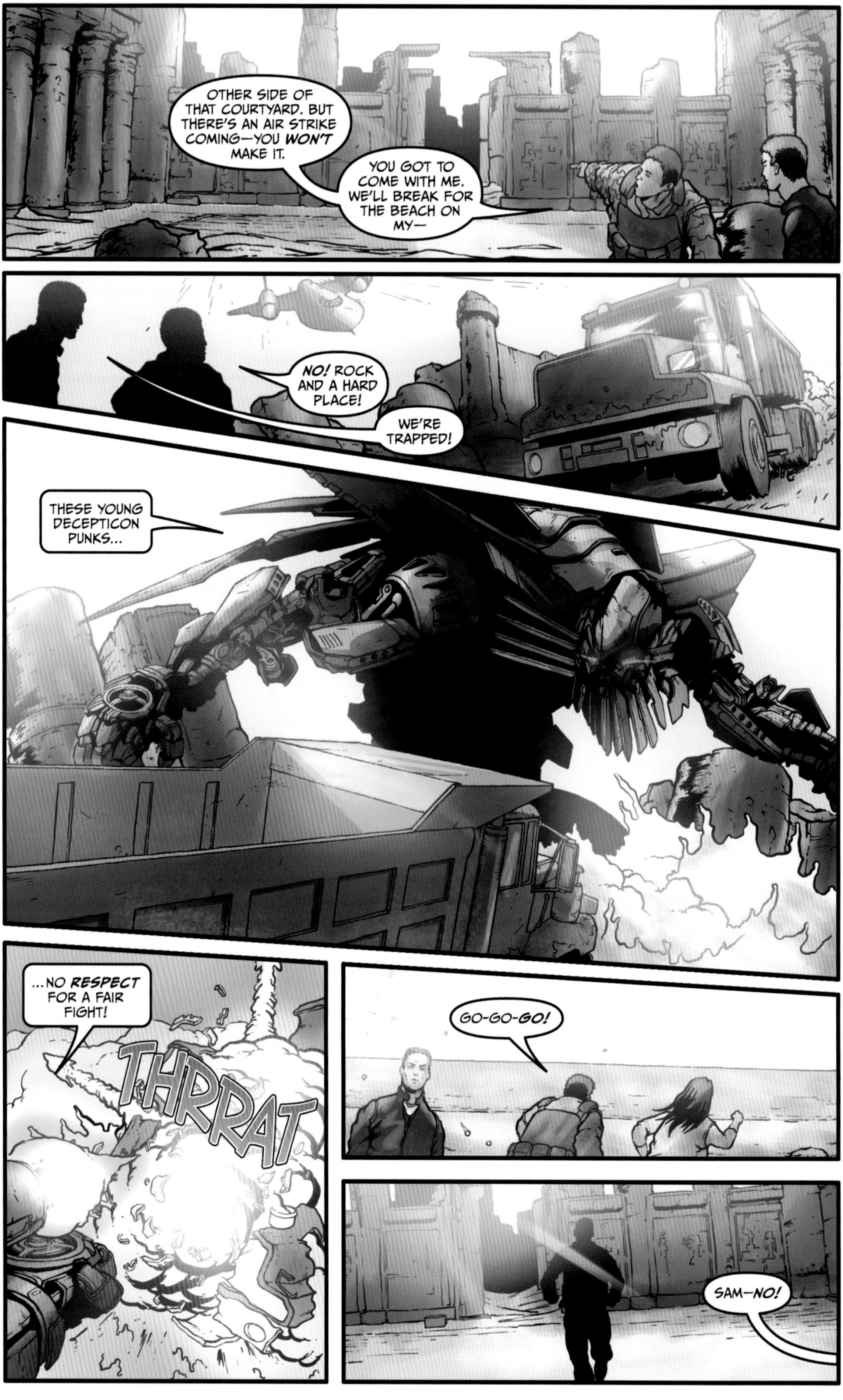
OTHER SIDE OF THAT COURTYARD. BUT THERE'S AN AIR STRIKE COMING—YOU WON'T MAKE IT.
YOU GOT TO COME WITH ME. WE'LL BREAK FOR THE BEACH ON MY—
NO! ROCK AND A HARD PLACE!
WE'RE TRAPPED!
THESE YOUNG DECEPTICON PUNKS...
...NO RESPECT FOR A FAIR FIGHT!
THRRAT
GO-GO-GO!
SAM—NO!

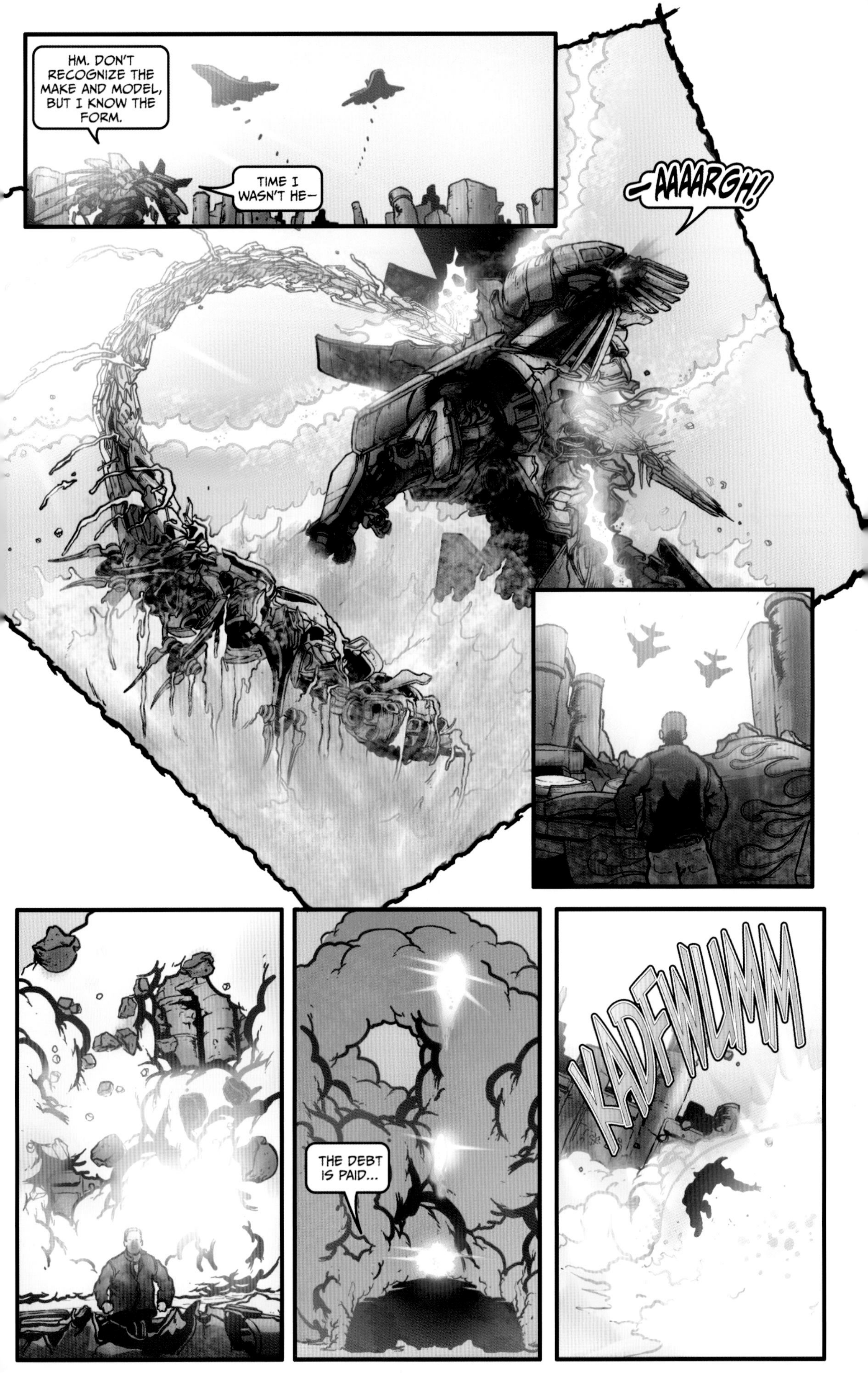

HM. DON'T RECOGNIZE THE MAKE AND MODEL, BUT I KNOW THE FORM.
TIME I WASN'T HE—
—AAAARGH!
THE DEBT IS PAID...
KADFWUMM

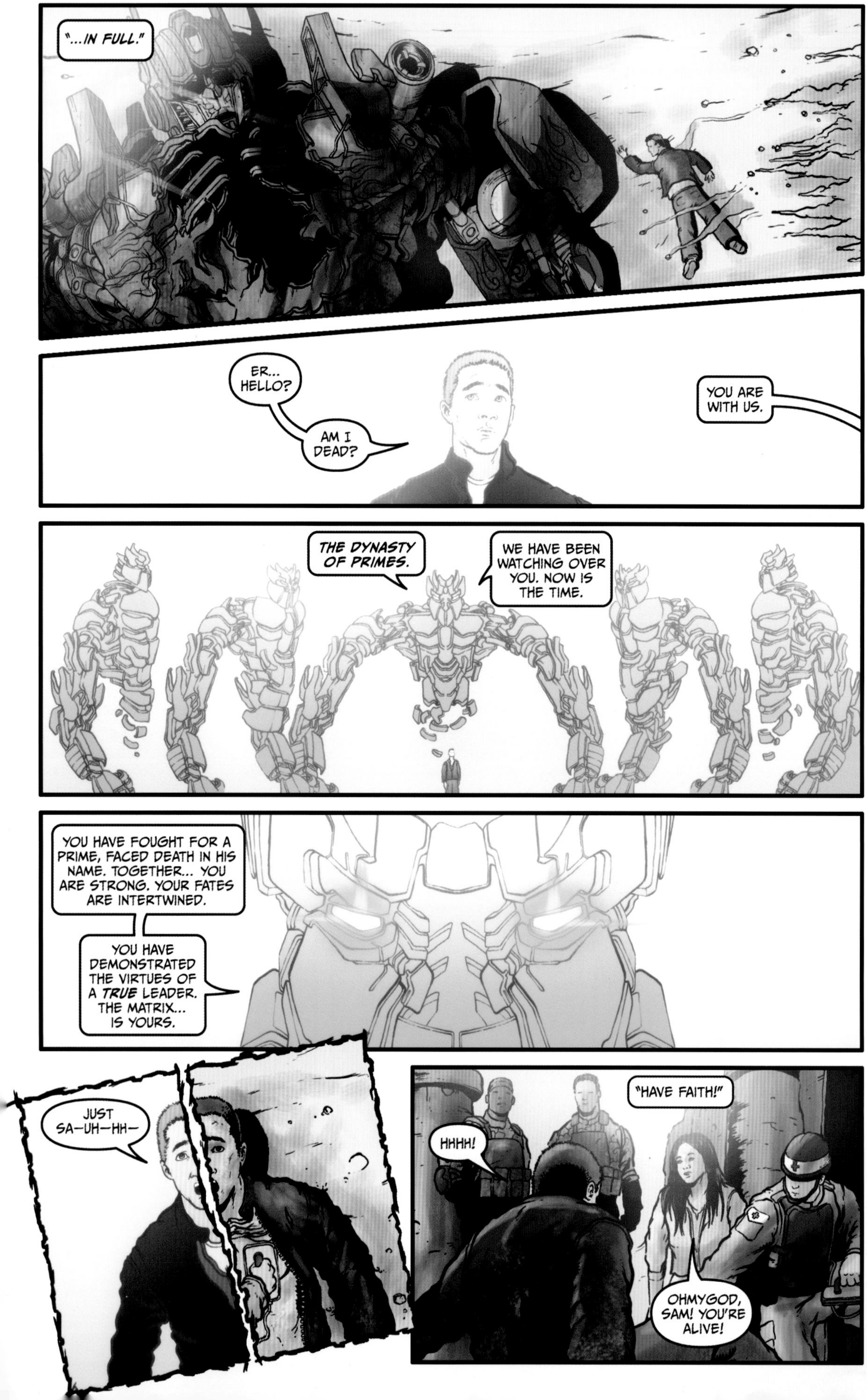
"...IN FULL."
ER... HELLO?
AM I DEAD?
YOU ARE WITH US.
THE DYNASTY OF PRIMES.
WE HAVE BEEN WATCHING OVER YOU. NOW IS THE TIME.
YOU HAVE FOUGHT FOR A PRIME, FACED DEATH IN HIS NAME. TOGETHER... YOU ARE STRONG. YOUR FATES ARE INTERTWINED.
YOU HAVE DEMONSTRATED THE VIRTUES OF A TRUE LEADER. THE MATRIX... IS YOURS.
JUST SA-UH-HH-
"HAVE FAITH!"
HHHH!
OHMYGOD, SAM! YOU'RE ALIVE!

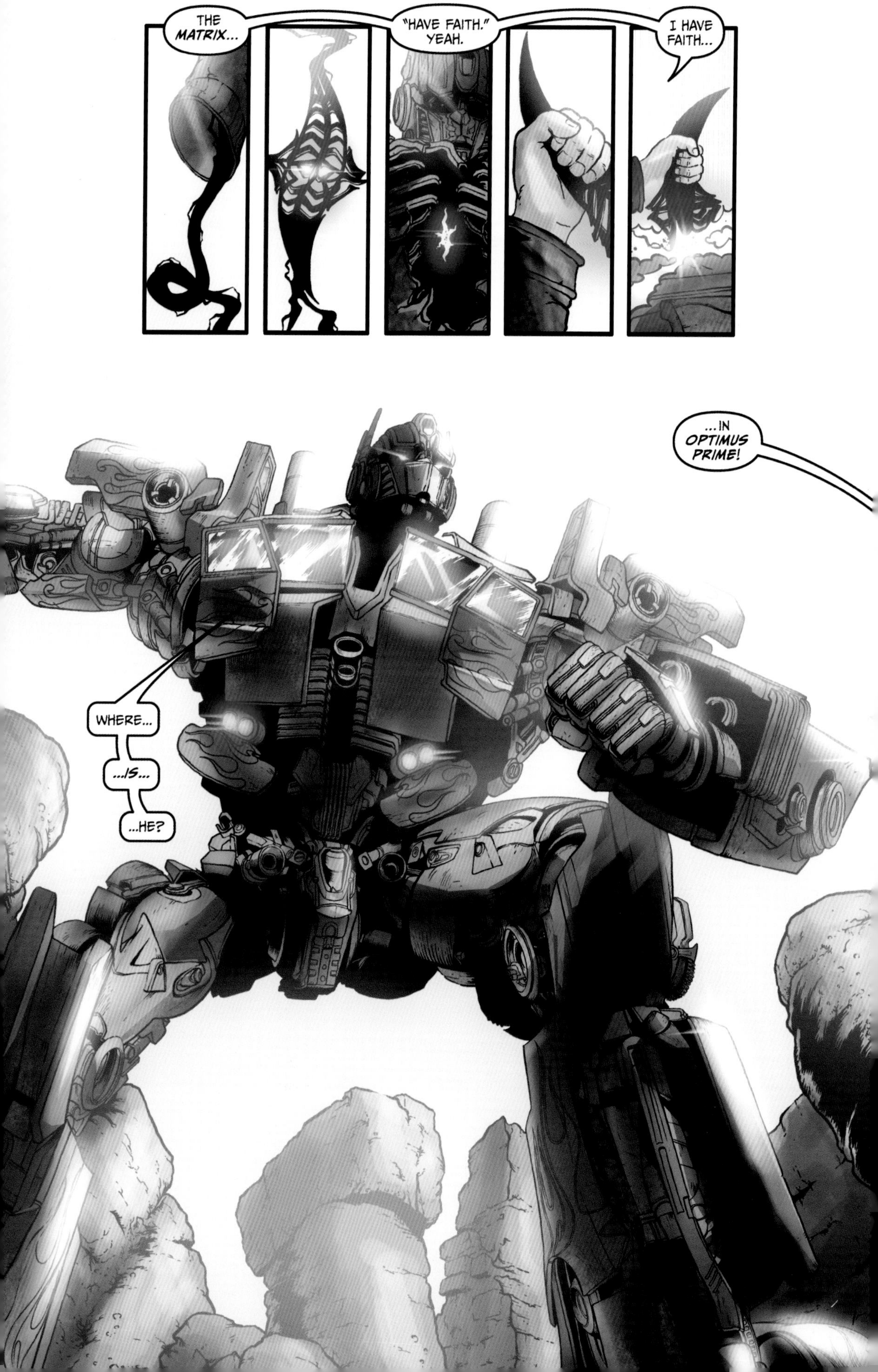

THE MATRIX...
"HAVE FAITH." YEAH.
I HAVE FAITH...
...IN OPTIMUS PRIME!
WHERE...
...IS...
...HE?

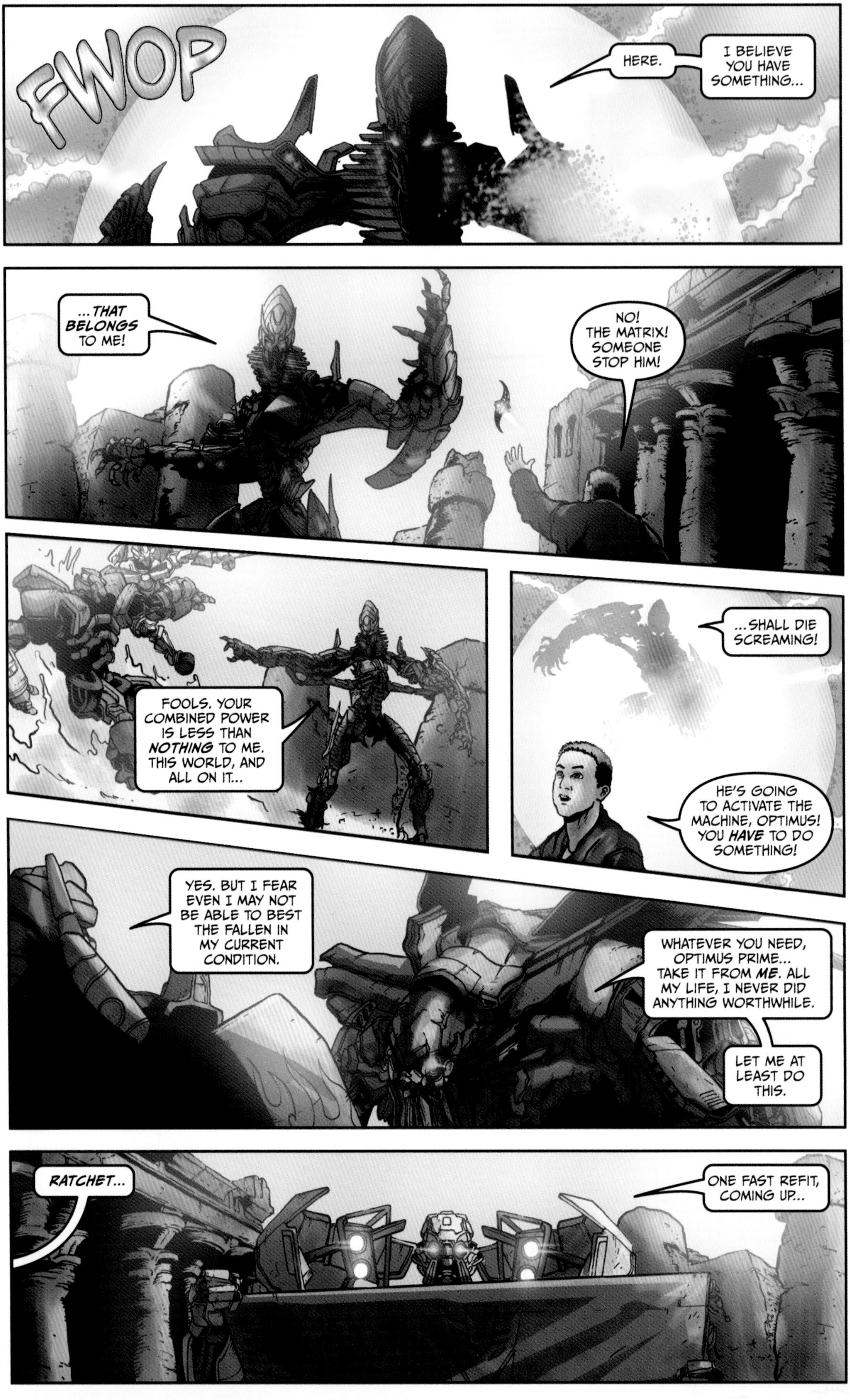
FWOP
HERE.
I BELIEVE YOU HAVE SOMETHING...
...THAT BELONGS TO ME!
NO! THE MATRIX! SOMEONE STOP HIM!
FOOLS. YOUR COMBINED POWER IS LESS THAN NOTHING TO ME. THIS WORLD, AND ALL ON IT...
...SHALL DIE SCREAMING!
HE'S GOING TO ACTIVATE THE MACHINE, OPTIMUS! YOU HAVE TO DO SOMETHING!
YES. BUT I FEAR EVEN I MAY NOT BE ABLE TO BEST THE FALLEN IN MY CURRENT CONDITION.
WHATEVER YOU NEED, OPTIMUS PRIME... TAKE IT FROM ME. ALL MY LIFE, I NEVER DID ANYTHING WORTHWHILE.
LET ME AT LEAST DO THIS.
RATCHET...
ONE FAST REFIT, COMING UP...

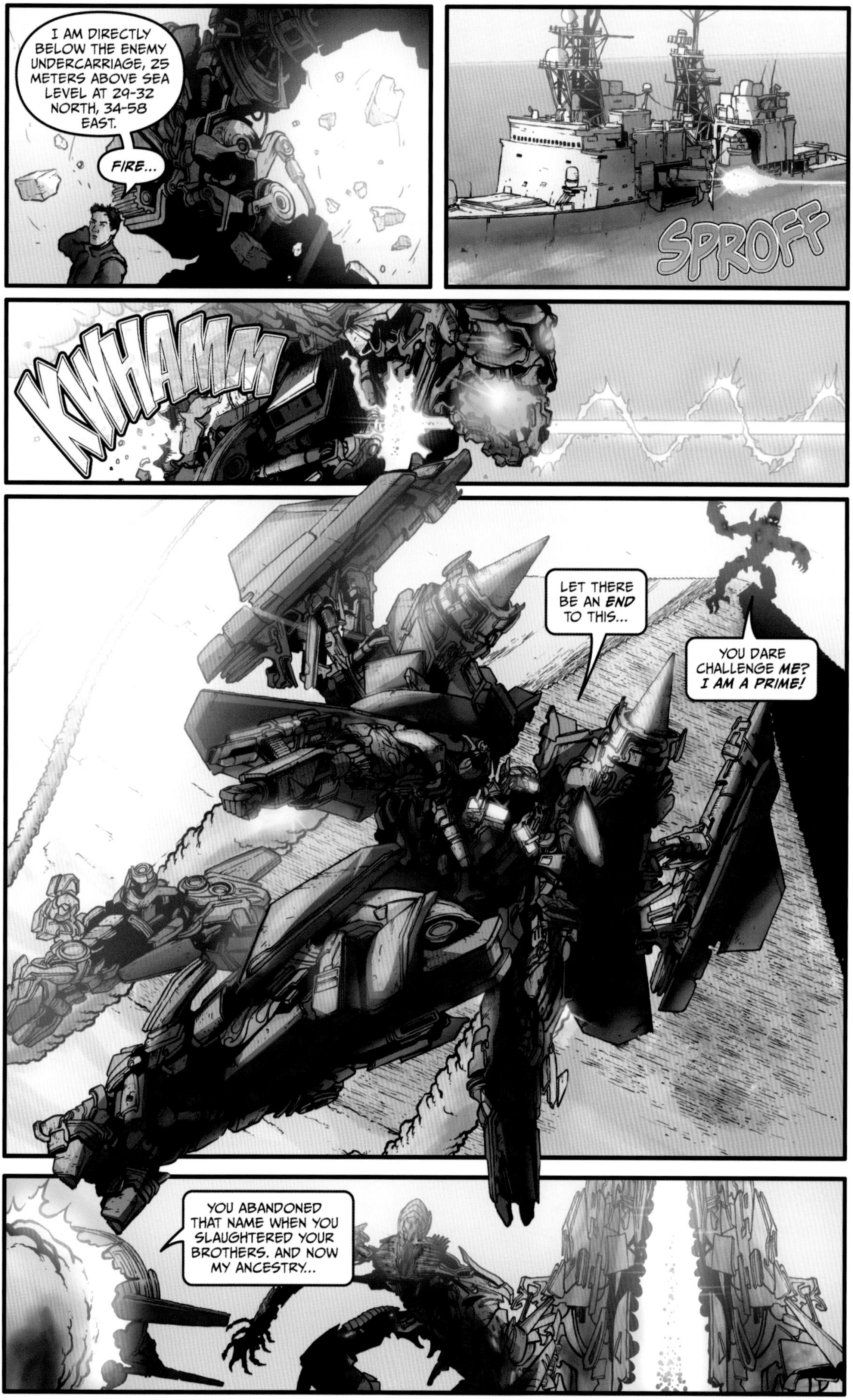
I AM DIRECTLY BELOW THE ENEMY UNDERCARRIAGE, 25 METERS ABOVE SEA LEVEL AT 29-32 NORTH, 34-58 EAST.
FIRE...
SPROFF
KWHAMM
LET THERE BE AN END TO THIS...
YOU DARE CHALLENGE ME? I AM A PRIME!
YOU ABANDONED THAT NAME WHEN YOU SLAUGHTERED YOUR BROTHERS. AND NOW MY ANCESTRY...

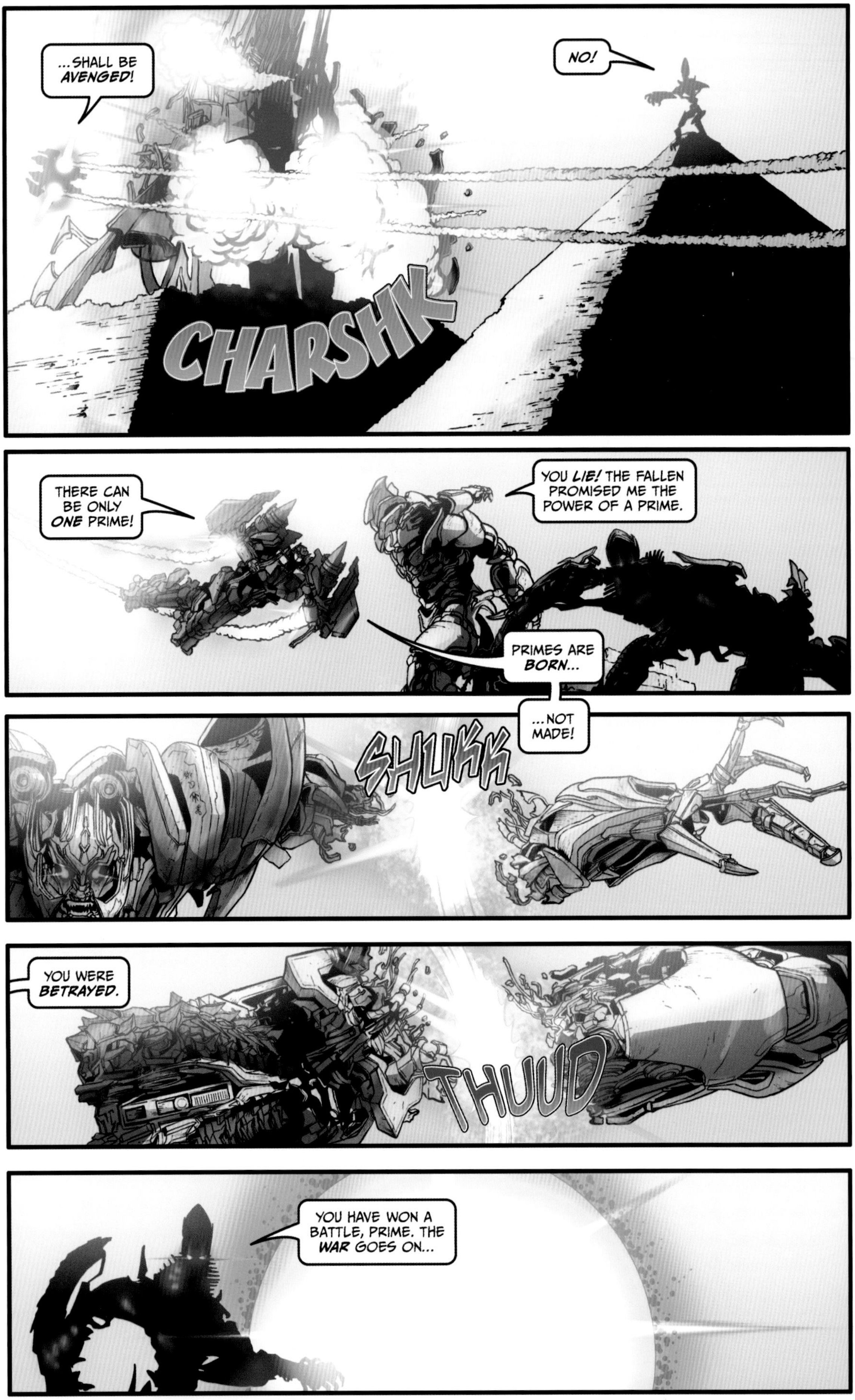
...SHALL BE AVENGED!
NO!
CHARSHK
THERE CAN BE ONLY ONE PRIME!
YOU LIE! THE FALLEN PROMISED ME THE POWER OF A PRIME.
PRIMES ARE BORN...
...NOT MADE!
SHUKK
YOU WERE BETRAYED.
THUUD
YOU HAVE WON A BATTLE, PRIME. THE WAR GOES ON...

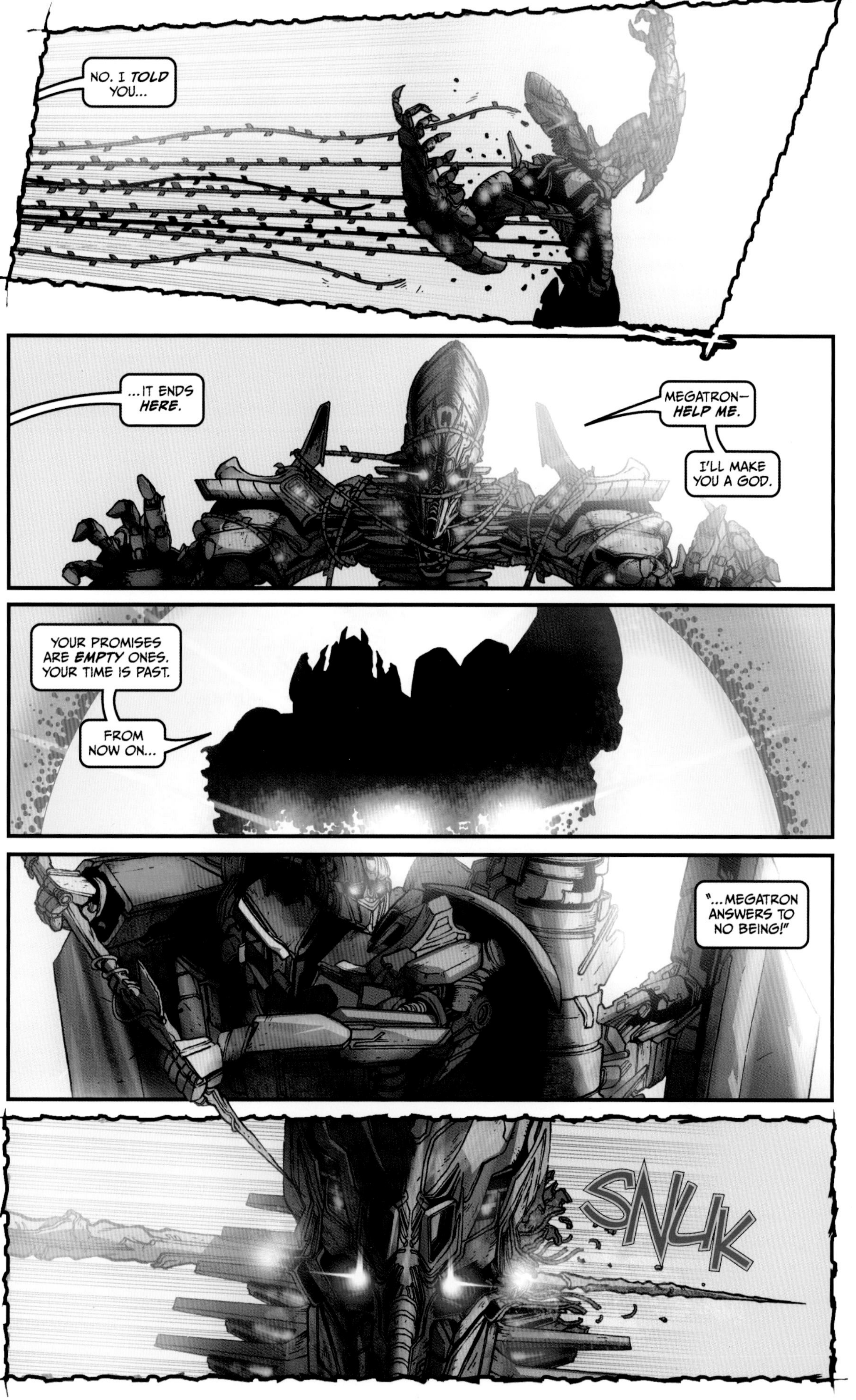

NO. I TOLD YOU...
...IT ENDS HERE.
MEGATRON— HELP ME.
I'LL MAKE YOU A GOD.
YOUR PROMISES ARE EMPTY ONES. YOUR TIME IS PAST.
FROM NOW ON...
"...MEGATRON ANSWERS TO NO BEING!"
SNUK

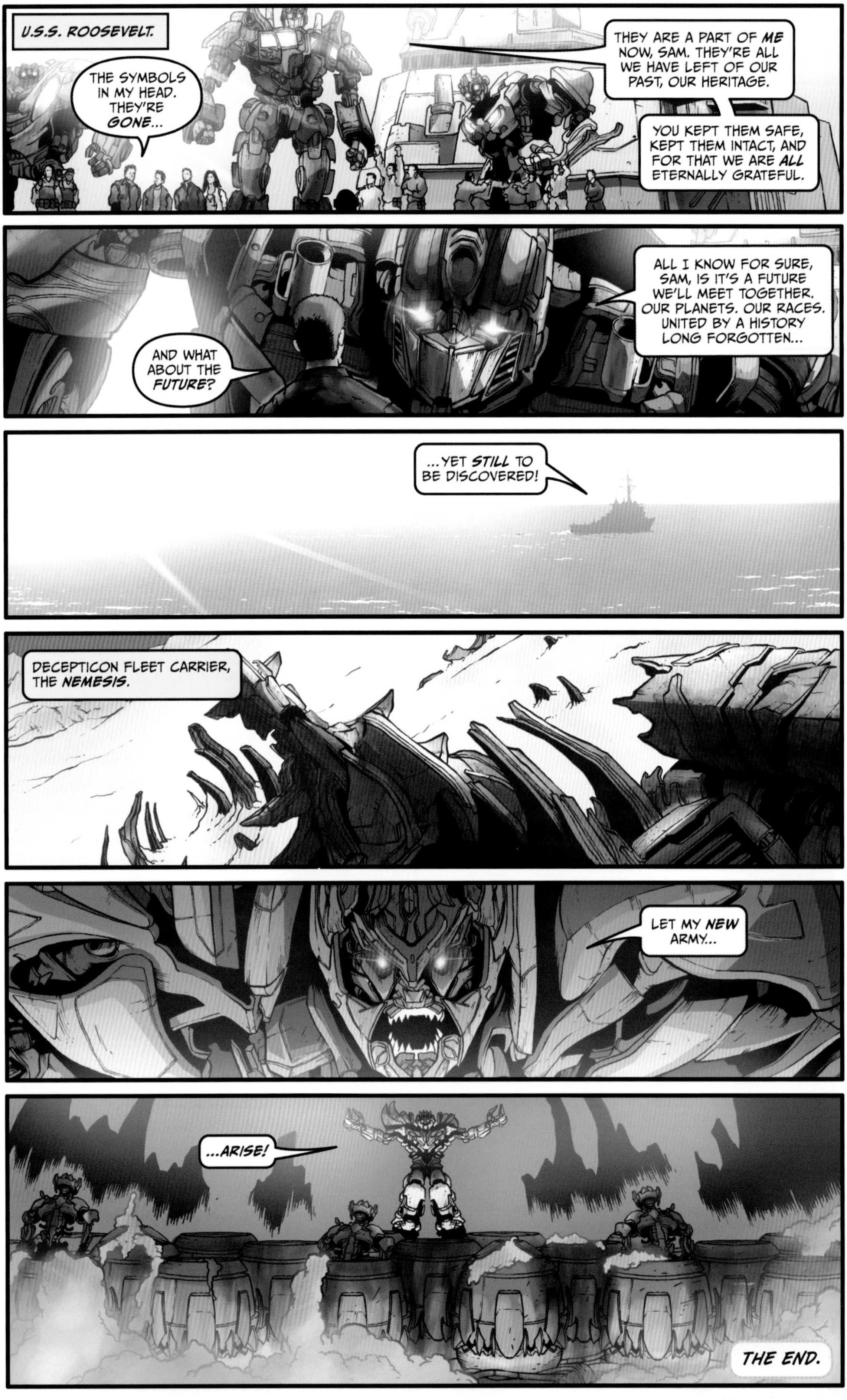
U.S.S. ROOSEVELT.
THE SYMBOLS IN MY HEAD. THEY'RE GONE...
THEY ARE A PART OF ME NOW, SAM. THEY'RE ALL WE HAVE LEFT OF OUR PAST, OUR HERITAGE.
YOU KEPT THEM SAFE, KEPT THEM INTACT, AND FOR THAT WE ARE ALL ETERNALLY GRATEFUL.
AND WHAT ABOUT THE FUTURE?
ALL I KNOW FOR SURE, SAM, IS IT'S A FUTURE WE'LL MEET TOGETHER. OUR PLANETS. OUR RACES. UNITED BY A HISTORY LONG FORGOTTEN...
...YET STILL TO BE DISCOVERED!
DECEPTICON FLEET CARRIER, THE NEMESIS.
LET MY NEW ARMY...
...ARISE!
THE END.

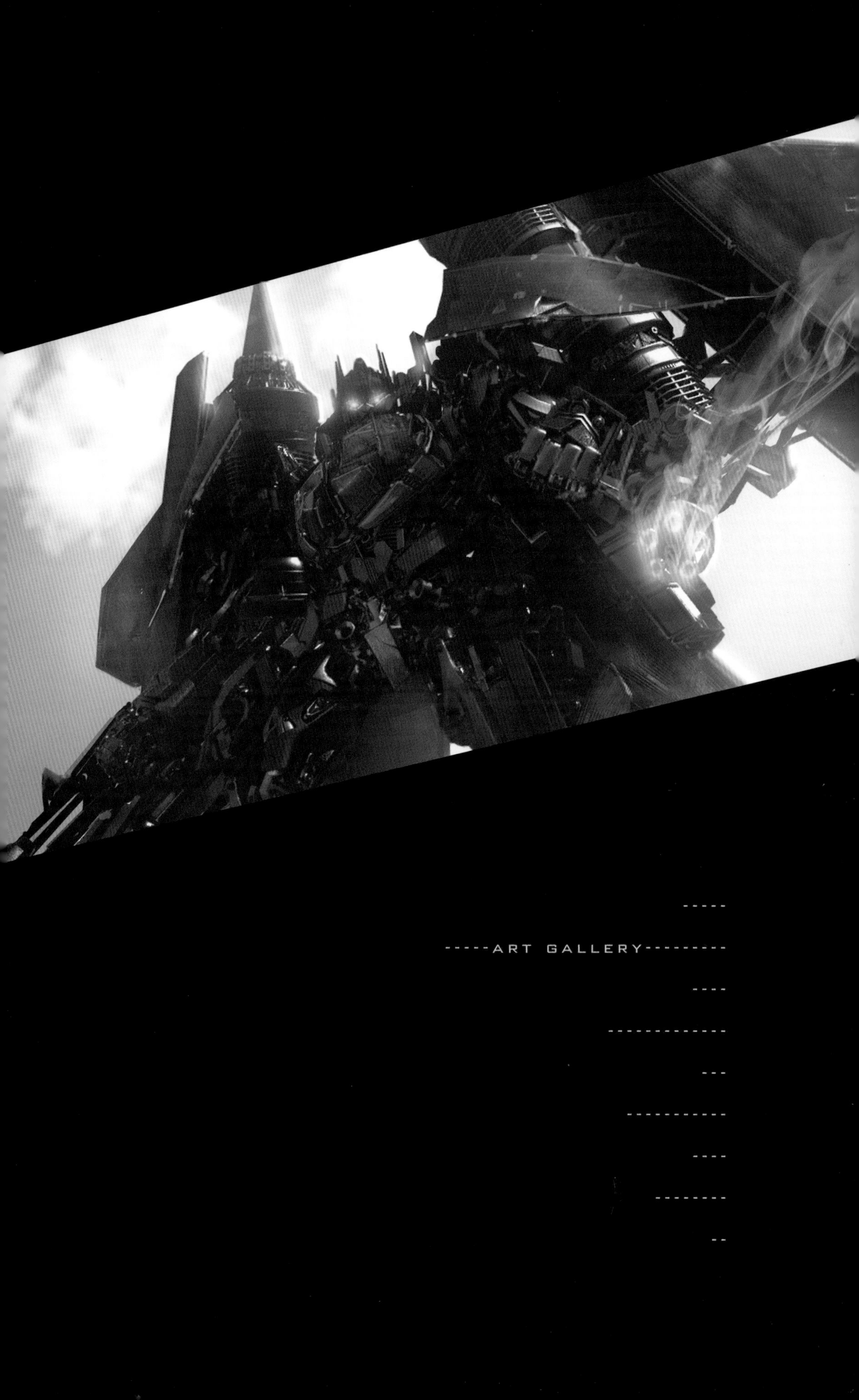

ART GALLERY

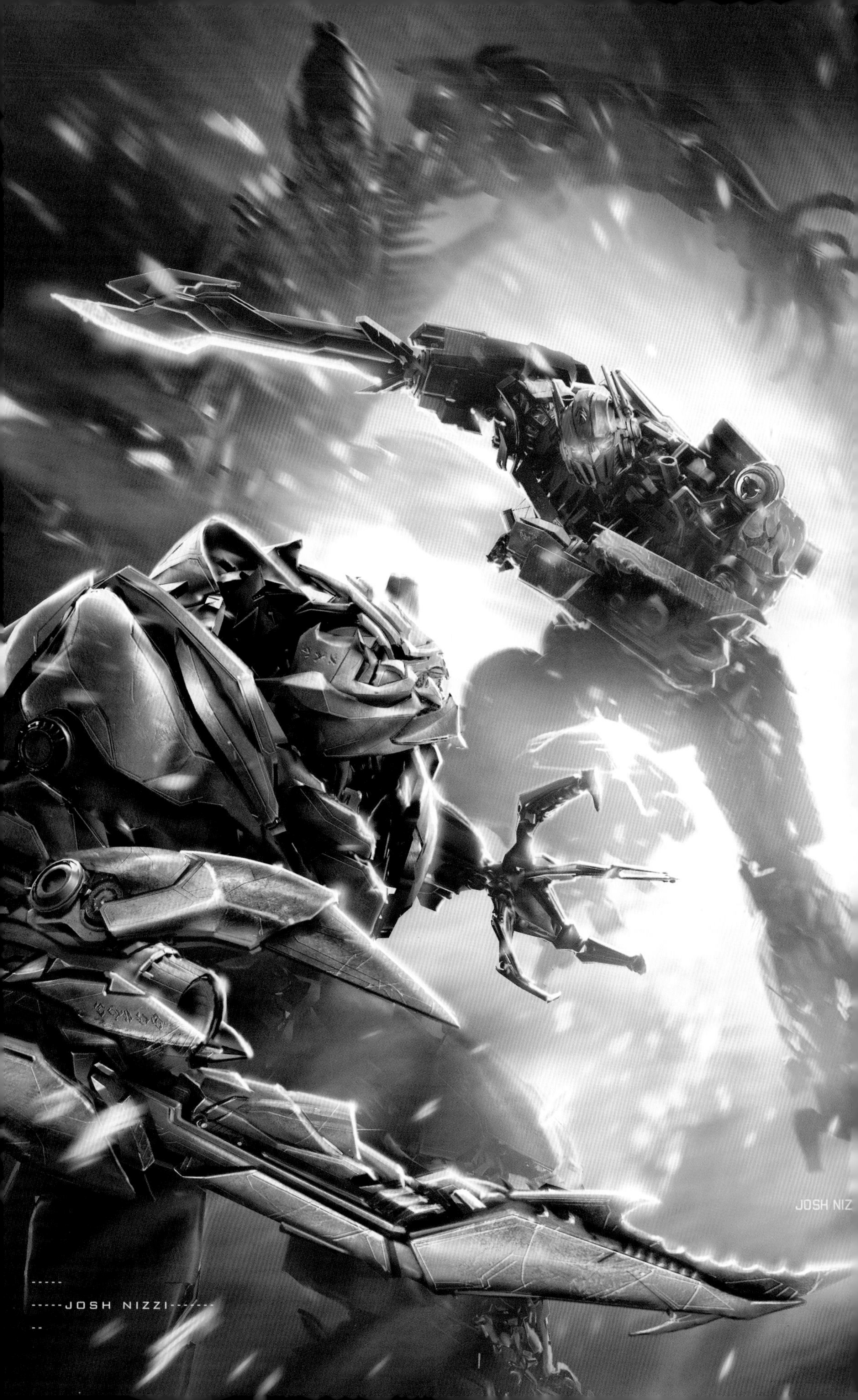
JOSH NIZ

JOSH NIZZI

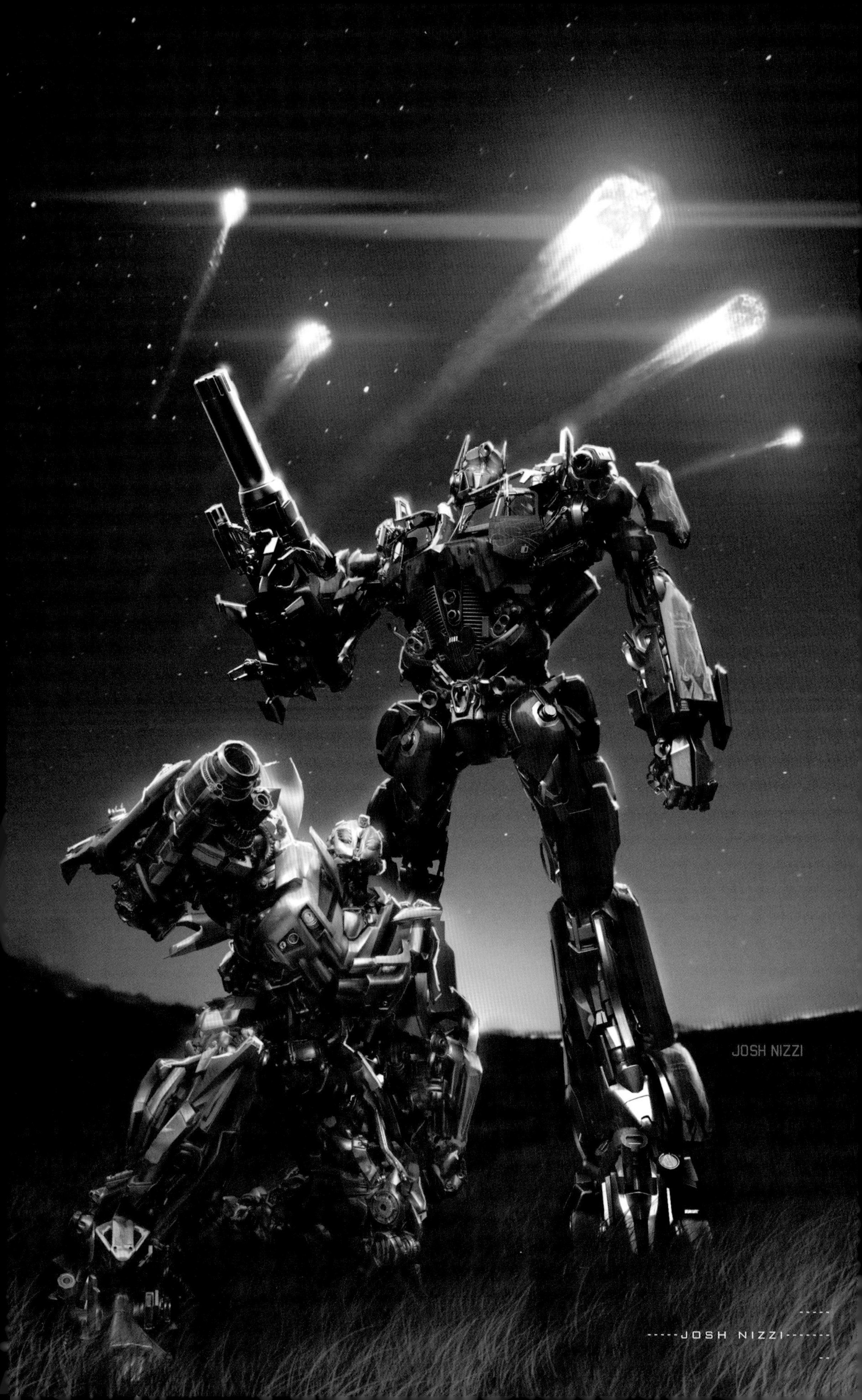
JOSH NIZZI

-----JOSH NIZZI-------

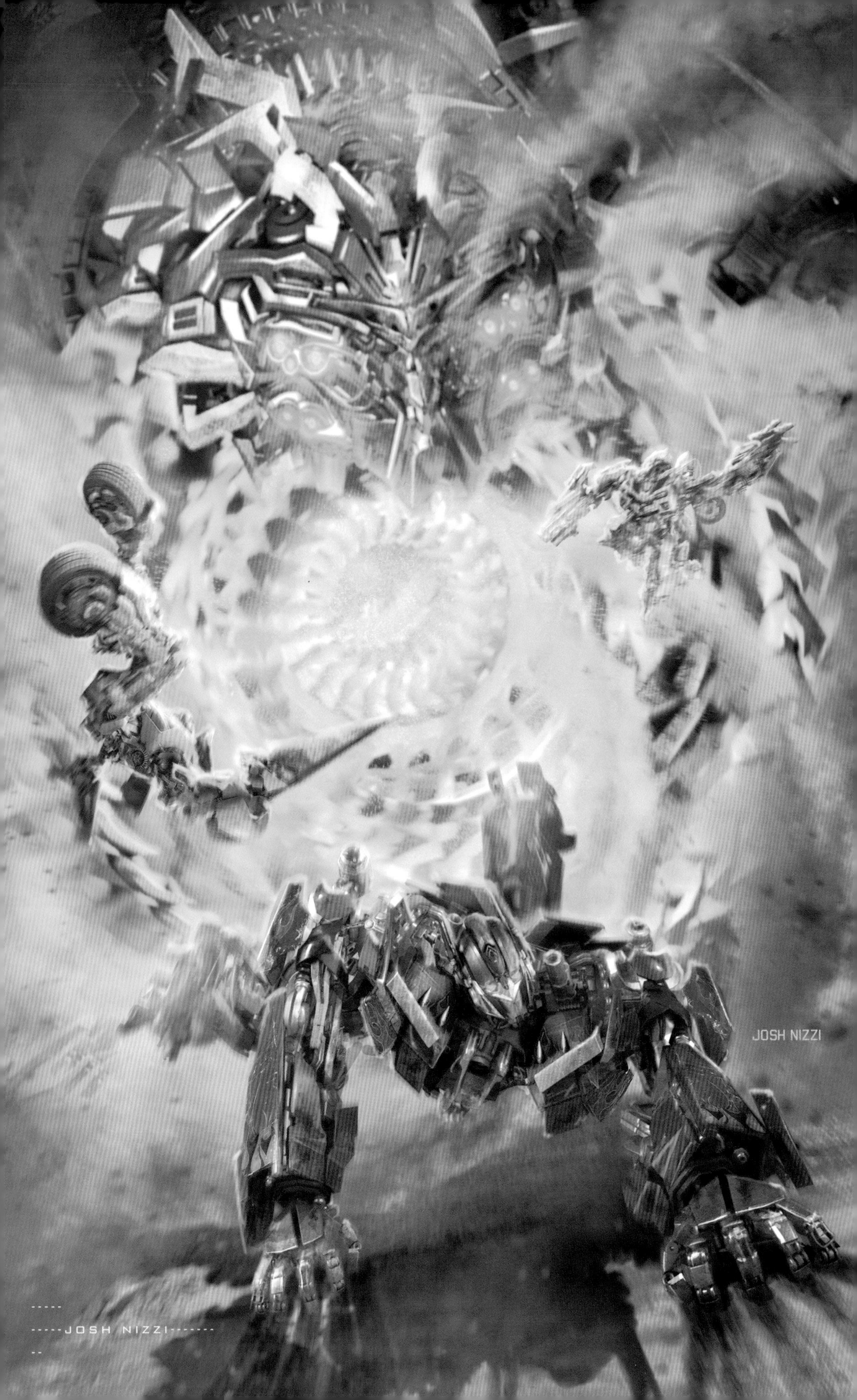
JOSH NIZZI

JOSH NIZZI

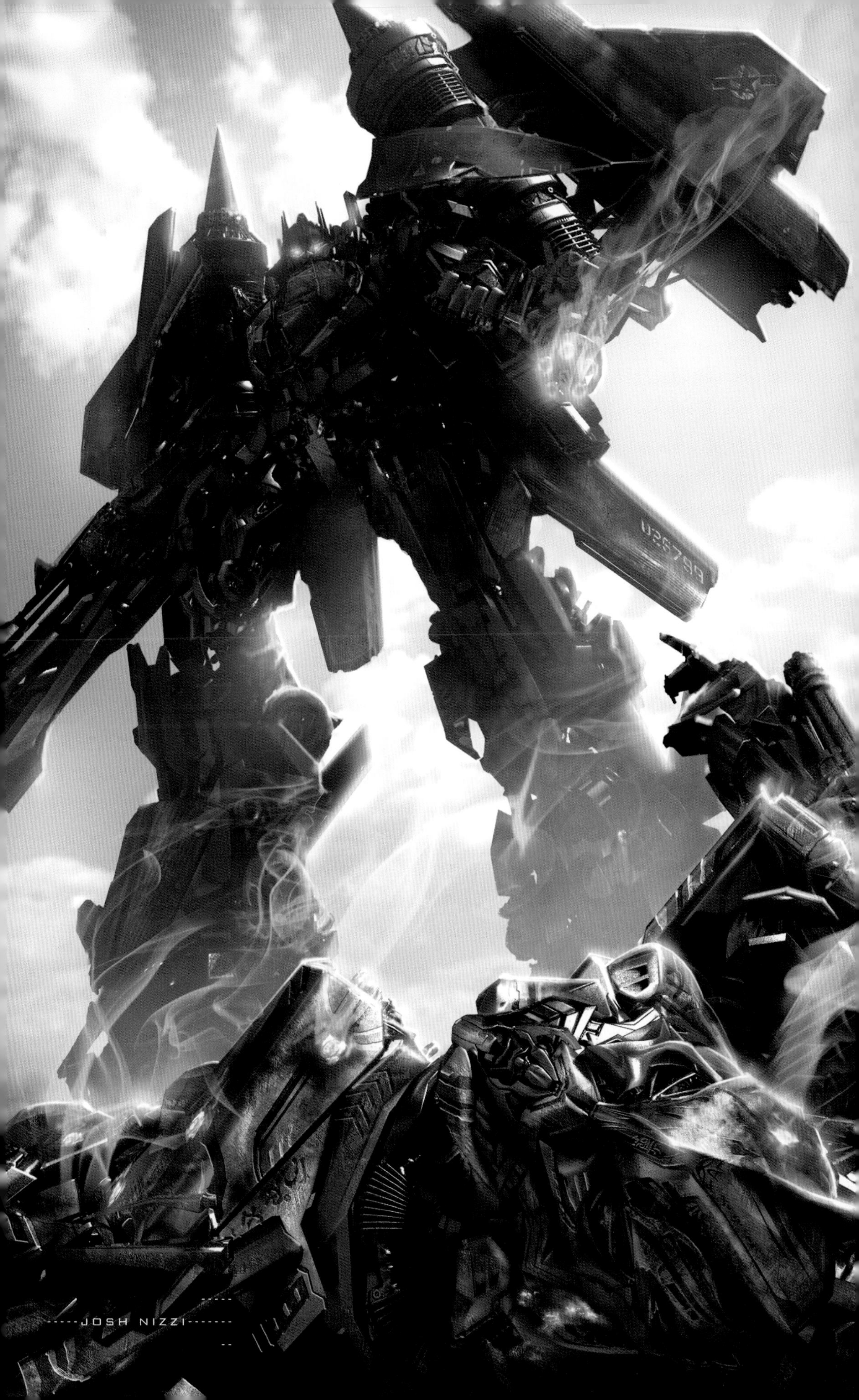

JOSH NIZZI

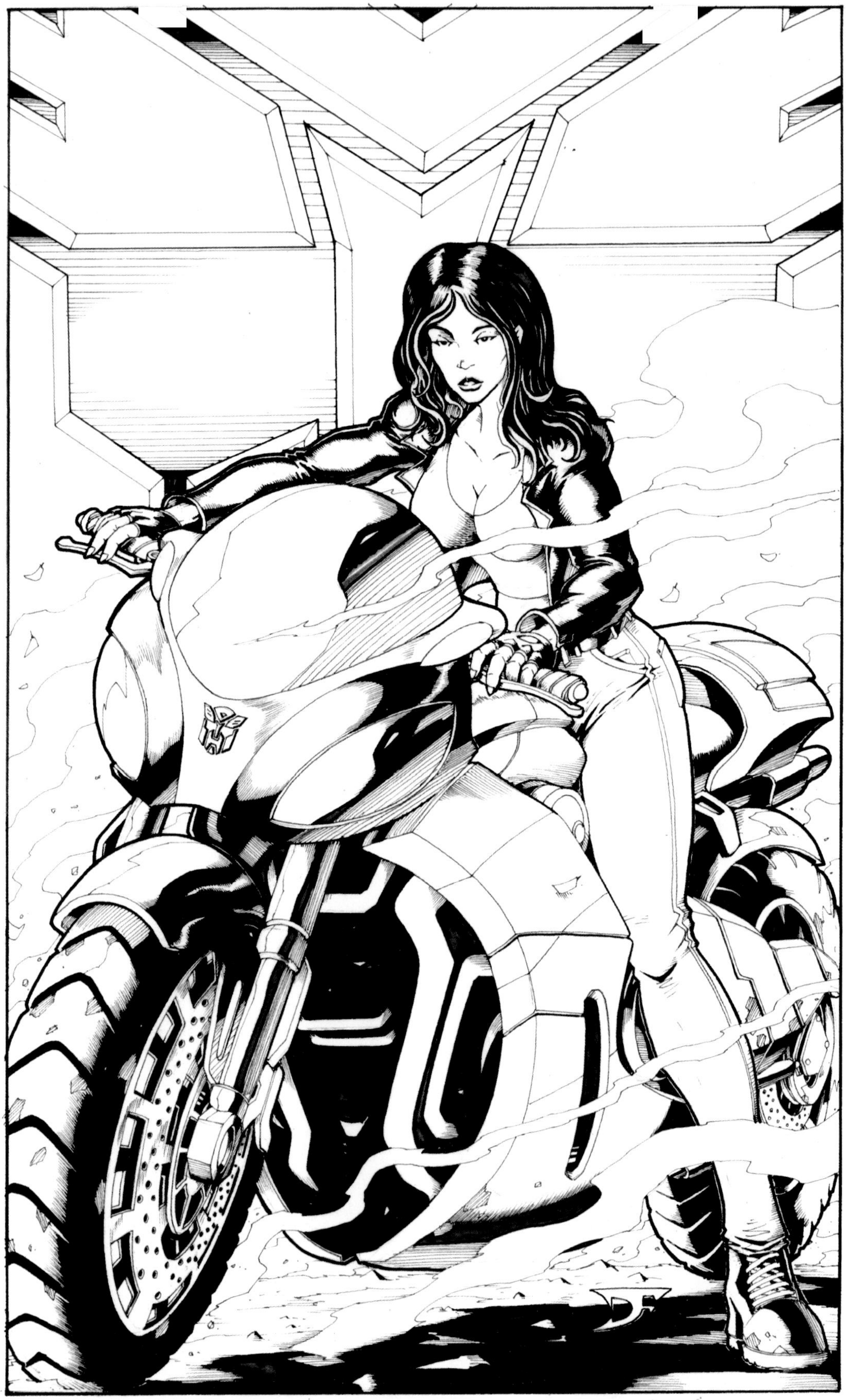

-----DON FIGUEROA-------

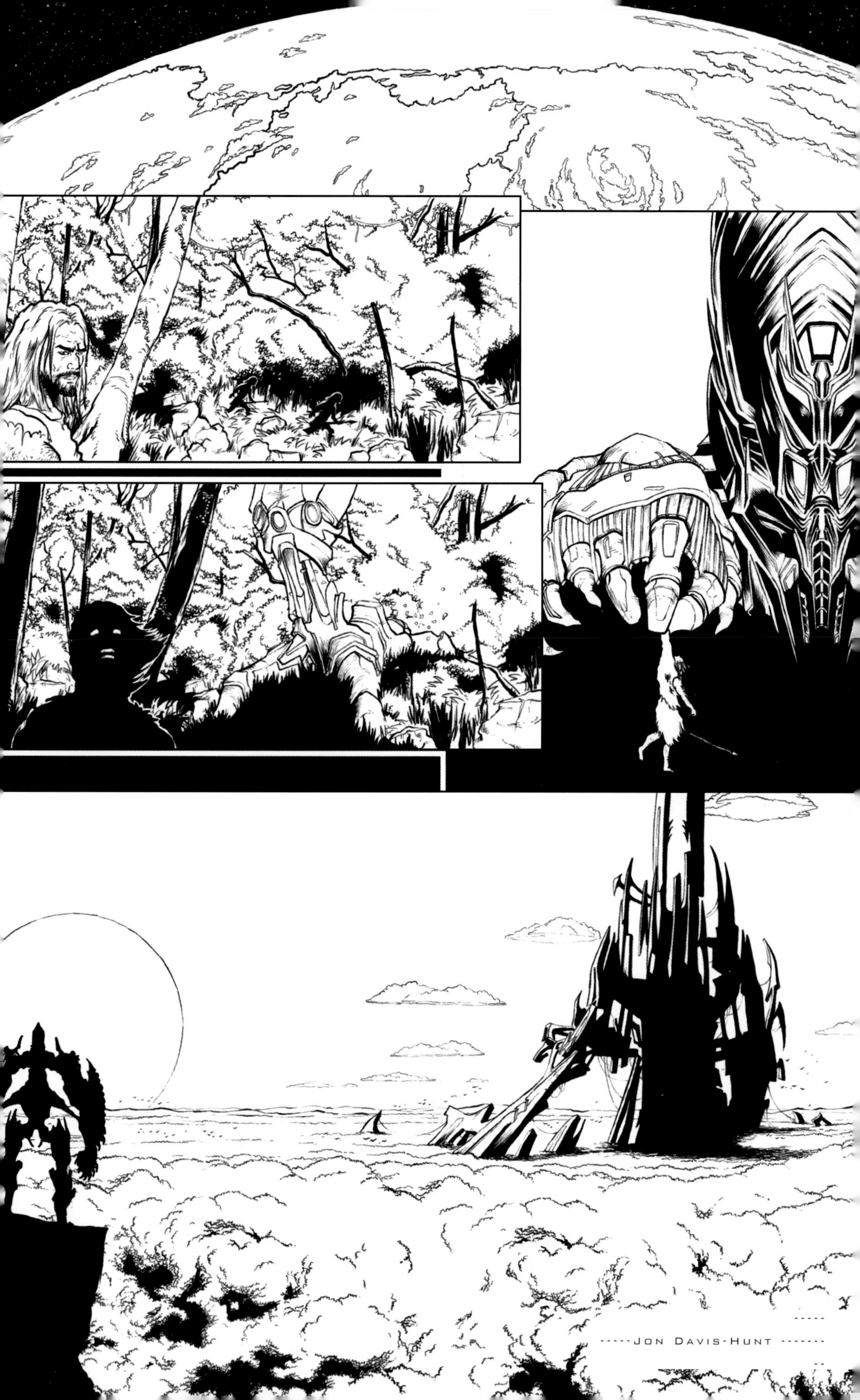
JON DAVIS-HUNT

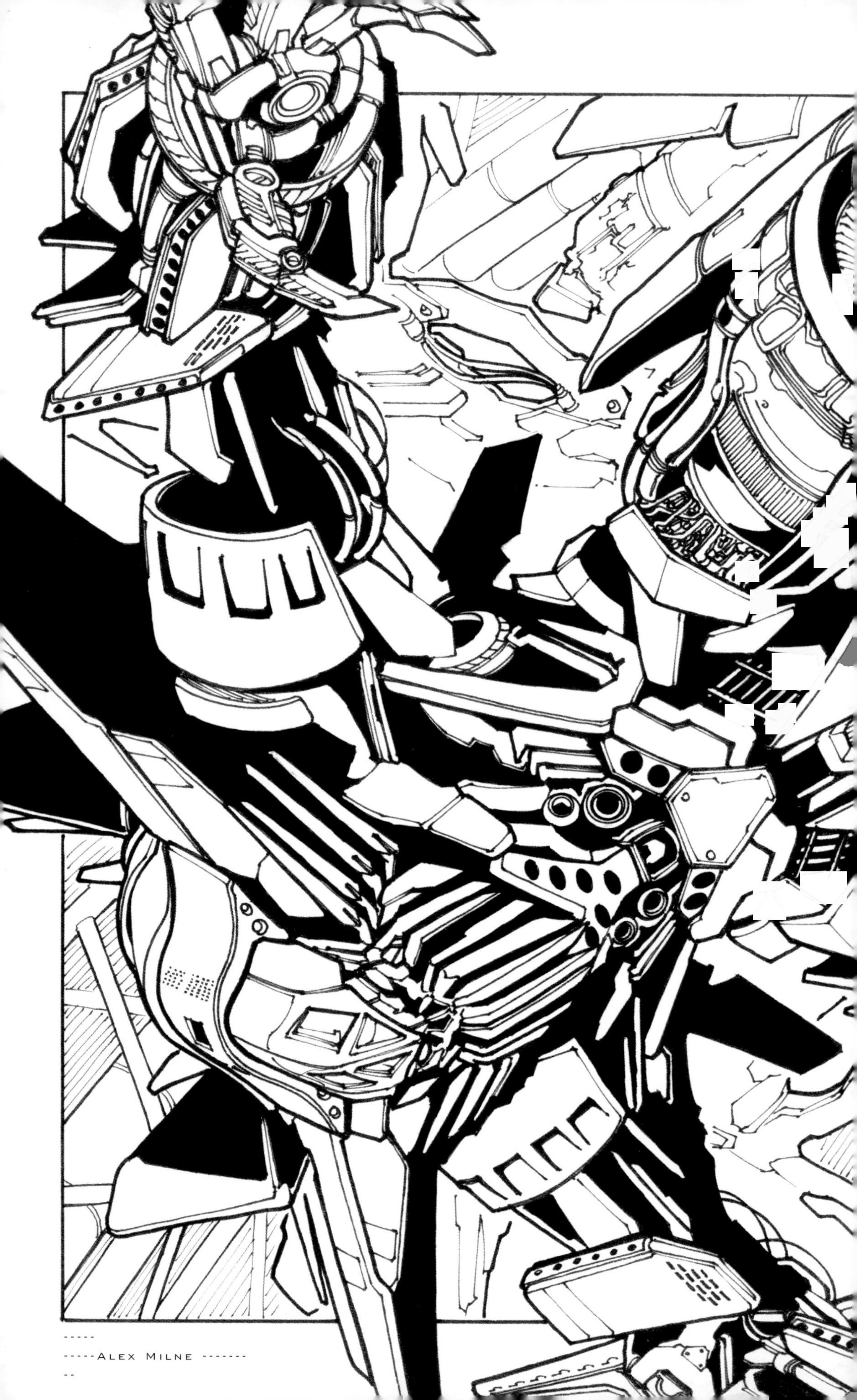

-----Alex Milne -------

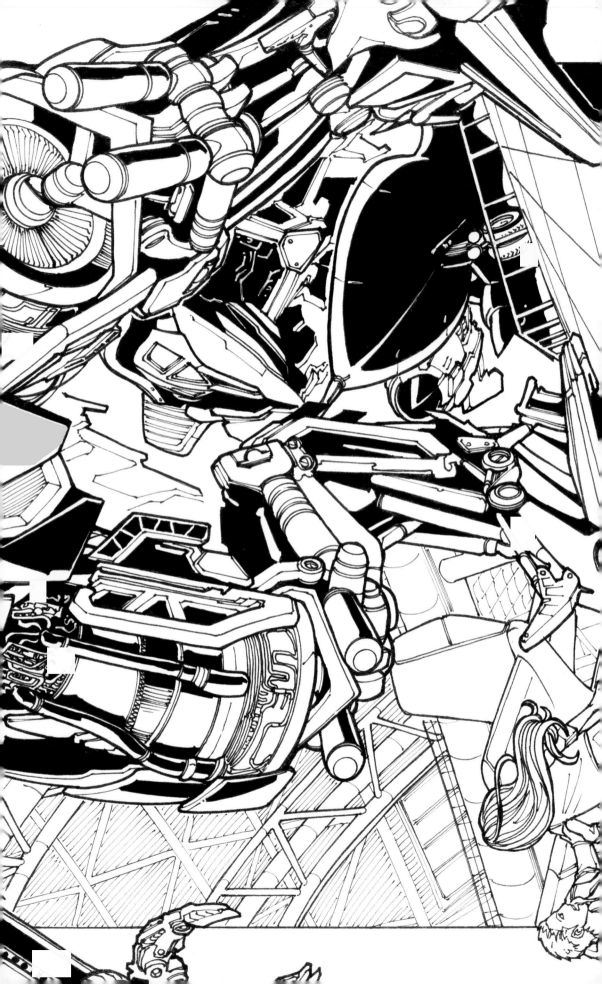

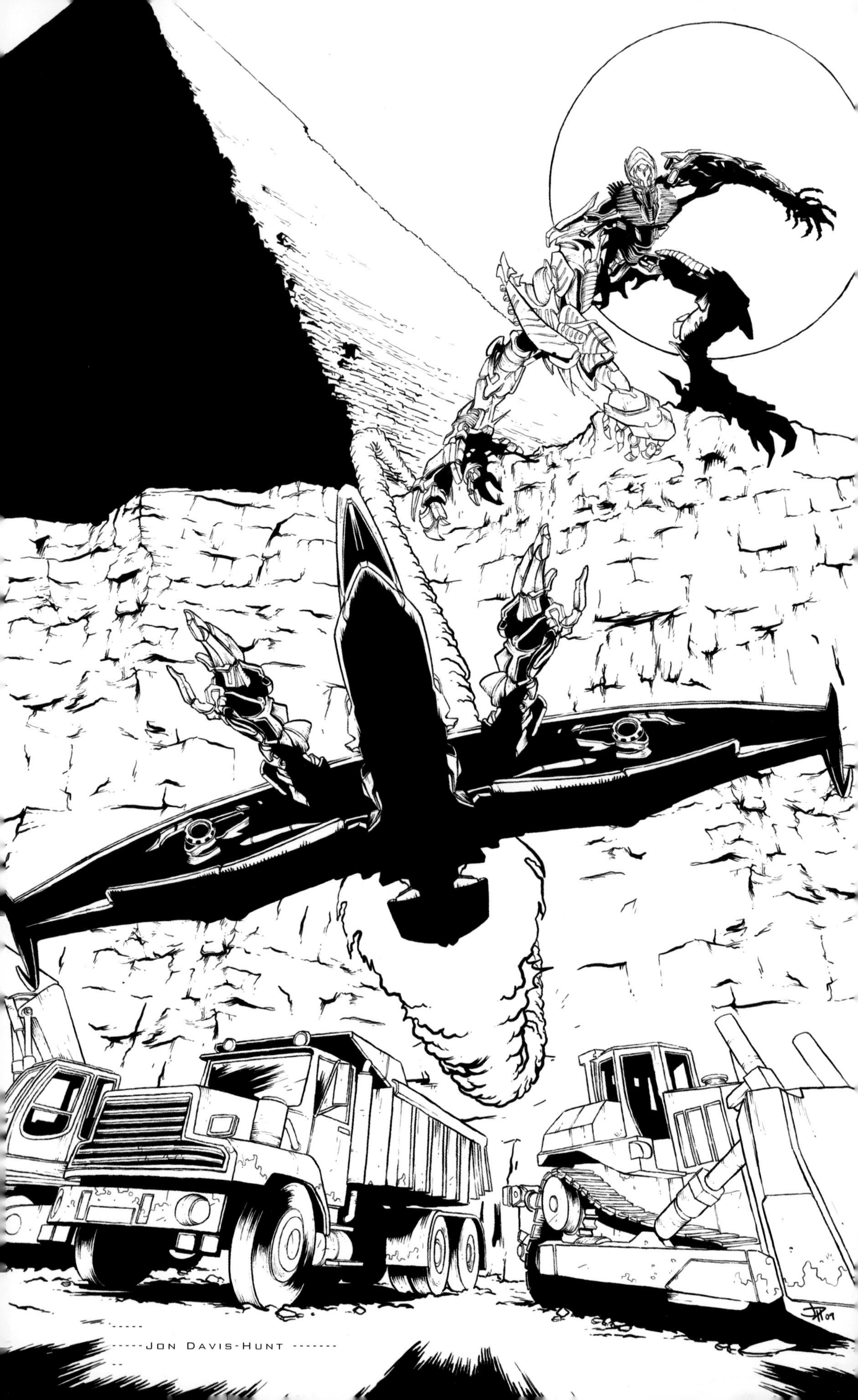

Jon Davis-Hunt

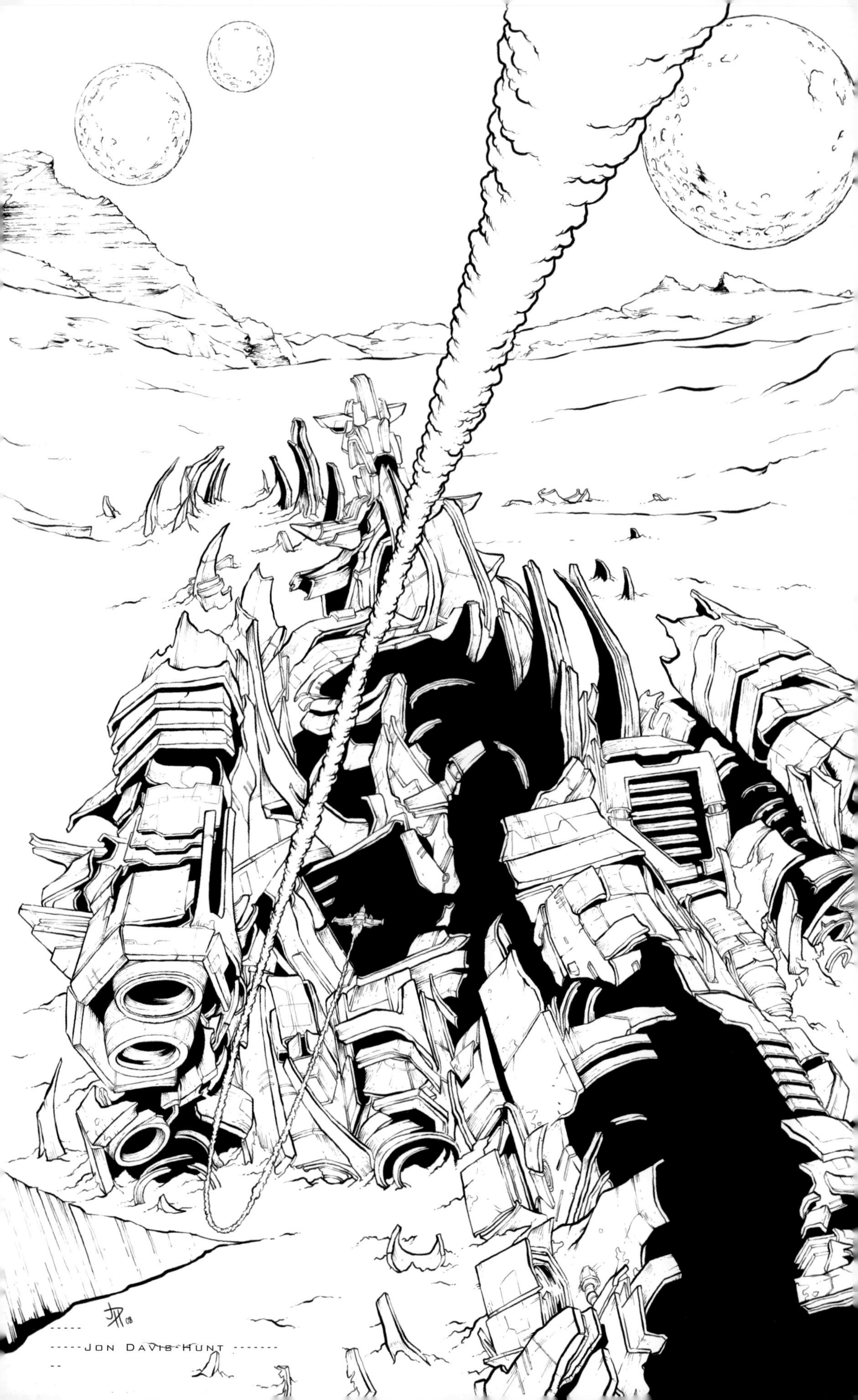

JDH 08
JON DAVIS-HUNT

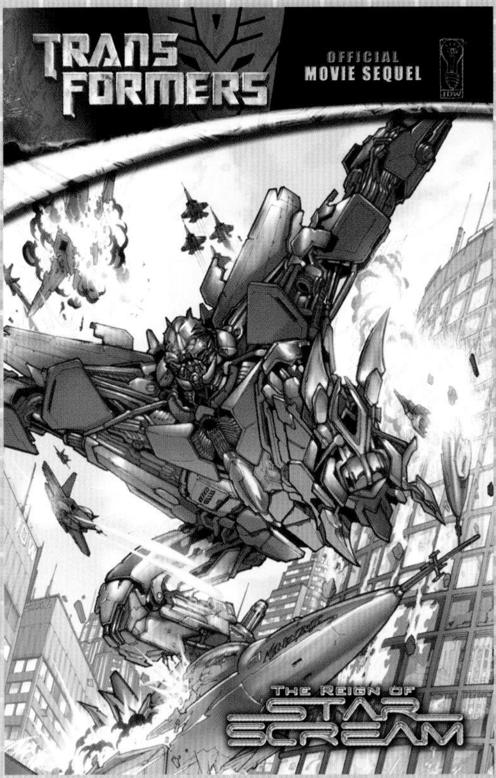
TRANSFORMERS
OFFICIAL MOVIE SEQUEL
IDW
THE REIGN OF
STAR SCREAM

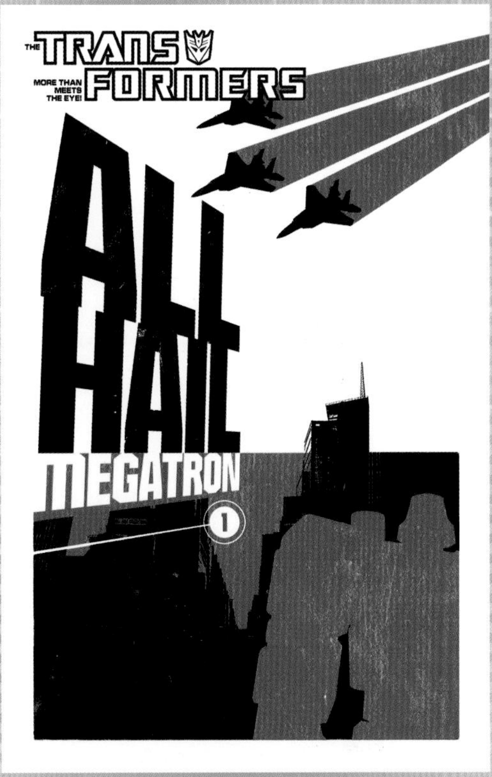
THE TRANSFORMERS
MORE THAN MEETS THE EYE!
ALL HAIL
MEGATRON
1

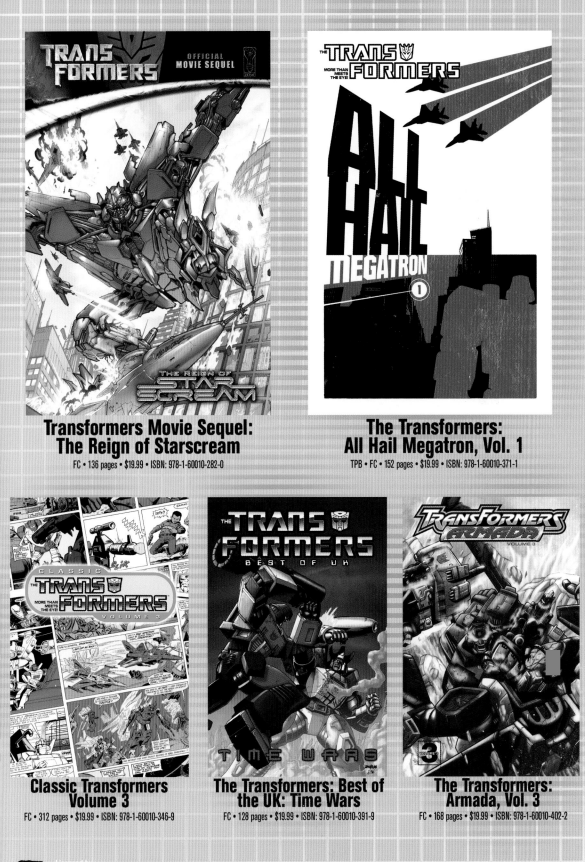

Transformers Movie Sequel: The Reign of Starscream
FC • 136 pages • $19.99 • ISBN: 978-1-60010-282-0

The Transformers: All Hail Megatron, Vol. 1
TPB • FC • 152 pages • $19.99 • ISBN: 978-1-60010-371-1

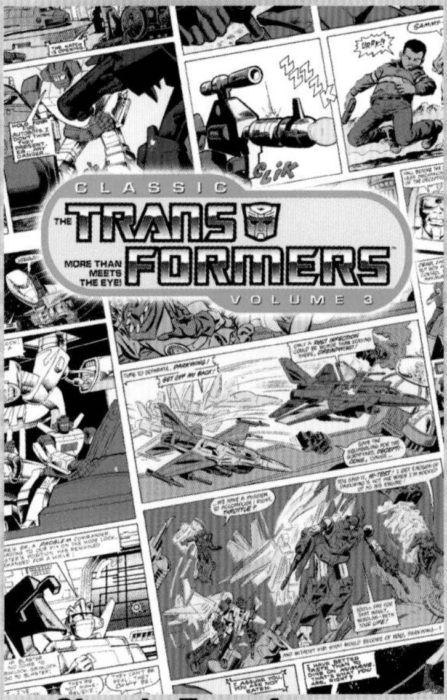
CLASSIC
THE TRANSFORMERS
MORE THAN MEETS THE EYE!
VOLUME 3

Classic Transformers Volume 3
FC • 312 pages • $19.99 • ISBN: 978-1-60010-346-9

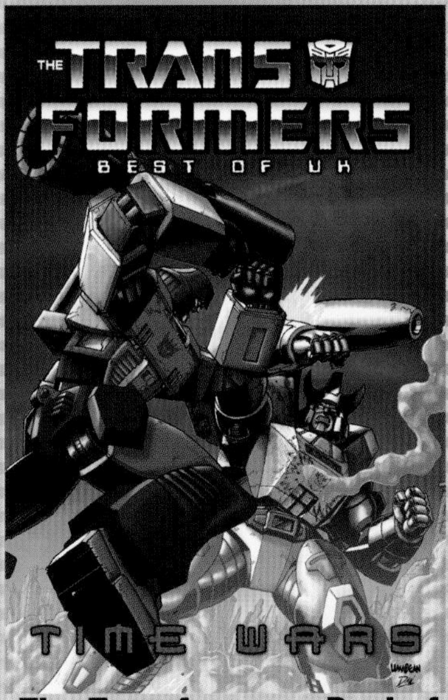
THE TRANSFORMERS
BEST OF UK
TIME WARS

The Transformers: Best of the UK: Time Wars
FC • 128 pages • $19.99 • ISBN: 978-1-60010-391-9

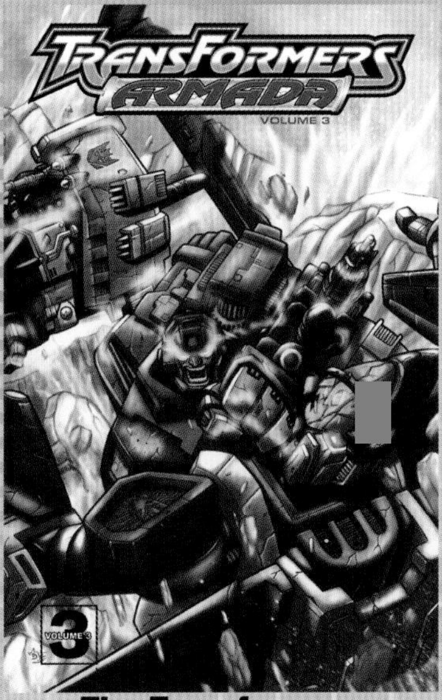
TRANSFORMERS
ARMADA
VOLUME 3

The Transformers: Armada, Vol. 3
FC • 168 pages • $19.99 • ISBN: 978-1-60010-402-2

TRANSFORMERS

REVENGE OF THE FALLEN

IDW
PUBLISHING

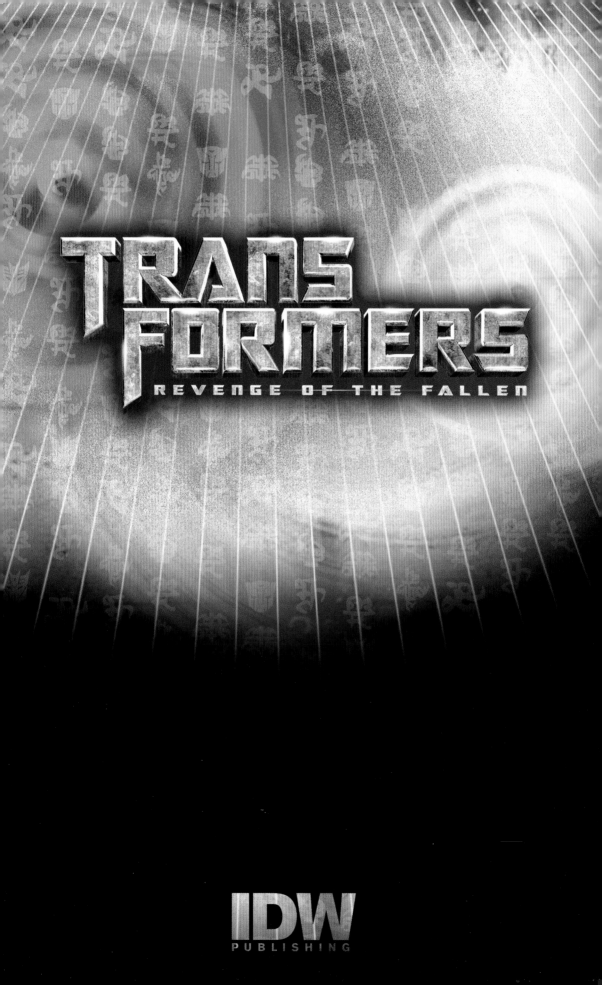